A JOHN CATT
PUBLICA

THE
MISSING PIECE
THE ESSENTIAL SKILLS THAT EDUCATION FORGOT

TOM RAVENSCROFT

First Published 2017

by John Catt Educational Ltd,
12 Deben Mill Business Centre, Old Maltings Approach,
Melton, Woodbridge IP12 1BL

Tel: +44 (0) 1394 389850 Fax: +44 (0) 1394 386893
Email: enquiries@johncatt.com
Website: www.johncatt.com

ISBN: 978 1 1911382393

Set and designed by John Catt Educational Limited

Praise for *The Missing Piece*

"This timely book captures what has made Enabling Enterprise with Tom's great leadership so successful over the last decade. It sets an ambitious vision of how we could support every child and young person to build the essential skills and understanding of the world to succeed - and then shares the practical steps to get there. It will be invaluable for businesses, employers and all those who want to make a real difference for those they support."

Dame Julia Cleverdon, Vice-President, Business in the Community

"No one is better placed than Tom Ravenscroft to write about the essential skills that our youngsters are failing to learn while at our schools and colleges. The Missing Piece is a clarion call, a well reasoned treatise that no one involved in the teaching of young people can afford to ignore if we are to develop a workforce fit for the 21st Century."

Jo Owen, Co-Founder and Trustee, Teaching Leaders, Future Leaders, and Achievement For All

"This is a bold and ambitious book, founded on a fundamental belief that no child's success needs to be limited by their socio-economic background and that essential skills are teachable.

"Tom brings lots of passion and commitment, real experience of the front line and lots of practice through Enabling Enterprise to life in this great book.

"The Missing Piece is widely researched and full of real experience that is ultimately packaged into practical advice focused on each stage of a child's development."

Paul Drechsler, President, The Confederation of British Industry (CBI)

"The Missing Piece is a powerful argument for the elevation of 'essential skills' in our education policy. As Tom states clearly and eloquently, these skills are the enablers of social mobility and will set children up for future success in the 21st century. There is a decade of insight behind this book, and it shows."

Brett Wigdortz, Chief Executive Officer & Founder, Teach First

Contents

For everyone who has helped build Enabling Enterprise.

Preface

A fundamental piece of education is missing. Knowledge and good grades are important but insufficient. Building character is powerful, but it still leaves a gap.

We as adults need to know a lot. We need to make good choices. But we also need to be able to *do*. All of us, whatever we do, need a core set of skills – to work with others, to manage ourselves, to communicate effectively, and to creatively solve problems. We might call these skills different things – soft skills, life skills or employability skills – but we draw on them as much as numeracy or literacy. I have known them as enterprise skills, but have come to see that they are best termed 'essential skills'. If we need them, our children and young people need them even more.

They underpin effective learning in the classroom. They stop students dropping out of university. They are more highly valued by employers than academic grades. They are a foundation for successful entrepreneurship. They are the enablers of civic engagement and social mobility.

When we look to the next decades, in a world of increased automation, fragmented jobs and the need for constant learning it is these skills that will really set our children and young people up for future success.

Yet as an education system, we behave as if they cannot or should not be taught.

But they can be, and they must be.

I am writing this almost a decade after I set up a social enterprise, called Enabling Enterprise. I was a secondary school teacher and the Enabling Enterprise programme was for the students in my inner-city classroom. They were not learning enough in school, and were in no sense set up for the rest of their lives.

Over the last ten years, I've had the enormous privilege of leading a brilliant team of teachers. We have worked with thousands of classroom teachers and volunteers and over 200,000 students. We have seen these children and young people, often from the most disadvantaged backgrounds, build those essential skills with the same rigour and focus as any other academic learning. They can become compelling communicators, they can balance logic and creativity, they can lead and be led, and they can set their own goals and stay on the path to achieving them. When these essential skills are mastered, we truly enable our students to achieve their potential.

This is not just another volley in the ever-rolling education debate, or picking sides in the false choice between prioritising skills, knowledge or character; they are a trio, and are all vital.

This book is partly my journey as a teacher and social entrepreneur; it is what our team at Enabling Enterprise have learnt the hard way; and it is also a manifesto for the future.

It is driven by the experience of teachers, parents, employers and our children and young people themselves and our collective insights about how we can all work together to fill this gap. Along the way, we draw from research and thinking across the educational spectrum, as well as from business and management academia.

I want for every child exactly what I wanted for my own students, and what I want for my own children: to have the essential skills to thrive in the classroom and to excel in whatever they want to do with the rest of their lives. Because this is possible for every child.

This book is a decade's accumulated insight and experience on how to do it.

Tom Ravenscroft
July 2017

Introduction

The rumble was the warning. It started as do the warning signs of a distant storm, building into the roar of a half-time crowd. The noise ricocheted down the white-tiled corridor, and my spine stiffened. I dug my nails into my hands.

The class stormed in, charging over tables, chairs and one another. Bags were swung, the desks scraped across the tired floors – their scratched and worn surfaces bearing the scars of a thousand other battles.

We settled with some effort. There was a seating plan which had been put together with the care of a diplomat, and then constantly rearranged to reflect shifting friendships and enmities lest hostilities break out. They still broke out, to the extent that some students were effectively isolated.

The fragile peace was a masterpiece of careful planning and the constant deployment of an array of distractive tactics. No one willing to put up their hands to answer a question – then I'll call on individuals at random. No answers – then I will give you time to think individually before coming back to you. I never came back to them.

Unable to get work done on time? Then I will build trackers to let you know exactly what you need to do next. Unable to structure your thoughts? Then I will create frameworks to the fullest extent allowed to help construct those ideas for you. Is your work just copied out? I will gently bring you up on that, and help you find your own words.

These students were on the verge of leaving school. Meanwhile, we crept, lesson by lesson, towards the targets I had dutifully written into my planner for each student.

And one day, everything came into focus. It might have been because we were writing an invoice for the third lesson in a row. That was the coursework assignment, and we had five taught hours to complete it.

I realised that these students were 15 or 16 years old. They were on the verge of going to college, apprenticeships or sixth form. Many of them wouldn't make it, and in 2008 would join the nearly one million young people who were not in education, employment or training.

I was doing everything I possibly could to get them their grades. And in the process I was preventing them developing the very skills that they would need in just a few months' time. They were unable to work together, they could not communicate effectively and they gave up easily. They had never been asked to set their own goals – I had set them.

I looked around and realised that this couldn't be what we were here for.

It was a scene that could have been in any one of thousands of classrooms that day. Classrooms where we had accepted that we had to get through, rather than get ahead. Where motivated, dedicated teachers feel that the long march to successful futures can only be directed through a set of grades.

While I worried about my students on the verge of leaving school, in other classrooms teachers were just as worried about their 11-year-olds' readiness for secondary school, their 8-year-olds' refusal to try again, or their 5-year-olds' inability to get on with each other.

Beyond our classrooms, my fellow teachers and I noticed concern too. Employers were perhaps the most vocal. It was while I was teaching, a decade ago in 2008, that the CBI published its first survey of business views on education and skills. The results made clear that employers had concerns about the basic skills of their joiners – including functional numeracy, literacy and IT skills. But they were also concerned about the employability skills that 86% of employers said were most important. Employability skills like teamwork, self-management, problem-solving and communication[1].

In 2009, the UK Commission on Education and Skills (UKCES) published a critical report on the vital importance of employability skills – describing the 'burning platform' for employers who were not seeing those skills in school leavers[2]. This wave of business concern was nothing compared to the reality that the financial crash brought with soaring youth unemployment which was to end up topping one million before the recession receded.

But it was not just about employment. Universities were also concerned about their undergraduates, who they felt lacked the basic skills to thrive in an environment with less structure and individual support. This was reflected in a high drop-out rate.

Finally, the third main route of school leavers – entrepreneurship. High level of business failure was a sad hallmark of the entrepreneurial scene. Some vital skills seemed to be missing.

What is missing?

So, what was going wrong?

Over the last 15 years, growing recognition of the problem has led different education ministers to apply different ideas to filling the gap – whether using enterprise education, introducing personal learning and thinking skills, emphasising social and emotional aspects of learning, or character education.

The reality is that under a broad and ever re-branded banner can be found everything policymakers thought students should know to be ready for real life that didn't fit elsewhere, everything that employers wanted that didn't fit neatly into the wider curriculum, and the individual philosophies of the teachers trying to do the best for their students.

In the resulting mess could be found: risk-taking, communication, resilience, financial literacy, commercial awareness, honesty, interpersonal skills, reliability and self-management. We confuse things further when we interchangeably use terms including life skills, soft skills, entrepreneurship, employability, 21st century skills, achievement virtues, or character strengths.

But whatever we call them, much of the difference is semantic – after sifting through the confusion, we can clearly identify communication skills, interpersonal skills, problem-solving skills, and self-management skills.

To reflect these four critical domains at Enabling Enterprise we settled on eight skills, balancing nuance with pragmatism. The two communication skills are presenting and listening and understanding. The interpersonal skills are teamwork and leadership. Problem-solving skills are divided into the pair of problem-solving (where the problem is pre-defined) and creativity (where it is not). Self-management has the two components of aiming high to set goals, and then staying positive to stick at achieving them.

And once we remove the noise, the evidence is clear that each of these eight skills is an enabler of future success, and learning in school. Each has a rich pedagogical background.

Importantly, this is not about whether all learning should be forced through the prism of building skills or whether these skills are a replacement for academic knowledge or rigour. It is about making a concerted effort to develop each of these skills as part of the whole curriculum.

This is not a new idea. Take presenting as just one example. What we call presenting would have been called rhetoric back in Ancient Greece and remained a priority through to the re-focusing of education on economic outcomes during Victorian times. It lives on today as debating in many of our schools, or 'oracy' in others and can be coached and trained to high levels of achievement.

Or take staying positive. We talk increasingly about resilience but staying positive is about equipping students with tools and tactics for sticking at things and adapting plans when they see setbacks – practical things that they can learn and implement, not just a mind-set.

We dig into each of these in Part 2, and it's fascinating to discover the richness of the individual skills – and their learnability and teachability.

So why aren't we teaching them?
It might be intellectually interesting that we are tying ourselves in definitional knots, but not particularly helpful for our children and young people.

To actually fill the gap and restore our trio of knowledge, character and skills, we need to fundamentally believe that these essential skills are teachable. This is a big step. Both experience and research indicate three broad responses to the idea of teaching these skills. I'm thinking here of teachers I've worked with, but research suggests it is a fairly consistent view across parents and school leavers too.

The first group see essential skills as innate and natural to their students – they proudly identify the natural leaders, team players or presenters. By extension, there are a lot of students, perhaps even the majority, for whom these skills will remain out of reach.

The second group believe that these skills are formed by everything in a student's life to the extent that a teacher can have very minimal impact. To this group, it is only a process of osmosis that will build the students' skills – and so a bountiful supply of activities is useful but with limited expectations of the effectiveness of any particular activity, or indeed the whole roster of activities given that students are only in class for five hours each day.

The third group view essential skills as lying latent until inspired into existence. We can spark an interest or ignite a passion but the mechanism seems mysterious. The onus remains on the individual to pursue this passion and realise their own potential.

In Chapter 7, I dig into each of these misperceptions and how they have hindered serious thinking about building essential skills.

A philosophical leap

The eighth chapter makes the greatest leap. Over the last eight years at Enabling Enterprise we have been ruthless about building our impact – seeking always to be as rigorous as possible, and being unemotional about cutting what doesn't work. We have seen that we have to think differently in order to make the breakthrough our students need: we have to build these essential skills alongside literacy and numeracy.

We've learned the hard way that occasional enterprise days, competitions or after-school clubs are not enough. We have tried all of these approaches.

I am keenly aware of the many claims out there for educational pet projects to be seen to be as essential as numeracy and literacy. It is slightly embarrassing to be trying to jockey for that turf.

However, when we look dispassionately at the characteristics of the basic skills of literacy and numeracy, we see four key things:

- They are primarily about doing something, not knowing something.
- They are useful throughout life in many different settings.
- They are tools to unlock and access further knowledge.
- While they are applied with contextual knowledge, they are transferable.

These characteristics absolutely apply to our essential skills.

Reimagining essential skills

Across the country, hundreds of Enabling Enterprise schools are now embracing this shift towards making essential skills a core pillar of learning, alongside literacy and numeracy. These schools work with children from as young as 3 through to 18-year-olds. Some are remote and rural, others in the heart of our cities. Some have more than a thousand students – and some less than 50. The majority of these schools serve children in the most disadvantaged neighbourhoods in the country, according to the Income Deprivation Affecting Children Index (IDACI).

All of them have made this transformation by implementing six key principles.

- **To keep it simple:** Rather than being overwhelmed by the complexity of trying to prepare students for all aspects of their future lives, these schools embrace a clear set of essential skills, and use them consistently.

- **To start early:** We rightly identify numeracy and literacy as the building blocks of education – and so we start young – and then we keep going. These schools also think about students' essential skills in the same way, rather than ignoring them after nursery age until the point they are about to leave school.

- **To measure it:** We are often led to believe that measurement is very difficult or a distraction from what we are trying to achieve. Schools who are excelling here find that by being precise about outcomes they become measurable – and that measurability drives better learning and better progress.

- **To focus tightly:** Whilst much teaching of enterprise or employability relies on presenting a smorgasbord of activities, we wouldn't expect students to learn to read by simply letting them loose in a library. Instead, these schools use essential skill levels to make sure students are working on activities that stretch them, akin to the way we use reading levels when developing literacy. We need focus and rigour, and to teach each of the essential skills explicitly and carefully.

- **To keep practising:** With literacy and numeracy we recognise the need to reinforce these key enablers elsewhere in the curriculum – a notion reinforced through initiatives highlighting that every teacher is also a teacher of English, for example. Similarly, while proper time is needed to develop essential skills in their own right, these schools reinforce it by highlighting the deployment and development of those skills everywhere else.

- **To bring it to life:** Finally, these schools apply the skills to real-life challenges – both to highlight their relevance and boost motivation and also to increase their transferability later on.

In the third part of this book, I explore how each of these principles actually runs counter to current mainstream practice. I look at what the evidence is for each principle and then what it looks like in practice. Along the way, it is illuminating to see how this group of pioneering schools are transforming their students' learning in school and prospects for the future.

A different future

I write this book with great optimism about the future. The plans and proposals here are ambitious, but they are achievable. They are already working in hundreds of schools today.

Through our experience at Enabling Enterprise, we can see the change for individual students, whole classes and entire schools. There are other programmes working in this field too. I know, though, that whilst Enabling Enterprise is working with over 85,000 students this year, our reach into 1.2% of English schools is just a small foothold on the challenge.

Ultimately, to ensure that all of our students are set up for the rest of their lives we will need to achieve three things. Firstly, to build a consensus that these skills are essential for our students' future success. Secondly, a shared belief that they are completely teachable. Finally, that we have a common language and goals around those skills to help all students to reach their potential.

Taking this from hundreds of schools to thousands will be achieved if we focus on making four big changes at a systemic level:

- Firstly, by doing a lot more to *train and support teachers and teaching assistants* who may never have received any training on how to build the essential skills. We need expert teachers with deep understanding, as well as a basic grounding for all teachers.

- Secondly, by *creating and maintaining a shared language and expectations for essential skills* to bring coherence to the range of activities and programmes out there. By having a single shared framework, individual programmes can add up to at least the sum of their parts, with the same skills reinforced consistently.

- Thirdly, by *ensuring that value is placed on essential skills in the education system*. This includes the school inspectorate Ofsted ensuring an emphasis on provision of structured, age-appropriate opportunities for students to build these skills at all levels in the curriculum. Alongside, there are other policy levers the Department of Education could use, including making essential skills a core requirement, clearer up-to-date guidance, dedicated funding and stronger destination data of where students end up beyond formal schooling.

- Finally, by *properly engaging parents*. As we do with numeracy and literacy, providing parents with the information and tools to support the development of their children's skills, from the youngest to the oldest.

Some distance still to go
The development of literacy and numeracy over the last couple of centuries should give grounds for optimism. From a shaky start, the developed world has seen almost universal basic literacy and numeracy achieved, with wave after wave of innovation helping to further those goals – whether standardised grammar, reading ages, or newer technological tools.

As the essential skills become an expectation of schooling we will continue to increase our effectiveness in building them together. We will learn and share best practice internationally. We will collectively refine the skills frameworks, furthering our understanding of any interdependencies and the long-term impacts of different programmes. As a result, we will continue to innovate around how we build the skills, and might expect to see twice the current rates of learning in a decade's time. Finally, we will harness the opportunities that new technology presents – whether to capture or record progress, to use simulations to build the skills, or artificial intelligence to hone them.

The final chapter makes clear that we will need to keep innovating because these skills are only going to become more important. Automation and algorithms will reduce job opportunities for anyone without an adaptable skill set, as even complex tasks may no longer require human workers. Similarly, there are clear trends in the nature of employment towards self-employment and gig work – needing a lot more self-direction and management than ever before. Our children and young people will need to be constantly learning and re-learning over their longer careers if they are to succeed.

But these changes will also provide huge opportunities, including careers focused on solving some of humanity's most intractable challenges, from the environment to global development and health. To capitalise on these opportunities we need all our school leavers to be equipped with the essential skills to really grapple with these challenges.

Let's get going

Through the work of Enabling Enterprise and others there is a growing body of evidence in schools across the country that this approach works, that we can teach essential skills as a core enabler of our students.

There are primary and secondary schools in very different areas across the country where every child can tell you what the skills mean for them, and where their parents regularly join them to better understand how the skills are built and how they can support them at home. I walk down these corridors and see how each class is strategically, incrementally building the eight skills that they need for success. I talk to children who can tell me exactly what they find invigorating and frustrating about leading others, will say how they're trying to become better listeners or presenters or recommend me a strategy for staying positive.

More than a couple of times I have given a speech only for an audience member to stand up to ask a question and to declare that their child has done Enabling

Enterprise. And when they do, my stomach constricts a little. Then inevitably they will blow me away that their child professed to adoring the activities that they have been doing – whether a trip to an employer like Birmingham Airport or an NHS hospital, or during their regular enterprise lessons in school. But what means the most is when the parents says that it's not just the activity – it's the change in their children. And that they wish they had had the same opportunity in school themselves.

I talk to our teachers a lot. Before they've started to implement the approach, they start in different places: some excited, some cynical, some unsure how they will find the time, and many sagely identifying the students who are their 'naturals'. Once they've started, they keep going because they see the difference in their students.

We can see the difference in the data too: students, even from the most disadvantaged backgrounds, can make progress in their skills at a rate that puts them on the trajectory for future success. It is unsurprising that students start in different places – and unsurprising that the majority are behind where they should be. It is exciting to see that student background is uncorrelated with the progress they subsequently make and that the gap can close. This can be done.

But let's start at the beginning.

Part 1:
What is the Gap?

He thumped the pile of coursework folders down with a satisfying smack on the desk. To emphasise his triumph he pushed his chair back and threw his fists into the air.

There was a murmur of congratulations from the other teachers as they looked up. Someone handed him a congratulatory cup of tea from the urn in the corner of the staff room.

'All done?'
'Yup – all done'
'How were they?'
'Alright…' A smile. 'Good enough anyway'
'They're set for life now, eh?'
A roll of the eyes, a smirk and a snort of laughter.
'If only.'

Chapter 1:
The Gap

Our schools are churning out the unemployable. So ran one memorable headline when I was teaching ten years ago. Students, it reported, were leaving school ill-equipped for the real world or work: unable to organise or apply themselves, work with others, or overcome setbacks.

We know this story well, but what is less well appreciated is that this same fundamental challenge undermines learning at university and makes entrepreneurial failure more likely. It is even a barrier to learning in school.

It was, and is, a huge constraint on the UK's growth, productivity and future prosperity. It is a tragic waste of individual talent and potential, and particularly affects children and young people from the most disadvantaged backgrounds.

Before we can fix the gap, we have to first look into it and understand why it has grown so wide.

My classroom
I first saw this in my own classroom.

I was 21 years old and just three months earlier had been completing my university finals in economics and management. I had had a very privileged educational experience for which I was rightly grateful – growing up in Buckinghamshire, attending the local grammar school and then on to the University of Oxford. It was quite a different experience, after training which was intense but brief, to be tasked with a roster of classes in a challenging secondary school in Hackney, in East London. My degree, majoring on economics, drove my passion to be a business studies teacher.

That I found teaching challenging initially would be unsurprising. But what really marked those early months was the sense of something missing. It was more of a background dissonance than any single moment; more of that rumbling sense of growing hunger than anything explosive. What troubled me most was quite mundane. When I asked my students to work in teams and they refused to work in the groups I set them. When I asked questions, and rather than suggest an answer, students would prefer to shrug and maintain a blank look. There were the critical coursework deadlines that passed without making any impression on the students themselves.

That was the dissonance. After a few months in the classroom by many measures my class were actually doing fine. I had created Excel trackers which automatically changed colour as coursework was completed. The students were making good progress, more or less on time, towards completing all of their coursework to an acceptable standard and all at least passing. I had created structures and frameworks to help them structure their thinking, help them complete their coursework and provide the evidence that the exam board were looking for.

But my awarenes was growing that my students' apparent progress was actually a thin veneer on reality. And the veneer was already cracking.

The gap in other classrooms

I was not alone in my fears. During my first year of teaching I shared a house with three other new teachers, teaching across different schools in North and East London. Our dinner chat frequently came back to the same set of issues. We were shocked by how little ownership our students felt over their learning and how much of the responsibility rested squarely on the shoulders of us as their teachers – a phenomenon that had turned students into passive recipients of knowledge. We shared notes on how many of the basic skills that we would expect of much younger students seemed to be absent. I was not alone in worrying at how inarticulate my students could be, or at the level of animosity between different groups of students. I was not the only one who questioned why so little knowledge seemed to be retained between classes.

We talked too about what we wanted for our students. We weren't teaching just for the thrill of boosting a student's results by a grade. We wanted to build a depth of knowledge and understanding in our students that would help them appreciate and enjoy the world around them. We wanted them to feel what success felt like and be motivated to be ambitious for their own future achievements. We wanted them to go out into the world beyond school and thrive – to fashion their interests, passions and skills to build themselves a brilliant, fulfilling life.

When the grades don't add up

Back in school, staff meetings invariably oscillated around students' grades, predicted grades and any gap between the two. We talked endlessly about the proportion of students who were going to achieve their five A*-C GCSEs including English and maths – the basic benchmark of a good set of GCSEs. That is not to criticise the school – it would undoubtedly have been the same conversation in any other staff room in the country at that time. But it was a symptom and a cause of what was happening in our classrooms.

Sadly, this approach was not even succeeding at achieving those five good GCSEs. In 2009 only half of students achieved those indicators[3]. In the schools serving the most financially disadvantaged part of the population, as mine was, the proportion was much lower still.

In 2016, only one in three students from low-income backgrounds achieved five good GCSEs including maths and English[4].

We weren't getting the grades the students needed, and as we worked harder and harder at getting those grades we realised something else: we weren't getting them ready for life beyond school either.

Also a gap at primary school

This awareness is by no means limited to secondary school teachers. One of Enabling Enterprise's primary school headteachers articulated a very similar set of fears for his students. As he said, 'Year on year, I am honoured to be working with children and teachers who overcome many challenges to high academic achievement. When they come to the end of Year 6 we have an assembly. The children sit on the stage, their parents and the other children in the audience, and I stand up and talk about how proud I am of their academic achievements – and I am. Every single word of that is true.' He went on to question though, how ready they really were for the next stage of their education journeys.

I've had the same conversation with dozens of primary school teachers – their fears that their children aren't ready for the next stage in their lives and for the shift that secondary school represents.

Our classroom challenge in the data

To see the problem in the classroom more neatly, we asked teachers to observe their students over a period of up to four weeks and look for whether a student regularly displays the behaviours that evidence a particular skill.

I should caution that this is not a representative sample of all students – in 2016, over 65% of our schools served the most deprived 20% of communities according to the IDACI index[5]. But a few examples bring to life what the challenge is[6]:

- When students are 6 or 7 years old we might expect that they can articulate their emotions in simple terms – but from a sample of 1498 students their teachers found that only 64% were able to.
- When children are 7 or 8 years old, their teachers reported that only 49% of the 1743 student assessed were generally able to listen to other students, and ask follow-up questions on what they heard.
- In terms of staying positive, by Year 3, when they are 8 or 9 years old, we would expect that students are able to stay calm when something goes wrong, without becoming uncontrollably angry or distressed. Their teachers reported that this was only the case for 56% of the 1742 students they assessed. What's even more concerning is that by the time they were 11 or 12 years old, their teachers felt that 16% of the students in their classes were still unable to do this.
- When students are aged 11 and starting secondary school, their teachers judged that only 2% could take notes effectively. Something is missing if teachers themselves can see little sign of.

Something is missing if teachers themselves can see little sign of some of these essential skills for learning and life in their classroom.

Beyond the school gates

Beyond the proverbial school gates, the future was looking grim for our students in 2008 and 2009. While we worried about the students in our classrooms, there was good reason to be nervous about what we were preparing our students for – whether that was employment, university or entrepreneurship.

(i) Beyond the school gates: Employers

Businesses and other employers were beginning to make clear that while we in our classrooms might be concerned about how our students were building their subject knowledge and qualifications, they were concerned at the prospect of employing them.

Businesses looking for qualifications and basic skills

In 2008, the CBI (Confederation of British Industry) ran its first annual survey of members' views on skills and education[7]. One of the clear points was unsurprising: it found that members wanted a well-qualified workforce, with an increased need for graduate-level qualifications – around one-third of jobs required degree-level skills or qualifications. There were particular shortages of students with science, technology, engineering and maths (STEM) backgrounds. There were also gaps around the foreign language skills of their newer recruits.

Among their less-skilled workforce, there were more acute problems. The 2008 CBI survey highlighted that almost half of adults in the UK 'have difficulty with numbers'. The basic expectations of businesses include multiplication, percentages, ratios, fractions, decimals, converting units and calculating odds and probabilities.

The survey also highlighted that one in seven (5 million adults) were not functionally literate. In terms of literacy, some of the expectations were legible handwriting, comprehension of basic texts and being able to communicate orally.

It is hard to argue with the notion that mastering basic numeracy and literacy has to be key – a priority reflected in the government's decision back when I was teaching that the five key GCSEs measure should explicitly include English and maths. I saw in my classroom that the students' ability to engage with more complex ideas of cash flow or break-even points depended on basic numeracy. Similarly, the focus on written coursework immediately disadvantaged many students who lacked the literacy to engage.

There were also problems in another area of basic skills: the IT skills of the workforce, which registered as a concern for more than half of employers (56%). In my first year of teaching, three spare hours on my timetable were filled by a purgatory of three Year 9 IT lessons. After that experience as an IT teacher, businesses' concerns in this area do not surprise me – even in 2008 before the widespread uptake of smartphones, students were fantastic at finding and sharing obscure but entertaining websites, and remarkably overwhelmed by the basics of the core Office applications like PowerPoint, Word and Excel.

As one small example, as the students were working on their coursework I was confused by how sporadic progress was – until I realised that they had never been taught how to name or save their files properly. As a result, after keying in whatever random phrase they thought was amusing at that moment, they promptly lost their lesson's work. Whilst fixable in a classroom context, I can imagine an employer being rather underwhelmed by a new recruit with this approach.

All of this would seem to reinforce the notion that schools are right to drive for mastering the three key basic skill areas of numeracy, literacy and IT. They should then push for good qualifications, and work towards university entrance – this is what employers need.

Businesses also prioritising employability skills

However, the survey also reflected the discomfort that we felt as teachers: qualifications alone were not enough. The CBI survey in 2008 highlighted that even at degree level, only 30% of graduate-level jobs relied on a particular course of study. What mattered to most firms (86%) were the more generic employability skills, including self-management, teamwork, business and customer awareness, problem-solving and communication, including listening and questioning others.

The UK Commission on Employability and Skills (UKCES) was also set up in 2008, with a focus on employability skills. In 2009 they printed an interesting report called The Employability Challenge[8]. The foreword from Sir Mike Rake, the Chair, is worth quoting: 'By working together well, individuals contribute to the productivity of the economy and success of society, improve the lives of colleagues and customers, and realise their own creative potential. This is enabled by everyone coming out of the public employment and skills system being able to work in a team, communicate clearly, listen well, be interested and keen to learn, take criticism, solve problems, read, write and add.' He further added that 'these employability skills are the lubricant of our increasingly complex and inter-connected workplace. They are not a substitute for specific knowledge and skills but they make the difference between being good at a subject and being good at doing a job.'

The Learning and Skills Network ran a similar survey in 2008[9]. They asked 1137 employers what they would be looking for and numeracy and literacy of course came up as critical for candidates. However, they highlighted that without 'enthusiasm, commitment and time-keeping' half of respondents would not make a job offer to candidates who were strong in their numeracy and literacy alone.

I look back to that period of 2008 and 2009 as this was the context of my class of students. To reassure you that this is no historical anomaly, the latest Skills & Education survey from CBI and Pearson in 2016 showed exactly the same pattern – that 89% of respondents would prioritise the employability skills and attitudes of the school and college leavers they recruit; just 23% would prioritise their qualifications and grades[10].

Businesses not finding the employability skills they sought

Sadly, as Sir Mike Rake noted 'In 2009, too few people have these skills...' despite the fact 'business has been asking for them for twenty years'. This is reference to the CBI's 1989 report, 'Towards a Skills Revolution', which emphasised the essential nature of employability skills[11].

Indeed, this has been the constant refrain of the CBI's annual surveys – not just that these skills matter to employers but that they are found lacking. In 2008, the CBI were highlighting particular deficiencies around communication skills. They also highlighted the need for a well-rounded set of capacities including self-management, teamwork, customer and business awareness, problem-solving, and communication skills alongside the ability to apply literacy, numeracy and IT to the work context.

There was no particular shift in the intervening years. A study led by McKinsey in 2014 found that skills that employers valued but felt were lacking in young people included spoken communication skills, work ethic, teamwork, and problem-solving[12]. What they pointed out was particularly galling – that despite high youth unemployment, employers were struggling to find young people with the skills they needed.

Finally, in 2016 the CBI's survey was clear that 'school and college is not equipping all young people with what they need to succeed'. They added that about half of respondents reported that they were not satisfied with skills in communication (50%), analysis including problem-solving (50%) or self-management (48%). The only relative chink of light was that only a quarter of respondents were concerned about school and college leavers' teamwork (26%) – fractionally better than concerns around literacy (32%) and basic numeracy (29%).

The result of this is perhaps reflected in the 365,000 young people, aged 16-24, who were unemployed in the last quarter, from February to April 2017 – a total of 10.7% of young people that age[13].

We are only going to need more skills in the future
It has become fashionable to highlight how much about the future is unknown. I have lost track of the number of times I have been sagely advised many of the jobs our children and young people will do in ten years haven't been invented yet. I can well believe that the content of roles and jobs will continue to evolve – ten years ago, social media was almost unknown and yet has spawned whole industries – not just of professional tweeters and the online marketing that goes with it, but changing personal and professional interactions in many fields and generating new possibilities for big data.

This is certainly the view of the CBI who cite that 77% of respondents believe that they will need a more-skilled workforce in the future. The final chapter looks to the future to explore exactly this point – with the trends of increased automation, the gig economy and rise of self-employment, the need to re-learn and to focus on larger and more intractable challenges.

That is aside from the concerns that are emerging around the UK's imminent departure from the European Union – which Ofsted itself has highlighted might make the development of skills increasingly important as the country relies more and more on home-grown skills[14]. Even the All-Party Parliamentary Group (APPG) for Education, a cross-cutting group of politicians, reflected that, 'the world of work and the labour market is changing and the education system is not keeping pace with developments'[15].

This is not just about the future, although I rather think that education should have an eye on what's coming. It is about what is happening in our classrooms today.

(ii) Beyond the school gates: University

By highlighting the concerns of employers, I am not presuming that the sole or even primary purpose of education is to create economic producers for industry. Do recall that I started with despair at what was happening in my classroom.

When I was teaching, the holy grail of success was university admission. The Tony Blair era might have come to an end before I stood in front of my class, but his goal that half of young people should go to university was still influential.

Some schools started to explicitly make access to university a stated goal for their students from the outset. Impressive schools like King Solomon Academy in London have a stated goal that they want all of their students to experience a university education[16]. This reflects the Charter School movement in the USA, many of whom make acceptance onto a four-year college course a guiding principle and expectation for all their students.

Grades become the main focus
The challenge with this goal is that overwhelmingly the focus to realise this ambition is on the grades that the students achieve. This is particularly the case when universities broadly acknowledge that there is often little to differentiate students on the basis of personal statements – whereas grades are a much clearer and less disputable metric of comparison.

In many cases, this then supercharges exactly the same behaviours that seemed so destructive in my classroom – the close focus on measures of progress and the securing of grades and results over the mastery of knowledge and wider skills. This well-meaning structuring in the classroom was complemented by wrap-around support.

For my students, this meant minimal responsibility for maintaining their own coursework folders – as I never let them out of my room for fear they would be lost. It meant that when deadlines were missed I immediately swung into action by keeping them back after lessons or after school to get the work done under my supervision. It meant that their learning was broken down into chunks which were ticked off as we progressed. The nature of the course I was teaching allowed that to happen.

Universities' perspectives on their undergraduates
Of course the reality is that this was wildly different from the experience that most undergraduates had on arrival at university. The wrap-around support was replaced by lectures, labs and occasional seminars or check-ins with their tutors.

The essays that they had to write were not structured into short questions – there was no single textbook to read before replicating an answer. Instead, reading lists were wider, questions more open and required structuring.

University, students quickly found, required enormous self-discipline. No one checked that they attended lectures, and the temptations of freedom were often overwhelming. The contact time they had in the form of seminars was often impersonal as part of a group with a lecturer or tutor who would rather be doing their own research.

The students of mine who I kept in touch with also reflected that they were surprised by the level of collaboration required. Arts students were often expected to discuss their ideas before the more formal seminars. Sciences students often had problem sets to work through together – helping and supporting one another to reach the right answers.

This did not go unnoticed. A study by the Cambridge Assessment exam board found that many students experience a major 'culture shock' between leaving school and starting their university study. As one academic reflected, 'we try our best to help them make the transition from being spoon-fed to being able to design a spoon and then feed themselves'[17].

The study included 633 academics, around half of whom believed that first-year students were not prepared for the demands of higher education. Many said that they had to compensate through extra remedial classes – both on study skills but also more independent skills.

The result of all of this is that each year, 1 in 12 freshers from a low-income background drops out of university[18].

So, what do universities want?

Universities are clear that they want a passion for the subject that is being studied. They are looking for the ability to read, absorb information, think creatively, and write persuasively. In the sciences, a high level of understanding is required, built on robust foundations. This includes a strong background in mathematics, and an understanding of its underlying principles.

But to thrive in the university environment, they also need study skills. The University of Cambridge emphasises four critical skills that are critical to the university experience[19]:

- Intellectual skills: These include thinking critically and analysing, synthesising different ideas together and also problem-solving.
- Communication skills: This of course includes producing formal written work of the highest quality. More than that, they also particularly highlight oral and non-verbal communication skills and active listening.
- Interpersonal skills: This is about working with others and also being able to motivate others – a reflection of a leadership role. They also cited flexibility and adaptability as key.
- Organisational skills: This includes the ability to work independently, to take initiative, for students to manage their own finances and time, and balancing different commitments – both academic and social.

These are skills that can be honed through the process of completing a degree, and the extracurricular activities and enterprise education support that a university setting makes available. But they are also the critical enablers of success along the way – and without them students are unlikely to be successful.

Different universities have similar frameworks. As another example, the University of Birmingham highlights similar skills to prospective undergraduate applicants to its law courses[20]. These are intellectual ability, communication skills, the ability to think and work under pressure, and study skills – including self-motivation, self-direction, and time management.

If any final evidence is needed that academic achievement is not enough, even prospective academics are warned by the University of Manchester that a good PhD alone will not be enough. Successful academics also need the ability to network, to manage their time, to be resilient, to present effectively and need leadership and management skills[21].

So, grades are not even enough here

We can move on then from the idea that if you are smart enough then grades and qualifications alone will get you to success. It turns out that even if you make it into university, some other skills remain critical.

It also turns out that if you don't have them you are much more likely to drop out – and suffer the twin setback of debt and a wasted opportunity.

(iii) Beyond the school gates: Entrepreneurship

A third route for my students beyond the school gates could well have been entrepreneurship – and for some of them it was. Often, this was focused on supporting a family business – running a shop or café, or trading.

The idea of entrepreneurship seems to be increasingly aspirational for young people. Research in 2013 suggested that 55% of young people aspired to set up their own businesses[22]. As someone who is now nearly a decade into building a social enterprise and has had more than a few conversations with people keen to 'take the plunge' who never do, I am rather sceptical about whether that statistic really means anything.

There is evidence of an uptick though. Research from Enterprise Nation looked at the number of company formations in 2006 versus 2013[23]. They found that over that period the number of founders under the age of 35 rose from 145,104 to 247,049. Particular areas of focus for these new businesses were business and management consultancy, IT, architecture, restaurants, mail-order retail and 'artistic and literary creation'.

The challenges of business failure

We all know that the rate of business failure is substantial. Indeed, the number of new businesses being created within this period was outnumbered by the number of businesses failing.

Now, there are perfectly good reasons why not every business makes it. Some come to a close for perfectly good reasons – that the original goal of the business has been achieved (this is particularly the case for social enterprises), that the owner retires or moves onto a new project, or that the business is bought up and integrated into another organisation.

However, there are also plenty of businesses which are cut down prematurely or never get off the starting blocks. It is currently fashionable to embrace business failure – not just as a sign of creative destruction, but as a sign of growth and learning on the part of the entrepreneur. I can certainly cite plenty of mistakes I have made and things that have gone wrong – and they have indeed been great learning opportunities, properly digested and rectified.

It is quite different to embrace the idea of 'failing fast' on small things, and the real impact of business failure. I think particularly of my students who would not have the same safety nets as their wealthier peers and for whom failure in their entrepreneurial endeavours would have been much more disastrous.

Now, sometimes external events take over. Indeed, 2008 while I was standing in front of my class is a clear example of broader market forces, and particularly credit markets, strangling firms. More often failure comes about through some of these regularly cited setbacks:

- Inability to manage cash flow or model the business effectively
- Lack of vision beyond making money or focus on building a great product
- Inadequate knowledge or understanding of business basics
- Weak leadership or the inability to manage a team
- Poor management of risk – whether through taking too much risk or the fear of failure
- Inability to persuade or communicate the value of the product

There is a lot there about the responsibility of the entrepreneur. Few businesses really fail because the idea is wrong, when the right approach would give the time and space to refine and develop the idea by managing risk effectively.

What an entrepreneur needs to be able to do

Entrepreneurial skills are commonly understood. In 2015, the Department of Business, Innovation & Skills (BIS) reviewed the evidence around entrepreneurial success and found that in order to be effective, entrepreneurs had to identify and capitalise on opportunities[24]. These opportunities might come from identifying customer needs, technical opportunities or market opportunities.

They broke down the skills that entrepreneurs need into four areas[25]:

(1) Idea identification and creation: Generating or envisaging ideas, recognising opportunities, and being able to acquire relevant knowledge to be able to capitalise on that idea.

(2) Capitalising on ideas: Awareness of the environment and factors conducive to exploiting the opportunity, along with then being able to garner the necessary resources, being able to convince others of the

value of the opportunity and being able to use networks to capitalise on these ideas.

(3) Traits and behaviours: Having self-belief, self-awareness and trust in their own judgements as well as the ability to manage risk and take responsibility and the ability to cope with difficulties.

(4) Managerial and leadership skills: The ability to manage others, to overcome institutional and other constraints, to turn an idea into a commercial opportunity and the ability to take decisions.

While some of these skills seem quite domain-specific, there are also skills that seem more generic – like the ability to evaluate decisions, being able to work with others, and being able to create and see through plans, for example.

Not a direction for the faint hearted

If there is any residual sense that entrepreneurship was an easy escape route for students who had struggled to engage at school then that sense is clearly wrong. The great entrepreneurial myths spun around individuals like Lord Sugar or Sir Richard Branson – for whom weak academic performance was no hindrance – underestimate the wider skills that needed to be built for them to succeed.

Bringing it all together

There is an important extra dimension to understanding the gap in essential skills too: that the gap is much bigger for students from disadvantaged backgrounds. Recent studies from the Sutton Trust and the Social Mobility Commission have shown that more developed soft skills are an advantage and hallmark of more financially advantaged students. The Sutton Trust evaluated the impact of the Assisted Places scheme of 1980-1997 that saw disadvantaged students assisted to attend private schools they would not have otherwise have been able to access. It showed that those individuals saw much of their subsequent advantage over their peers as deriving from the development of soft skills like self-reliance, curiosity, communication, leadership and teamwork[26]. At the same time, the Social Mobility Commission found that more financially advantaged parents put more emphasis on building soft skills[27].

So, it would seem that the nervousness we felt in the classroom was reflected in the wider world. There was a gap in the skills that students needed to learn effectively in school, those that employers are looking for, those that universities sought, and those that would allow our students to have more entrepreneurial futures.

While I have focused on these three routes beyond school, these areas have overlaps with many other forms of civic and democratic engagement, and volunteering as well.

Summary

This chapter has focused on exposing the gap in our education system.

As a teacher, I and many of my fellow teachers felt we were missing something fundamental – both for our students' development as children and young people and to enable them to learn effectively. We saw the dissonance in the classroom when we focus on grades without an appreciation of the wider skills our students need to be successful. Indeed, the focus on these grades drives teaching approaches that detract from students developing these skills.

This gap undermines our hopes for our students' futures beyond the classroom. When we look beyond the classroom we see that whether our students aspire to employment, university study or entrepreneurship next, they are lacking some essential skills.

Now we see the gap, we need to understand why we haven't managed to fill it so far.

Chapter 2:
What are we doing wrong?

We've seen pretty starkly that there are meaningful gaps in what our students are getting out of their experience in school.

The gap is something that we intuitively saw as teachers in our own classrooms. It opened up while we focused on establishing ourselves as successful teachers in the eyes of our schools. That meant ensuring order in the classroom, covering the curriculum content efficiently, doing a blend of activities to stretch our pedagogical muscles, and then seeing all of that come together in the ultimate judgement on our abilities – the students' grades.

The tragic irony was that, through an obsession with their final grades, we were short-circuiting the very skills that would be the foundation for richer, deeper learning and future success.

The gap between what is covered in the classroom and what our children and young people really need for future success in employment is most frequently vocalised by business organisations like the CBI. But it is equally short-changing to young people, particularly those from more disadvantaged backgrounds, when they look to further education, university or entrepreneurship as their next step in the world.

So, before going further, it's worth looking at what has been tried before to build the skills for successful learning in the classroom and the future.

And why these attempts have all failed to fill the gap.

Enterprise Education: A brief history

In school, enterprise education is meant to tackle this challenge. The explicit need to develop skills can be traced back to 1976 when then Prime Minister James Callaghan reflected that 'I am concerned on my journeys to find complaints from industry that new recruits from the schools sometimes do not have the basic tools to do the job that is required'[28].

Most relevant to us though is the last 15 years, so let's fast-forward to 2001, when the Labour government declared that one of its key economic and educational objectives was to secure 'a skilled productive workforce, able to act in an enterprising way'. This was followed in 2002 by the pithily titled Davies Review of Enterprise and the Economy in Education which called for greater support from businesses in order to build enterprise capability in all young people[29]. The Review recognised that most secondary schools were offering some sort of business engagement, but little on building students' skills beyond these experiences.

Without delay the government allocated funds, rising to £60 million a year by 2005-06, 'to give every child the chance to spend, on average, five days over their school career engaging in quality enterprising activities'. In 2003, the then Department for Education and Skills (DfES) made work-related learning statutory whilst saying that since this would be delivered across the curriculum it would not need additional curriculum space.

So far, so promising. Yet in 2005 when Ofsted came to evaluate enterprise learning for Key Stage 4 students (aged 14-16) they found some progress, but many shortcomings[30]. The government continued to invest, with direct grants to fund enterprise activity in secondary schools. It subsequently extended this to both primary and tertiary education. By 2010, though, an evaluation of enterprise education commissioned by the Labour government highlighted that confusion persisted and that evidence of impact was 'patchy'[31].

As we know, in 2010 the Coalition Government came into power, determined to shake up the education system. By 2011 dedicated government funding for enterprise education ended, with schools no longer directly responsible for enterprise provision. Work-related learning stopped being a statutory requirement.

This was a tough few years for those of us in the enterprise education field. One of the largest enterprise education providers, Enterprise UK, promptly broke up and others worked to shore up their organisations.

Most recently, there seems to have been a small renaissance in enterprise education with the publication in 2014 of Lord Young's report, Enterprise for All[32]. In it he highlighted the importance of an enterprising attitude, particularly to a new world where self-reliance and creativity were key. Some of the practical ideas to come out of the report included giving teachers more training and support to build the enterprise and employability skills of their students. He also suggested more teaching on how to set up a company or be a sole trader, as well as creating an Enterprise Passport to better record what students had achieved.

This was backed by the launch of the Careers and Enterprise Company in 2015 with a remit to support careers and enterprise provision in secondary schools and colleges in England.

Personal Learning and Thinking Skills (PLTS)

Enterprise education is not the only attempt to try to prepare our children and young people for the rest of their lives.

One of the more ambitious visions of the last couple of decades was the Tomlinson Review of 14-19 education[33]. It was the result of two years of hard work, including drawing together a consensus in education for a major shift away from existing GCSE and A level provision. In his opening remarks, Mike Tomlinson argued that 'too many young people leave education lacking basic and personal skills' and that 'employers [are] having to spend large sums of money to teach the "basics"'. This is certainly a step towards recognition of the challenge we've identified.

He went on to highlight that all 14-19 learning should include the development of a range of common knowledge, skills and attributes such as personal awareness, problem-solving, creativity, team-working and moral and ethical awareness.

Some of these ideas were expected to be realised through the introduction of new Diplomas, which were launched in 2008. Of particular interest were the Personal Learning and Thinking Skills (PLTS), which were a core component of them. The Diplomas themselves were offered at different levels for students aged 14-19. They combined a broad knowledge about a particular area alongside functional maths, English and the PLTS framework. The Diplomas included 'Construction and the Built Environment', 'Engineering', and 'Creative and Media'.

In an innovative qualification, the PLTS framework still stood out. The framework combined six elements with the goal of ensuring that students became independent enquirers, team workers, effective participants, self-managers, reflective learners and creative thinkers. There is a lot that resonates here with the challenge that we discussed earlier.

Just to sketch out one example, 'team workers' included the ability to collaborate with others to work towards common goals. Students should also be able to reach agreements, managing discussions to achieve results, and adapt their behaviour to suit different roles and situations.

As another example, the 'self-management' element encouraged students to seek out challenges or new responsibilities and show flexibility when priorities change. It also encouraged perseverance and commitment towards achieving goals.

There is much to appreciate in this framework. At the time they were described as 'generic skills that are essential to life, learning and work'. They still live on in several guises – for example alongside some apprenticeships – but sadly didn't make it into mainstream schooling as the Diploma programme unwound. In 2010, the new Coalition government announced that the development of the final three Diplomas which would have started in September 2011 would be stopped and that students would no longer be entitled to study a Diploma.

Social and Emotional Aspects of Learning (SEAL)

Another approach which intuitively showed some promise was SEAL – that is, the Social and Emotional Aspects of Learning. The first pilots of SEAL took place in 2004-06, and it was promoted more widely to schools thereafter.

I remember this being introduced while I was teaching as the first item of an INSET day at the start of term. The whole school, bleary from the first day back gathered together in the hall as one of the senior staff introduced the concept and what it meant.

The goals of the approach were to underpin effective learning, positive behaviour, regular attendance, staff effectiveness and the emotional health and well-being of all who learn and work in schools. These are promising ideals, and seem to chime with the gap we have already highlighted.

The initiative aimed to ensure that children from the age of 3 through to 16 developed some critical personal and social skills: self-awareness, managing of feelings, motivation, empathy and social skills.

The idea was partly that these skills would be taught at primary school through an explicit curriculum. However, there was a sense too that a wider approach would be needed. Some ideas shared in the SEAL Community website[34] include school councils, buddying and peer mediation schemes, critical skills and values training for staff, and worry boxes.

At secondary school, the SEAL agenda would be delivered at a whole-school level, through the then-catchy 'quality first' approach to teaching and whole-school frameworks. It would be supplemented by small-group intervention for children needing extra support, and their families. Where necessary, individual interventions might also happen.

This was no small initiative – by the time it was evaluated in 2010 it was reported as being implemented in around 90% of primary schools and 70% of secondary schools.

Unfortunately, at secondary level the evaluation was lacklustre: the researchers found that SEAL did not have any significant impact on the students' social and emotional skills, general mental health or address pro-social behaviour or behavioural problems[35].

When looking at school-level outcome data the analyses indicated that SEAL failed to have a positive impact. School climate scores showed a mixed picture – pupils' trust and respect for teachers, liking for school, and feelings of classroom and school supportiveness actually fell during the implementation of SEAL. There was a more positive picture for students' feelings of autonomy and influence as well as specific improvements in behaviour, interpersonal skills, and relationships.

My own experience makes these results unsurprising: after it was introduced to us in that morning INSET session it was literally never mentioned again.

Character education

The new Coalition government appointed Michael Gove as Secretary of State at the Department for Education, as it was austerely renamed. A plethora of decisions emerged in rapid succession: the scrapping of the national strategies including SEAL, enterprise education requirements and the unwinding of Diploma qualifications.

Energies were actively refocused on a back-to-basics curriculum, promising more rigour and emphasising traditional subjects. Newer qualifications were pared back, and focus was placed anew on GCSEs and A levels which were reviewed and made more challenging and knowledge-based. Coursework was reduced. Schools focused more on GCSE outcomes, including new 'Progress Eight' measures and the English Baccalaureate.

Structures changed too with the rapid scaling of the academies programme and its growth at the primary school level. Free Schools, which could be launched by any approved group, started to emerge and other specialist types of school and college including Studio Schools and University Technical Colleges grew.

The replacement of Michael Gove by Nicky Morgan in July 2014 saw a slight rebalancing away from just the academic results to addressing some of the gap that we've seen.

The launch of the Careers & Enterprise Company we have already mentioned. Alongside it, the government announced its ambition that the UK should be a world leader in 'character education'. Fuelling this new approach was a character education fund and character education awards.

The awards held in February 2015 gave 27 schools and organisations £15,000 each in recognition of building key traits in students. It all sounded very exciting. Nicky Morgan recognised that 'teaching character not only benefits children at school – it also plays a vital role in ensuring young people leave school prepared for life in modern Britain'[36]. She explicitly highlighted the duality of not just supporting academic success but also improving job prospects.

Even the CBI, who we saw earlier can be relied on to worry about the skills gap, declared, 'the awards represent a step towards achieving what the CBI and businesses have long been calling for: an education system that develops young people who are rigorous, rounded and grounded – this means a focus not only on knowledge and skills, but also on the attitudes, characteristics and behaviours that will set them up for success outside the school gates'.

The schools and organisations cited in the press release were working on an inspiring array of personal characteristics: camaraderie, loyalty, discipline, respect, aspiration, responsibility, determination, friendship, passion, excellence, independence, self-management, honesty, kindness, perseverance, professionalism, grit, spark, eloquence, expertise and craftsmanship. That's before we mention resilience, resourcefulness, reciprocity, teamwork, effective communication, creativity, innovation, positivity, initiative, drive, confidence, ambition, consideration, respect, endeavour, and courage. And who would want to overlook tolerance, self-regulation, empathy, honourable purpose or compassion. Or achievement, self-awareness, and integrity.

These are all excellent things to be building and showcasing. The main approaches the award winners were taking included: 'passports' to capture experiences, activities and reflections; extracurricular activities; explicit recognition of these virtues in school life; and mentoring.

Could this fill the gap? These are all positive examples but they lacked hard evidence. Even prize-winning schools and supporting organisations only ever mentioned anecdotal observations of improved further outcomes. They also lacked any clear mechanism for spreading good practice to the other 24,000 schools in the country.

More fundamentally, I would argue that character is about the choices we make – not the abilities we have to do things. Character matters, but it alone cannot fill the gap.

Beyond the school gates

Finally, we should note that filling the gap need not just be the responsibility of schools. Indeed, there have been initiatives from universities, employers and other organisations too.

There are some great extracurricular programmes out there: The Duke of Edinburgh Awards scheme, for example, is much emulated – including through the new National Citizens Service programme. Organisations like Young Enterprise, Career Ready or Business in the Community (BITC) all have programmes that explicitly support the development of essential skills, albeit that they might be variously called life skills, enterprise skills or employability skills.

Others, including British Exploring or World Challenge, go even further to build skills through taking students on expeditions to far-flung parts of the world and presenting them with immersive challenges.

Many other extracurricular activities also highlight the positive effect that the main activity might have on what we call essential skills. This includes sports, drama, music, dance, or chess. In case you think I'm exaggerating, turn to the example of the government funding rugby players to come into school to build character amongst school children[37]. Or the government's NCS website which trumpets the chance to 'develop life skills like confidence, leadership and communication to boost your CV or UCAS personal statement'[38].

Other organisations like the Prince's Trust work explicitly to build enterprise and what they term life skills, as well as confidence. They particularly target their work at those young people who might be vulnerable, or who have already dropped out of the formal education system.

Employers already do a lot too. The latest CBI survey showed that four out of five respondents have at least some links with schools or colleges. Not only that, but there was positive momentum behind doing more – that over half of those already involved were looking to do more whereas just 6% were cutting back.

This is borne out by our experience at Enabling Enterprise – I have been amazed time and again by the level of enthusiasm shown by our employer partners. It is remarkably straightforward to engage employers with the importance of working with our students, to persuade them to host those students in their offices and to help build their skills and understanding of the wider world.

Most employers, the CBI survey highlights, primarily focus on work experience placements and careers advice and talks. These alone unfortunately, do not tackle the development of skills which take repeated development and practice – as will be explored further later on. But there is a willingness and opportunities to do more.

The problem remains

The overwhelming view of schools, employers and universities is that all of these efforts have not added up to any systemic solution to the gap we see.

This problem seems to be particularly acute for children and young people from more disadvantaged backgrounds. Studies from the Sutton Trust and the Commission for Social Mobility and Child Poverty have highlighted that independent schools and wealthier parents put a lot more emphasis on building their children's soft skills[39]. This was also the conclusion of an independent research report commissioned by Enabling Enterprise and conducted by LKMco which found that 'there is a sizeable body of evidence showing poorer children and young people tend to demonstrate lower levels of aptitude in skills enterprise education seeks to develop, such as communication, confidence and pro-social behaviour when they enter school. If unaddressed these gaps remain evident throughout schooling'[40].

The challenge is not just that students from poorer backgrounds tend to have fewer opportunities to develop these skills than their peers. It is that even if they overcome the odds to succeed academically, the absence of these skills means that they still earn less than their wealthier peers, and do not achieve as highly in their future careers[41].

To really understand the gap, we have to look at two critical questions:

- How should we define the skills we want to focus on, and the language we use around them?
- How should we differentiate between skills, knowledge and virtues?

Skills: What's in a name?

There are few areas of education where it seems so difficult to pin down exactly what we mean as it is with these skills. This is not just an intellectual puzzle, but a real problem.

After ten years of work in this arena, just some of the terms that I have seen used interchangeably are:

- Life Skills
- Soft Skills
- Essential Skills
- Entrepreneurial Skills
- Employability Skills
- 21st century Skills
- Achievement Virtues

Now, that is before we even consider the nuanced definitions and components that actually lie beneath these.

To illustrate, if we just take employability skills, the UKCES's 2009 report identified that there were dozens of working definitions of employability skills and explored 20 in depth[42]. Then throw in the character strengths that the Department for Education highlights as just some of the things that are worth building (of which there are 14 in their official definition, and a lot more cited in the award winners already highlighted). Then throw in study skills or PLTS or SEAL. Then throw in entrepreneurial attributes, and the enterprise education curriculum.

If this was a literal gap then you would imagine that the piling up of this lot would fill it. Sadly, words and frameworks are not the same as students actually being able to do stuff – like thrive in school, higher education, employment or entrepreneurship.

At an initial glance they all seem to have a similar and apparently complementary blend of virtues, skills, competencies and knowledge.

How is a teacher, school leader or parent to choose?

When is a skill not a skill?

The first critical point is that it is not harmless to blend character virtues, knowledge or understanding, and skills together. Although the language is often used interchangeably, these are distinctly different things, with different implications for how we develop them in children and young people.

(a) Character virtues

Virtues reflect attitudes and patterns of behaviours and are often linked to morality. For example, the Catholic Church identifies seven virtues in its doctrines – prudence, temperance, justice, courage, faith, hope and love or charity. The contrast in this case is with the seven deadly sins of hubris, greed, lust, envy, gluttony, anger and sloth.

There is a long history of seeing the development of virtues as a central part of education before a greater focus on grades rebalanced classroom learning more resolutely towards the acquisition of knowledge.

The Jubilee Centre for Character and Virtues at the University of Birmingham has done a lot of work in this area. They highlight that character can be tangible and can support human flourishing – that is, having both happiness and the achievement of potential[43].

They broadly split virtues into three areas. The first is Civic Character Virtues which they define as 'character virtues and skills that are necessary for engaged and responsible citizenship' including service, citizenship and volunteering. The second is Moral Character Virtues, defined as 'those character habits that enable us to respond well to stations in area of experience'. Some of the examples they share include courage, self-discipline, compassion, gratitude, justice, humility and honesty. The third and final strand are what they call 'performance virtues'. I am slightly less convinced these are really virtues and are actually skills or capabilities – for example, leadership and teamwork. Others include perseverance, grit and determination.

Critically, they emphasise that character is generally 'caught' as much as taught and so the main focus should be on the school culture and ethos. Practical steps to do this include affirming a commitment to strengthening students' character in its mission statement. They recommend selecting a small number of character virtues everywhere: 'on the playing fields, in classrooms, corridors, interactions between teachers and students, in assemblies, posters, headteacher messages and communications, staff training, and in relations with parents'[44].

The Jubilee Centre's model school puts a particular emphasis on extracurricular opportunities as the way to build character. As we saw when we looked at the DfE's Character Awards, the award-winning schools and organisations did not have a fixed character curriculum with taught content, but rather consistently reinforced key themes and ideals.

(b) Knowledge

Knowledge is the ability to recall, understand and explain. At the most basic level, this might mean things like times tables, historical chronologies, rock classifications, the names of scientific equipment or phonics sounds. At a more complex level it might mean knowing the causes of the First World War, the conjugations of verbs, or chemical equations.

When we talk about enterprise education, financial literacy has often been included as one aspect. Financial literacy might include how to set up a bank account, manage credit cards or get a mortgage. Economic understanding and consumer awareness also sometimes feature, as does some entrepreneurial knowledge like how to write a business plan or the principles of marketing.

Additionally, if we conflate enterprise and careers education, which is often referred to as Information, Advice and Guidance (IAG) we include a lot of knowledge about different industries and career routes. Plus practical knowledge like how a CV or covering letter is structured.

We are most comfortable with teaching knowledge – and that is what our school system has increasingly focused on – not least because it seems reassuringly straightforward to test knowledge.

We can build basic knowledge through didactic instruction, drilling and memorisation, or research and discovery. We can reinforce it through practice or application. We can further manipulate, reconcile or expand that knowledge through analysis and evaluation.

When teaching is focused on knowledge retention, it affects the activities that teachers select. These activities often aid students in committing to memory and reinforcing understanding.

(c) Skills

Competences or skills are the ability to do something – to successfully enact a repeatable process. Skills are an incredibly diverse bunch – from being able to safely chop a piece of wood, to successfully navigating a car into a parking space, or being able to re-wire a house. There are specific skills to being a brain surgeon, an airline pilot, a plumber, a cleaner, a receptionist or a coder.

Professor Bill Lucas at the University of Winchester makes the important point that we really only know if a skill is acquired when something is done[45]. Skills are often backed by theory but are primarily about being able to *do* – not just knowing how one could do something. Therefore, the real test is when faced with a scenario to be able to act effectively.

Skills are primarily taught through this combination of modelling, theory, application, reflection and continued practice. The relative emphasis on these elements varies, and copying and seeing a skill modelled is often very important too. However, just mimicking tends to produce a very shallow skill that cannot be transferred to different settings.

As just one example, I had a friend who lived on a busy street and had mastered a speedy parallel park – essential on a busy road where parking spaces were rare. Impressed, I asked how she did it – only to find out that she had been shown that if she followed a certain number of right and left turns of the wheel and edged back using the passenger pillar as a guide in that car she would always be fine. When she got a new car she had to start parking on a different street.

Skills can therefore vary considerably by the depth of understanding, how easily they can be mimicked and how transferable they are. Essentially though, they are all about *doing*.

So what are we talking about then?

If we go back to some of the different elements that get lumped in together, we see that we can come a long way by sifting them according to whether they are character virtues, knowledge and understanding, or skills.

Character virtues – **how we make choices**	• Honesty	• Determination	• Resilience
	• Courage	• Kindness	• Willingness to learn
	• Risk-taking	• Enthusiasm	• Passion
Knowledge and **understanding –** **what informs us**	• Financial Literacy	• Business Understanding	• Consumer awareness
	• CV Writing	• Economics	
Skills – **what we can do**	• Leadership	• Teamwork	• Time management
	• Customer service	• Presenting	• Delegation
	• Problem-solving	• Creativity	• Goal-setting

When we break these down, it becomes clear that throwing so many different elements into the mix is actively unhelpful, because each of these elements requires a different approach to its development.

As we've seen, virtues can be modelled but tend to be 'caught' as much as taught by being identified and reinforced through action. They affect the choices that individuals make. On the other hand, knowledge is taught through the acquisition, retention and recollection of facts, theories and intellectual frameworks. Skills are built through a combination of knowledge and modelling and are then developed through application and practice.

I am not seeking to put these in any sort of hierarchy.

But what is clear is that if we try to cover all three simultaneously, we end up with a bodge. This does not help teachers.

Instead, we should be building skills when this is the focus, and we should be building knowledge when this is the focus, with character and virtues being reinforced as a constant background track.

[handwritten: Different Set of words]

This is not the same as saying that understanding, behaviours and essential skills are never *deployed* together. They are – but to presume that their deployment together means that they should be taught together is to confuse the important work of practice with the game itself.

We have seen that the gap is about the students' ability to *do* – not what they know, or their character *per se*. So we can move on; let us now isolate skills.

Picking the skills

There are an endless number of skills that we might care about, but I am indebted to the UKCES who in 2009 helpfully highlighted several broad areas of skills:

- Communication
- Literacy ⟶
- Presentation
- Numeracy ⟶
- IT ⟶
- Reliability, responsibility
- Punctuality
- Positive Attitude
- Adaptability
- Self-management
- Work safely
- Problem-solving
- Creativity
- Team working
- Interpersonal skills

I am going to put literacy, numeracy and IT to one side as these are already taught as explicit key skills in school. There are a couple of skills which sound more specific to a particular workplace – such as working safely – which would be quite different in an operating theatre compared to a construction site.

If we focus now on the remaining skills, we can identify four main themes:

- Interpersonal skills: Working with others as a leader, team player, or a provider to customers

[handwritten: Are these clusters of the UKCES skills?]

- Communication skills: Including being able to interact with others and present
- Creative problem-solving: Being creative, innovative and solving problems
- Self-management: Taking responsibility, achieving goals, being adaptable, being resilient and demonstrating a positive attitude

We can now cross-check this against the other relevant frameworks including entrepreneurial skills, 21st century skills and study skills. We find that there is a surprisingly good fit.

The Cambridge University model of study skills added in students managing their own finances and time, and balancing academic and social commitments, but these are an extension of those same self-management skills, and having a solid knowledge of finance.

There are plenty of models of so-called '21st century skills', but a frequently used one refers to Collaboration, Creativity, Communication and Critical Thinking. Once again, these are all elements that are covered in the definition above but with self-management to bind them together.

This comes with a clear health warning though: Some of these skill sets, particularly 21st century skills, have become synonymous with an 'embedded skills' approach which can be presented as being an alternative to focusing teaching time on building knowledge. The fact that I think these are good skills to have does not presume that I agree with that method of teaching them – a point I will come back to later on.

Ultimately, we have to choose which skills to work on.

I'll talk a bit more about the benefits of simplicity later on, but there is no super-science to the eight we have chosen at Enabling Enterprise. We have found that most of the areas above have two key elements:

- **Interpersonal skills** have both an element of working with others as peers, and in a leadership position – so we have split them into *Working in a team* and *Leading others*.
- **Communication** is both giving and receiving, so we've split this into *Presenting* and *Listening & Understanding*.
- **Creative problem-solving** is really about two different situations – where there is a pre-existing problem to be solved which we've termed *Problem-Solving*, and where the solution is more open which we've termed *Creativity*.

- **Self-management** can mean lots of different things but the main elements are firstly to set clear goals and plans, which we call *Aiming High*, and then having strategies to stick at those to see them through to completion – which we've termed *Staying Positive*.

So, why call them essential skills?

The final question is what to call them? Now, it was tempting to come up with a completely new name – but then I realised I would just be adding to the existing chaos.

'Study skills' was out because the skills are important for life beyond academic study too. 'Employability skills' was out because that did not sufficiently recognise that these same skills are essential for children from their earliest years – and not just because of employability. '21st century skills' seemed timely but I appreciate the argument that these skills pre-exist the 21st century – and that history matters. That term also comes with a lot of pedagogical and ideological baggage. 'Entrepreneurial skills' would logically be skills for entrepreneurship – and that continues to be a niche pursuit.

At Enabling Enterprise, it will be unsurprising to hear, we originally used the language of 'enterprise skills'. The challenge that we have found is that enterprise also carries a lot of baggage. It is often seen as being skills to work in a business, or just seen through the lens of enterprise education. We'll see later on that enterprise education can still play an important role here, but there are plenty of organisations who contribute to, or draw off, these skills who would never see themselves as part of that sector. Because we use this language, in the later parts of this book we will sometimes refer to enterprise lessons – you can rest assured that these are focused on the same skills we are talking about.

Ultimately, we now think about 'essential skills for education, enterprise and employment'. This shortens neatly to 'essential skills'. For us, this captures the diverse usefulness of the skills and also their critical nature – as we saw in Chapter 1. Helpfully, the Education Endowment Foundation now use this language too. It's not perfect, but we can all work with it.

Summary

We've come a long way in this chapter. We set out with the conviction that there was a gap in the capabilities of our students that was hindering their ability to thrive in the classroom and in whatever they wanted to do in the future.

We asked the same question that I asked as a teacher of 15- and 16-year-olds – 'why has no one ever taught them this stuff?' What are we, collectively as an education system, doing wrong?

It's important to recognise that many attempts have been made to prepare our young people for the rest of their lives. In a whistle-stop tour we considered some of these: the long vintage of enterprise education, the idea of building personal learning and thinking skills into the 14-19 curriculum, wider roll-out of social and emotional aspects of learning (SEAL) at a similar time. Most recently, the character education agenda offered another chance to fill the gap.

The problem, of course, is that the gap has persisted as each of these approaches has been brought forward and then receded into the background again.

It's a bold move to spend so long worrying about definitions, and I certainly didn't spend so long worrying about them when I set up Enabling Enterprise. The last seven years have taught me that definitions really matter if we want to get stuff done. They matter because when trying to build students' capabilities to thrive we often talk about an apparently interchangeable set of knowledge and understanding, character virtues, and skills.

But each is distinctly different and is learnt and taught quite differently. By separating them out, we can use an appropriate teaching approach to each element.

We then refocused on skills – not because I'm against knowledge or because I think character is irrelevant but because the gap that we have seen universities, employers and teachers fretting about is their students' ability to *do* things.

We saw that there are four broad skills beyond literacy, numeracy and IT that are consistently called for to underpin students' success: interpersonal skills, communication skills, self-management skills, and problem-solving skills.

Now it's time to look at each of these skills in more detail to work out why they really matter and how they can best be built.

Part 2:
Reimagining Essential Skills

That there is a gap is incontestable. We see it as teachers in our classrooms. We see it as employers or as educators. We see it when young entrepreneurs falter. We sometimes see it as parents.

It is clear that academic achievement is necessary but insufficient. There are a set of skills, aside from knowledge and character strengths, that underpin the success of our children and young people – and indeed, all of us.

We have seen that efforts to fill the gap to date have been inadequate for the task. We have jumbled the skills, put them into artificial silos and then given them a dizzying array of different names.

But, as we have seen in the last chapter, there are four clear strands that seem to come up time and again: interpersonal skills, communication skills, creative problem-solving skills, and self-management skills. Now we will break these four strands down into eight teachable skills:

- Communication Skills: Listening and Presenting
- Interpersonal Skills: Teamwork and Leadership
- Self-Management Skills: Aiming High and Staying Positive
- Creativity and Problem-Solving

How are each of these skills built and what have we been doing wrong? In looking closer, we will find that they often have a rich pedagogical history and a promising, often inter-disciplinary evidence base behind them. From the Ancient Greeks to cutting-edge business theory we have a fascinating journey ahead of us.

But first, we pick up the story in my classroom a decade ago.

My classroom

My class were already 15 or 16 years old, and had barely a year before they were going to be leaving their compulsory time in school, and would have to face the wider world.

I wanted them to build skills to support their transition into sixth form, college or employment. I also wanted them to have some way of being able to make informed choices about their futures.

Into the world

My initial idea was to take them into the working world – to see what they could achieve, and the skills they would need to get there. This is where being a teacher in central London was a real boon – just a 25-minute bus ride away from the shining City of London. In less than half an hour we went from one of the most deprived areas of the country to one of the wealthiest.

I was thrilled when two City businesses – an investment bank and a law firm – were bold enough to welcome my students in. And I was still naïve enough not to be put off by the idea of trooping my gaggle of teenagers through the middle of the capital.

My students' responses were remarkable: any swaggers replaced with shyness in this completely unfamiliar situation. Whilst they were unnervingly quiet they were also engaged – leaning forwards as they were introduced to employees from those respective companies. The questions from the students invariably started with demanding to know how much everyone was paid but then became more nuanced – had they been to university, what grades had they needed, what did they want to do next? They asked about the day-to-day – what did they actually do on the computer, did it matter if they were late, how long were the days, what did they enjoy about their jobs, and what did they like the least? They tried to get their heads around their journeys to where they were today.

I knew my students well enough by this point though to know that they would not maintain this barrage of questioning indefinitely. I also wanted them to get something tangible out of the trips to be able to talk about in the future too – so I created a couple of games to get them working with the employee volunteers. It was nothing particularly sophisticated – just creating a business pitch or a simple construction challenge.

If they had been surprising on that first trip, the buzz on the bus home was staggering. And it lasted for at least two lessons. This was my first insight – that inspiration matters. I drew on that trip in the following couple of weeks from the theoretical ('What did David say were some of the challenges about being a manager?') to the applied ('Do you think that Lauren pokes her employees in the ribs when she's a bit bored?') to the threatening ('I can assure you now that no one, you included Billy, will be visiting a business again unless you can show business behaviours in my classroom'). But it also became clear that this alone could not fill the gap for my students.

Focusing on building skills

So, I got the students setting up and running their own small businesses, drawing inspiration from a course put together by the then Network for Teaching Entrepreneurship. As soon as we started, it became obvious that this was going to be a slow-motion car crash without a little more scaffolding. Students who were used to using their peers as distractions or light entertainment were not going to immediately transition to being collaborative colleagues.

While this should have been entirely predictable, it was confirmed in the next lesson when my first group fragmented – their company had lasted approximately 80 minutes.

It was becoming clear that I could neither just inspire the students into having better skills nor simply give them a project that needed the skills and hope they would discover them along the way. To really make progress, I would have to actually teach the skills directly.

That would only be possible by really thinking about exactly what skills they needed and breaking them down. Each lesson worked on building one of the eight essential skills in a small chunk, and then giving the students the space to apply that to their businesses. For example, in one session I introduced mind-mapping and word association as an approach for students to generate ideas before applying it to creating marketing ideas. Or in another, I introduced techniques for managing conflict by identifying opportunities for compromise before setting them the challenge of drawing up their business's organisational structure.

We started to make some progress: my students picked things up quickly. There were hiccups but they all managed to launch their businesses, they all made sales, and all of them were able to give a presentation at the end of the year about their businesses and what they had learnt.

Beyond my students

So far, this probably all sounds pleasant enough but hardly revolutionary. Having developed this programme for my students, by September 2008 I was happy to share it with other teachers in other schools. I didn't want to be *that* teacher who had developed some good resources but refused to share them with colleagues.

What we had then was a promising but embryonic programme – with the twist that it was being used not just by business studies teachers like myself, but also maths teachers, English teachers, science teachers and even a couple of French teachers.

A difficult decision, but not that difficult

In June 2009, I felt that there was enough in the Enabling Enterprise concept to turn it into something that could be used more widely. The motivation was two-fold. Firstly, my class had finished their course – not only had they visibly built their skills but when I got their results over half received a Distinction in their qualification, massively exceeding the school's and their own expectations and reinforcing my belief that there was something in what we were doing. That was further encouraged by what was going on in other schools – and the feedback that I was getting from teachers who were seeing a similar pick-up in their students' engagement and broader development.

It was a difficult decision – I loved teaching and I knew I would miss the students.

But I was also increasingly concerned that there was a fundamental gap between the expectations we had as a school system and what our students actually needed. As a teacher, I was broadly left alone so long as I fulfilled some basic requirements. Firstly, to ensure that students remained in the classroom, broadly stuck to school policies and no one got hurt. Secondly, to be up to date with the pattern of evaluating students – ensuring that the array of trackers, databases and reporting were up to date and compliant. Thirdly, and this was really only as a new teacher, was to deliver solidly good lessons when I was being observed, and to maintain notes in my planner for future lessons. And finally, to be achieving the target grades for my students.

Where was the preparation for the rest of their lives? Where was the development of the fundamental learning ability under the grades? Where was the systemic motivation to do anything that would positively support achievement beyond students' grades?

In the end it was not too difficult a decision.

Introducing our eight essential skills

Enabling Enterprise launched with an ambitious mission: to ensure that one day, all students build the essential skills, experiences of work and aspirations to succeed. The first thing to do was to make that tangible by pinning down exactly what we wanted to achieve.

The eight essential skills are what we collectively believe, borne out by the evidence, every student needs to be successful throughout education and in whatever they want to do in the future. Together they represent the missing piece.

In approaching how we think about these skills, we have aimed to minimise abstraction. That means avoiding broad attributes which might combine the skill with a personality trait, like confidence, sociability or resilience. Instead, we focus solely on the skill itself – an important distinction that we will revisit later through the work of the Brookings Institute[46].

Before we can make real progress, we have to really understand each of our eight skills. They might seem intuitively familiar but that can be deceptive. Over the coming chapters, we discover how the skills affect learning in the classroom and success beyond it, how they are built, and the evidence for their teachability and impact.

Chapter 3:
Communication Skills

Schools already invest considerably in building the literacy of their students – that is their ability to read and write. As such, let's leave that to one side and instead focus on oral communication, which is now sometimes referred to as 'oracy'.

There are two sides to such communication:

- *Listening:* the receiving, retaining and processing of information or ideas.
- *Presenting:* the oral transmission of information or ideas.

Of course, to listen or present effectively we have to also be doing a little of the other: transmitting when we are listening to show engagement and understanding (or not), and equally when we present we also need to be receiving some feedback in terms of our audience's reaction.

Both of these are worth exploring in depth.

(1) Listening

Listening is the first part of communicating – and the first essential skill to underpin everything else. This is how students move beyond passively hearing to become engaged learners.

It may seem simple – or such a fundamental skill that it should be developed in the home environment. But we know that it is often limited. And this undermines effective learning in school and is one of the skills that is always called for by employers.

The good news is that listening skills can be built effectively – throughout a child's time in school.

In the classroom

As teachers we often worry about whether our students are really taking in what's going on – I certainly did in my classroom.

Some people worry that teaching has become too didactic – that students are only there to absorb information. If this was the case, those same people would have twice the cause for concern because there was evidence that little of that information was actually being absorbed. I remember being disheartened when my Year 10 and 11 students were unable to take notes or to capture their own reflections.

Students who are unable to listen effectively will simply not get the full value out of being in the classroom. They may build and 'bake in' bad habits – like only listening to what they have decided is relevant to them. Or they may be easily distracted by thinking about their response, or even just a witty aside to a classmate. Or they might not be taking in information because they have already made assumptions, based on a pre-conceived view of the speaker.

This is reflected in the Skills Builder assessments that Enabling Enterprise teachers conduct of their students before they start their programme with us. They found that in Year 3, when the students are 7 or 8 years old, only 17% were able to generally listen in to class discussion and share an opinion when called upon. Meanwhile, secondary school teachers reported that only 23% of their new students were able to analyse how a speaker used language and gesture to engage an audience.

There is an implicit assumption that students can listen effectively in order to access what is going on in the classroom. But while aspects of listening are assessed in subjects like modern foreign languages or music, it is rarely taught explicitly as a skill.

It seems fundamental that if we are going to spend so much time teaching, we should first make the investment in building students' capacity to listen and understand. That is, to be engaged listeners and have the processes to ensure their own comprehension.

Beyond the classroom

It is not just in the classroom where listening matters of course. At college or university, a greater emphasis on lectures means that students need the tools to actively engage with what is being communicated to them.

This is even more the case in a work environment. Many jobs require the quick comprehension of instructions from a manager who might not be an effective teacher or have the patience to model how to do something repeatedly. Communication, specifically listening, has been highlighted for decades as one of the most important skills needed for the workplace; it is sought by employers in entry-level employees but also in those being promoted[47]. That's why almost every definition of employability skills reviewed by the UK Commission for Employment and Skills (UKCES) included oral communication.

Sadly however, it is also one of the skills most often reported lacking in new graduates looking to join the workforce. And for anyone who thinks that being a good talker will make up for being a good listener in the workplace, the evidence is not in their favour. The overwhelming message from business is that for effective sales, negotiation or management, being able to listen, digest, and respond to what is being said is more important than speaking[48].

Finally, there are strong arguments that being able to listen effectively is essential for being an active participant in society. For example, Deakin Crick *et al* suggest that skills including critically and thoughtfully listening to the ideas of others are fundamental in teaching young people to be active citizens[49]. In a political climate when the truth is not always clear, young people will benefit from being able to deconstruct and truly analyse and understand what they are hearing.

How it is built

It might seem an obvious cliché, but listening is not the same as hearing. Listening must be a more engaged process – and is sometimes referred to as 'active listening' as opposed to the passive.

We work with the youngest students to build their ability to hear, to recall and then to follow simple instructions. As they develop, they should be able to process and recall stories or more complex narratives. At this early stage, this means managing distractions (like fidgeting or seeing something else going on) and being patient enough to wait for their chance to speak.

Towards the age of 8 or 9, most students should become more critical analysts of what they have heard. They move beyond just being able to re-state a narrative, and instead are able to seek deeper meaning in the way that the information has been conveyed – including the speaker's use of language.

Alongside this, they will also be developing strategies for capturing more of what they hear – for example, making simple notes, or drawing out critical points, assertions and ideas. This is an essential step towards pulling out the meaning from the words and phrases that they are hearing.

As they transition towards secondary school, they become much more critical observers of a speaker. They start to identify how they are being drawn in as a listener, and to understand the underlying motivations of the speaker so they can critically evaluate what they are hearing. They become more able to hear two different perspectives, elicit their main ideas and adjudicate between them.

They are continuing to build their listening and understanding strategies too. These strategies will include note-taking and forming further questions. They should also be demonstrating that they are listening – for example, by showing positive body language like leaning in or nodding – and realise that their responses are a key part of this communication.

Ultimately, the highest achievers in this skill will be able to critically evaluate a speaker, including their language, omissions and ambiguity, and use different approaches to actively listen over an extended period and in different contexts.

Teachability and impact

When it comes to listening, we can see there is a set of strategies and practice that underpins listening effectively. Students need the ability to take notes, to structure how they gather their thoughts, and to structure their ideas. They need to understand concepts of bias, gesture, and emphasis.

Of course, when applied, listening skills will be significantly enhanced by a solid understanding of the context and content. We know that this is a pre-requisite for comprehension in reading, and it is the same for listening. But particularly beyond school the transfer of information is less structured into lessons and subject areas – and so school leavers will need to be able to navigate without such a clear framework to fit this new information into.

(2) Presenting

The complement to listening well is presenting or speaking well. Where listening is about receiving information, we define presenting as the transmission of information or ideas. That doesn't just mean a formal presentation but can include conversation or negotiation, particularly when the students are younger. Indeed, we often talk about this as 'sharing ideas' for the youngest students.

This side of communication is considered more often than listening, but of course the two are interdependent. Building students' ability to articulate their ideas is critical for their learning and to deepen their own understanding – as the Education Endowment Foundation make clear. The demand from employers is also incontestable.

By breaking this skill down into chunks, it is clear that progress can be made – with a significant positive impact for the students.

In the classroom

Enabling Enterprise teachers often report that their students struggle to share their ideas effectively – and as a result can be reluctant to offer any additional thoughts in class conversation. In my classroom, where students did offer ideas, these were rarely more than clichés which could not stand up to any further questioning. I quickly realised that whatever question I asked of one of the more enthusiastic business studies students, it was always answered by some variation of 'so they can make more money'.

If we want students to reach higher-order thinking, they need both a depth of knowledge *and* the skills to be able to express their own ideas too. That can be written, and generally is in school. But it is also essential to be able to express their ideas orally and that is often overlooked.

This is a point that School 21, an innovative 4-19 school in East London, think is critical. In their school, they have introduced 'oracy' as a key additional element in their curriculum – which is defined as the development and application of a set of skills associated with effective spoken communication[50].

Our own Skills Builder teacher assessments show a similar challenge across hundreds of other classrooms. Only 61% of students joining secondary school were able to put their points in a logical order when sharing their ideas – something that we would expect of students two years younger.

Beyond the classroom

We have already seen that there is compelling evidence that communication skills are highly valued by employers – they were highlighted by the CBI Education & Skills survey which found that 50% of businesses were not satisfied with school leavers' communication skills[51].

We also know that employers are quick to make judgements at the interview stage – and one of the earliest things they can judge is the communication skills of applicants. Work by the Commission for Social Mobility has highlighted that students from more disadvantaged backgrounds are often undermined at this point because their communication skills do not suggest the 'polish' that their wealthier peers might have honed, despite equal academic achievements[52]. The ability to present effectively at an early stage in a career is an important signalling mechanism of high potential.

In the context of university, discussion and debate plays an important part – and the need to articulate one's own ideas is critical. While in school rote learning, instruction and exposition can be effective ways of internalising basic knowledge, this is much less the focus of undergraduate learning.

For entrepreneurship, the ability to pitch and talk compellingly is fundamental.

How it is built

For the youngest students, aged just four or five years old, sharing ideas is likely to be just about making their own needs known – often to an adult who structures that conversation. As they advance, it is about being able to communicate their thoughts and ideas to another child and then to a small group. Anyone who has seen groups of children playing together at this age will see that they are practising sharing ideas – their games appear to be continuous narratives of make-believe which are long on description and direction and short of very much actually happening.

It is intuitive that this is essential, and the 'Chatter Matters' guidance from speech and language charity I CAN[53] highlights that 'proficiency in speech, language and communication is critical to the development of a child's cognitive, social and emotional well-being'. Where children haven't mastered these skills, interacting with their peers and teachers becomes a frustrating experience – as those of us with two-year-olds who struggle to make themselves understood can attest to.

As they develop, the complexity of what students can communicate should increase. They should start to be able to introduce some structure to their ideas and be confident in sharing these ideas with their class and wider groups of their peers. This ability to articulate is essential for the students to start building more complex ideas. As School 21 and Voice 21 argue, 'it is through speaking and listening that we develop our views, apply knowledge and extend our capacity to think critically'[54].

After building this foundation, presenting begins in earnest – firstly just being able to share ideas clearly and then being able to vary tone, expressions and gestures to keep an audience engaged.

As they enter secondary school, students should use examples to bring their points to life. It is only once they are about 12 years old that we would expect students to start really engaging with their audiences. At the most basic, this means picking the right tone for the audience – knowing, for example, that their headteacher is a different audience to their peers and that what is judged appropriate by those audiences is likely to vary. As we talk about presenting here, we are thinking not only of formal presentations with one person standing at the front of a room, but also sharing ideas in a meeting or being persuasive in a negotiation (coupled here, of course, with listening effectively).

The more accomplished students will start to become more aware of their audiences as they present – modifying their language, tone and expression according to the reactions they receive. They will also start being able to anticipate the reactions that they might get and have thought of potential alternatives in advance.

Ultimately, we can be very confident in our school leavers if they are accomplished, confident communicators and presenters who are able to adapt to the reactions of the audience.

Teachability and impact

The cultivation of presenting skills has a rich history. From antiquity and into the early 19th century, the teaching of rhetoric was seen as a critical pillar of a good education. That is, the ability to build and deliver convincing arguments.

The Roman politician Cicero, back in the first century BCE, was arguing that oratory, in the right hands, was the highest form of the expression of humanity[55]. This was no simple matter – he identified the need for a strong body of knowledge on the subject matter, the ability to arrange and choose words well, to have a sense of humour, to be quick yet sensitive, and to have a great memory. He saw these skills as a rarity – as indeed they probably were at that time.

What would surprise our ancestors is how little we formally structure and build this skill now. At primary school, we might encourage students to 'show and tell' or take part in school plays, dance or music but these rarely push them to improve their presenting skills. As a new parent myself, I can tell that I will not be a particularly stretching critic if my son is ever in any similar performances.

There is a skill set to being an effective communicator which is separate from being knowledgeable on the topic. This includes a separate band of knowledge and practice which holds useful whatever the content that is being communicated. For example, a range of ways of structuring a presentation and other devices like rhetoric are applicable in different settings. Similarly, for some of our teenaged students we reinforce simple concepts like the 'Five Ss' as the key elements of effective performance: Stride purposefully up onto the stage, Stand firmly, Smile at the audience, Speak carefully, and Seek eye contact. Although a simple example, this is something that exists as a skill whatever the content.

Indeed, one of the reasons that rhetoric got a bad name was that these techniques could be used to create the illusion of knowledge and deep thought without them necessarily existing. We could probably all cite examples of those who appear fully confident in their assertions but whose assertions seem to rest on very little at all.

Recently, there has been an uptick of interest in this area, evidenced in a recent report from LKMco in partnership with Voice 21[56]. They found that 68% of teachers they surveyed felt that it was very important that they helped develop their students' oracy skills. The barriers were a shortage of teacher training and confidence in building these skills, but also a sense that finding space to focus on building these speaking skills was limited. We will revisit some of these barriers in the next chapter.

On the other hand, in the LKMco report, teachers highlighted that there were positive impacts on both the students' social and emotional development and their confidence to engage in learning as they build their oracy skills[57].

Similarly, research by the Education Endowment Foundation highlights that oral language interventions can be highly effective[58] where they explicitly target extending students' spoken vocabulary and use questioning to help expand students' comprehension.

Chapter 4:
Interpersonal Skills

A lot of possible attributes could be captured under interpersonal skills. We might want to consider customer service, peer feedback, teamwork and leading others.

For us, though, teamwork and leadership are the two that are universal, irrelevant of the setting. There are of course a myriad of competing possible definitions for teamwork and leadership, but we have sought to keep them simple enough to be meaningful and memorable for both teachers and students:

- *Teamwork:* working cooperatively with others towards achieving a shared goal.
- *Leadership:* supporting, encouraging, and motivating others to achieve a shared goal.

Let's look at this duo in more depth.

(3) Teamwork

Teamwork and collaboration have become surprisingly polarising in education – but often because their development has been conflated with just doing more group work. The reality is that beyond the pursuit of individual learning in the classroom, much of wider life does at least require cooperation.

Through our work, we have found that even students who initially seem the least promising collaborators can become active participants. Of course, building this teamwork skill requires a much more thoughtful and focused approach than just putting the students in groups.

Once mastered, there is strong evidence that this skill is not only valued by employers and universities but that it can underpin effective classroom learning too.

In the classroom

In my classroom, I underestimated the challenge of getting my students to work in teams to set up their small business projects. I naïvely hoped that the profit motive would overcome their initial resistance. When it quickly became clear that they would not be working in teams of my choosing, I decided to give up that particular battle for the sake of the war.

What was striking was how little focus there had been on actually equipping students to be able to work with one another. This is something that comes up a lot in my conversation with Enabling Enterprise teachers. Essentially, since primary school almost all day-to-day work had been an individual pursuit and any group work was an unstructured supplement to that. Beyond the football team, few of my students had had opportunities to build their teamwork skills.

Beyond the classroom

In my classroom, the lack of teamwork skills made key ways of learning impossible. A proponent of didactic teaching might shrug this off, but at university level it is a standard expectation that alongside lectures, students should also collaborate – whether on a presentation, piece of research, or in completing problem sets.

Employers and entrepreneurs are certainly not complacent – both consistently highlight the ability to work with others as a critical factor for success. It is nearly impossible to conceive of a job that doesn't involve working with others. Even apparently isolated roles like artists or coders have to deal with others. The legal structure of being a 'sole trader' can also give the misleading sense that if you are your own boss then interpersonal skills are less important. But you're unlikely to secure many customers without interpersonal skills.

The CBI and Pearson's Education and Skills Survey in 2016 showed that 26% of employers saw a deficit in their new joiners' teamwork skills. This ability to work with others is also reflected in colleagues' perceptions of their wider attitude to work – an attitude which 89% of employers say is a critical consideration when making choices in recruiting school and college leavers[59].

This is also reflected in a 2002 study, where some of the critical elements to being an effective team member included understanding goals, contributing to a positive environment, being enthusiastic in contributions, encouraging others and staying focused[60].

How it is built

Our definition might sound simple – that teamwork is working cooperatively with others towards a shared goal. However, this simple-sounding concept is obviously underpinned by a lot more – even cooperation is a spectrum from the grudging through to the more active.

For the youngest children, we are really talking about the basics of social interaction – for example, something as simple as being able to take turns with one another and to share. Anyone who is aware that this is an expectation of five- and six-year-olds will be surprised at the battles in secondary school over limited calculators in a maths classroom, but we have to start somewhere.

As children develop they become more aware of the concept of working together in a team, and how it requires different skills from just working by themselves. This is likely to include thinking about what the advantages of teamwork can be, and when teamwork or individual working is better.

By the time they are 8 or 9, we aim that students can work in a team on a collaborative task and have some simple strategies like voting to help overcome obstacles. As their thinking becomes more sophisticated, rather than making binary choices, they are more likely to reach compromises by merging different options together.

If this is already sounding challenging, there is still a lot more to do to be on the trajectory to employers' and universities' expectations: the focus switches to how to include all team members in discussions and actively building consensus and a sense of inclusion.

So far, lots of the activities that we would expect students to be working on are based around group conversation and are self-contained. In the wider world, of course, many collaborations with colleagues, undergraduates or customers are much more open-ended.

In this context, older students benefit from being able to understand that other team members are likely to have a different set of strengths and weaknesses, and are mindful of how best to draw on these. They should also become more aware of the performance of the team, and start using these insights to influence the performance of the team – perhaps even playing their role to support the leader or other team members as best they can.

Teachability and impact

I have sometimes heard or read that teamwork and the ability to collaborate is innate – or that we are all social animals. I have variously seen the building of the Pyramids or the Great Wall of China cited as examples that we have always been able to work in teams.

I would argue that these are particularly weak examples given the possible use of forced labour. Indeed, the definition of teamwork that we've been using would not recognise an outcome achieved in that way. This point is not a facetious one – organisations are less hierarchical and linear than they once were and need a much greater level of skill to navigate. Teams are often created for shorter projects and then disbanded, or require working in matrix structures with less formal power to hold them together. We have all seen teams that are effective and those that are not.

Of course an effective team needs to have knowledge about what they are doing. An F1 team that can perform a pit stop in seconds is not going to be easily substituted. And clearly a good football team needs more than strong relationships and ways of working together.

But alongside individual performance there are skills and knowledge that underpin effective teamwork. Some of these elements include self-awareness to understand how to make an individual contribution, the ability to work in different organisational structures, and emotional awareness of others. These things are distinct and transferable to many different situations.

In building these skills, we also allow students to access learning more widely. For example, collaborative learning can be useful – but in their book, *Educating Ruby*, Professors Guy Claxton and Bill Lucas make the point that 'one of the reasons that learning in groups … can be ineffective is simply because the children have never been shown how to'[61]. A study by Webb back in 1985 found that 'collaborative learning teams attain higher level thinking and preserve information for longer than students working individually'[62].

Similarly, the Education Endowment Foundation found a reliable, positive impact to collaborative working. They added that 'evidence about the benefits of collaborative learning has been found consistently for over 40 years and a number of systematic reviews and meta-analyses of research studies have been completed'[63]. At the same time, they found this learning approach can be low cost too. But of course, to access these potentially beneficial approaches to learning, the students need to have a basic set of teamwork and collaborative skills in place.

(4) Leadership

Alongside teamwork sits leadership. We have already defined leadership as 'being able to support, encourage and motivate others to achieve a goal'. That is not uncontroversial – each week in *The Times* an interviewed business leader is asked to provide their own definition and there is enough variation to keep that particular question interesting.

This skill is particularly susceptible to being seen as innate – that an individual is either a natural leader or not. This is short-sighted as there is good evidence that teachable skills underpin being an effective leader. And once those skills are mastered, students can work even more effectively in collaborative settings.

What's more, there are big pay-offs to building leadership skills beyond the classroom.

In the classroom

In my secondary school classroom, it was initially difficult to get volunteers to take leadership positions – even for very minor acts of leadership like facilitating a group discussion. I can picture now the shrugs that were the stock response to requests for someone in a group to take a lead.

The alternative reaction that I have seen with younger students is that the loudest student becomes the leader every time and then tells the others what to do. Over time, these students see themselves as the natural leaders – with the effect that they do not try to become better leaders, as their gifts feel innate. At the same time, those other students see leaders as someone other than themselves.

Beyond the classroom

We read a lot into who takes the role of leading when the opportunity is presented. It is a signalling device not just of leadership skills, but of wider abilities and potential.

Leadership is often seen as aspirational. This is reflected not only in the language that is used by institutions like business schools (Harvard Business School's mission – 'to educate leaders who make a difference in the world'), but also in pay structures. With a few exceptions, leaders are paid more than their followers.

For our school-leavers employers are likely to have higher regard for those who have some evidence of taking on leadership positions. Even right back to being captain of a school sports team. The students themselves will have much more confidence to take these positions if they have started to build their leadership skills early.

How it is built

You might argue that children of 4 or 5 are too young to be leaders – although it is evident that some have a preference for taking charge and imposing their view of how things should be on their peers. This is not actually the most solid basis for building a high level of competency in leadership skills.

Rather, for the youngest students the focus is understanding others. This is not an innate trait. That's why with 4- and 5-year-olds we are modelling how to articulate their feelings and then to identify the feelings of others. This might be as simple as flashcards of facial expressions, or discussing scenarios and how the characters might feel at different points in a story.

We move on by the time the students are 7- or 8-years-old to how they can start organising simple tasks between those they are leading. They learn to identify when their peers might need support or assistance, and then provide basic encouragement to motivate each other to complete those tasks. They will subsequently need to be able to defuse disagreements or have tools to encourage their groups to reach a consensus.

As they continue to develop, they should start building a deeper understanding of their own strengths and weaknesses to build their leadership style as well as some basic management tools.

By the time they are 14- or 15-years-old they should be able to, albeit in a basic way, apply their understanding of their peers' strengths and interests to allocate tasks in a justifiable way between them. Later on, they think more about how they can draw on strategies to increase motivation and engagement amongst their teams.

The students who go the furthest will have a good grounding in different styles of leadership and be able to judge and moderate their own preferences – whether they love a good consensus or prefer the strong grip of the autocrat. The moderation comes from recognising the dark side to leadership and challenges that might arise.

Teachability and impact

It's interesting that employers recognise that these skills need to be developed and invest huge resources into building effective teams and building leadership in their workforces.

Critics might argue that leadership depends on expertise or expert knowledge. That is interesting, and would seem to make some sense in that some academic institutions are led by those with the most expertise. But in many cases it is not the case that she or he who knows the most is automatically the leader. There is some evidence that a leader will tend to have a level of intelligence greater than the average of their followers[64] but that this tends to be a threshold requirement[65] – that is, once a minimum is achieved, it is no longer significant. Goleman compared the impact of purely technical skills, cognitive skills (including analytical reasoning and problem-solving, which we will come to) and emotional intelligence attributes. Throughout organisations, emotional intelligence had twice the impact on individual effectiveness of technical skills or cognitive skills – and by the most senior levels in the organisation, individual success was 90% explained by those emotional intelligence attributes.

Others argue that leadership skills are natural gifts. This view underpinned much of leadership research in the early- to mid-20th century, as researchers sought to find the combination of traits or characteristics which predicted leadership success. Some of the characteristics that were highlighted included vitality and endurance, decisiveness, persuasiveness, responsibility and intellectual capital[66]. These developed further into what is often referred to as the 'Big Five' model – extroversion, agreeableness, conscientiousness, emotional stability, and openness to experience.

The challenge is that these models are better at predicting who will come forward as a leader than differentiating between those who are effective and ineffective. Jim Collins has explored effective leadership through a long-term examination of company performance, and found that quieter, determined and focused long-term leaders outperformed others[67].

A balanced view of the literature is that character does have an impact on how effective a leader is in different situations – and that the relevant characteristics will vary by situation[68]. It also highlights that there is a high degree to which these skills can be built.

This includes knowledge about how to structure tasks, to understand the motivations of their team and simple things like how to organise and chair meetings effectively. It is also built through practice so that, in situations of high stress, a leader can perform more highly by relying on this practiced instinct.

There is a lot that is teachable here.

Chapter 5:
Self-Management Skills

At Enabling Enterprise, we have broken the concept of self-management down into two parts: the setting of goals and planning how to achieve them, and then the strategies to stay on track with those plans, adapting them as required, but seeing them through to completion.

Self-management is one of those areas that can quickly become mixed up with character. For example, we might equate self-management with being resilient, or visionary, or self-aware.

For our purposes, though, we are focusing on the teachable skills. That is why we are eschewing the language of resilience and instead thinking about two things:

- *Aiming High:* the ability to set clear, tangible goals and devise a robust route to achieving them.
- *Staying Positive:* the ability to use tactics and strategies to overcome setbacks to achieve goals.

This is a powerful pair.

(5) Aiming High

We use the slightly more clunky formulation of 'aiming high' rather than 'high aspirations' for good reason. Too often high aspirations are associated with just setting the most ambitious goal possible – whether footballer, X Factor winner, astronaut, prime minister or US President. Most children clock on pretty quickly to what are perceived to be the 'best' things to do.

Discussion with teachers has often highlighted that there is no meaningful difference in the levels of ambition between those students in the poorest communities and their wealthier peers. The reality though is that their wealthier peers are hugely more likely to achieve their aspirations.

Therefore, we instead talk about aiming high. This is both having an ambitious set of goals for the future, but also ensuring that those are grounded in reality and that there is a clear plan to achieve them – with clear actions, steps, and intermediate targets.

In the classroom

As a teacher, I often worried that we were undermining our students' responsibility and ownership of their goals and work. I never let coursework folders out of my sight, I tracked completion and chased down work as deadlines approached. Not doing so seemed too much of a risk when we felt straitjacketed by accountability measures.

In schools teachers generally set the students' targets for them. These expectations ought to be based on individual student potential, but in practice are also heavily influenced by government targets. This means minimal proportions of students achieving the expected level in SATS at primary school or five good GCSE passes, including English and maths, at secondary school. Or they may be focused on progression – whether from starting primary school or the Progress 8 measure which tracks students' progress across eight subjects from the age of 11 through to 16.

The result when we set targets this way is that students rarely feel any meaningful ownership of those targets or responsibility for charting the course to achieve them. This resulting passivity is a wasted opportunity in the classroom and undermining of future potential.

Beyond the classroom

In the workplace, we know that effective management means giving individuals the space to develop their own goals and plans within a framework of organisational strategy and values. There is evidence that giving that space actually results in much more ambitious plans and a greater level of achievement than if those goals were simply set by management. This is unsurprising – as humans we are generally motivated by feeling in control and having a sense of purpose.

That aside, most medium- or high-skilled roles require that the individual post-holder takes the lead in creating their own plans and steps to achieve what they have been asked to do. It is only lower-skilled and lower-paid roles where this sort of self-structuring is not required.

We will look more at future trends in the final part of the book, but a couple of trends are particularly important to building our students' ability to aim high. The first is that employers are clear that they will be needing more employees with higher skills including management and leadership skills in the future. The CBI's annual employer survey highlighted that 69% of employers expect to need more people with leadership and management skills with just 2% expecting to need fewer. This is a long-term positive trend, with this 'net demand' figure running at above 60% since the economic recovery started in 2010[69].

Beyond any single employer though, the career paths of individuals leaving our schools are becoming more entrepreneurial. Fewer people have a linear route through their careers – instead, managing their own careers, moving between roles and organisations. This will require self-management skills to set goals, find opportunities and make plans.

How it is built

For the youngest students, aiming high starts with the simple concept of 'trying their best', and having a sense of what that means, why it matters and why hard work and persistence will be important. Until they're about 7 or 8 years old this is the focus – seeking out challenge, trying something new and taking pride in their achievements.

As they get into the older years at primary school, the emphasis then becomes starting to set simple targets for themselves. This will probably need quite a lot of support and structuring from their teacher or a parent initially.

By the time students start secondary school, they should be taking a lot more of the lead on setting and articulating their goals. This includes being able to identify a logical series of steps that they will need to take to achieve their bigger goals and intermediate measures of success. They will probably learn to use SMART targets (that is, those that are specific, measurable, achievable, relevant and time-limited).

This is important, because by the time they are in Year 11 at the age of 15 or 16 they need to be making serious decisions about their future routes, and their longer term plans and goals for themselves.

Of course, planning and aiming high doesn't stop once students have left the school gates – throughout careers, or in achieving wider life goals, the ability to set realistic goals and plans to achieve them remains essential.

Teachability and impact

It is challenging to directly teach 'high aspirations'. This is a classic example of the combining of knowledge, behaviour and the skill: the knowledge of what is out there, and what progression routes through education and employment look like; the behaviour of choosing to seek out the most stretching opportunities; and the skill of being able to develop realistic plans. Separating out these elements in building them is essential, and it is the skill element that we focus on here.

The skill of aiming high has several underpinning elements – each of which is teachable. We need students to have the ability to accurately self-reflect to understand their own strengths and weaknesses. Here we can introduce self-evaluation tools and the use of benchmarks of performance. We also need them to be able to seek out information and guidance from appropriate sources. This can be taught through building awareness of different research routes and how to talk to adults to glean the information they seek. Finally, we need them to be able to turn the understanding they glean from applying these elements of the skill to creating realistic plans.

Once these plans and goals are in place, there is good evidence that these well-founded aspirations lead to greater motivation and subsequently higher education attainment[70]. A review from the Education Endowment Foundation showed that while the causal link between aspirations and academic attainment was difficult to prove conclusively, positive effects were seen most clearly for low-attaining pupils[71]. There is also evidence that educational and career aspirations developed while students are adolescents in schools, for example between 11 and 14, can have lifelong significance[72].

(6) Staying Positive

The importance of resilience is often discussed in schools. Carol Dweck's work on Growth Mindset[73], and to a lesser extent Angela Duckworth's work on Grit[74], has permeated schools. Once again, though, we found that these terms have become catch-alls for a diverse set of approaches – and focused on the character trait of choosing to stick at something difficult.

We focus here on the learnable strategies that help students to work through setbacks, barriers or mistakes – whilst capitalising on what they learn along the way. We call this skillset 'staying positive'.

It is this ability to keep at something that is most highly prized by employers, and widely cited by entrepreneurs as the driver of their success. In fields as disparate as elite sports or science, the ability to keep making progress in the face of adversity is what separates those who ultimately succeed with those who do not.

And we can teach it.

In the classroom

In my classroom, I was frequently concerned by the number of students who would promptly give up when faced with a challenge. It didn't have to be a significant challenge – perhaps as simple as not having the correct equipment with them, making an early mistake or not understanding part of an explanation. Our teachers have shared examples of students giving up pre-emptively – not even getting to the challenge because they have decided they are unlikely to succeed.

As I was teaching a subject which was primarily assessed through coursework this was particularly evident because trying to get students to the end of a piece of work could be a battle. And the idea that they might want to redraft or improve that work was an alien concept at the beginning of the year.

Without this ability to stick at something it is unsurprising that the potential for progress was capped. When our teachers assessed their students at the outset of secondary school before an Enabling Enterprise programme, only 60% of them were deemed to be happy to try something that would be stretching for them.

It is telling that the government's 2016 white paper 'Educational Excellence Everywhere' highlighted the importance of students 'being resilient and knowing how to persevere, how to bounce back if faced with failure'[75].

Beyond the classroom

The CBI found in their survey of employers that the most valued attribute for hires who were school or college-leavers was their attitude, including positivity and the ability to self-manage[76].

This is mirrored in conversation with our employers – those employees who really stand out and then thrive in the long-run are those who are stretching themselves and developing. Without this self-motivated progress there is little justification for promotion – and without the willingness to stick at difficult, stretching stuff there is little chance of that progress.

This is also the case at university – where grappling with more complex academic concepts requires sticking at work, and also being able to maintain effort on larger pieces of work, like essays or dissertations, over a substantial period of time.

Entrepreneurship or self-employment is defined by the ability to self-motivate and overcome barriers. Many entrepreneurs have their stories of highs, lows and setbacks along the road to success.

How it is built

To stay positive first requires a level of self-awareness. Without understanding our own feelings when faced with challenges, it is very hard to manage or adapt to those feelings. So for our youngest students, they simply need to be able to articulate and identify their emotions and link them to their own experience. For example, they might understand where frustration comes from and how that can lead to feelings of anger or upset.

Building off that as 6- or 7-year-olds, it would be good if they can start to understand not only that those feelings exist, but that they can be damaging or exacerbate setbacks – and instead start to practise the idea of staying calm and managing disappointment.

If we stopped there, though, we would run the risk that students just worked harder to avoid situations that seemed too challenging or pushed them outside their comfort zone.

Instead, we continue to ensure that students can respond positively when faced with setbacks by finding the alternative solutions, or making the most of the new opportunities that open up as a result.

By the time students are reaching the end of their time in primary school, they should be not giving up in the face of setbacks – but are responding by deliberately applying the strategies that they have learnt. This may not yet be an automatic behaviour but is gradually becoming so. This might feel artificial, but there is plenty of evidence that reactions that initially might be contrived can eventually become automatic.

In the same way, we see students building their ability to take on a challenge and try to identify both the positive opportunities that arise from it and the appropriate next steps. As they reach 15 or 16 years old, we hope that students are able to seek challenge – and approach these challenges able to understand the inherent risks, and to manage them.

The students who achieve real mastery in this area will leave school not only with their own bank of strategies and tactics to stay positive in challenging situations, but with a positive attitude to seeking out challenge and encouraging others to do the same.

Teachability and impact

Students of equal academic ability can respond very differently to perceived challenge. One might relish the opportunity to overcome the obstacle and learn in the process. The other might become discouraged and admit defeat.

Research shows that this ability to tackle challenges can significantly affect school and life outcomes for young people, including academic success. Furthermore, these skills can be learned, measured, and have lasting effects on academic performance.

A study in Martin Seligman's *The Optimistic Child* (1995) found that a student's inability to demonstrate self-discipline was as crucial a factor in academic underachievement as inadequate teaching[77].

A more recent longitudinal study by Scales *et al* (2006) in the US found that higher levels of resilience are strongly correlated with higher grade point averages (GPAs) among middle and high school students[78]. These findings hold true over time, so that students reporting more resiliency characteristics early in the study had higher GPAs three years later, compared to students with lower resilience levels at the start.

What can be applied consistently though are these strategies for staying positive, even when facing challenges. Over time this might build up to the disposition of being resilient, but it is much more effective to focus on teachable strategies.

Chapter 6:
Creativity and
Problem-Solving Skills

Our final pair of skills are a critical piece of the puzzle but are also open to debate and strong differences of opinion, as we will see. At Enabling Enterprise we have found that there are teachable elements of both creativity and problem-solving.

The two definitions that we will be working with are:

- *Creativity:* the use of imagination and the generation of new ideas.
- *Problem-solving:* the ability to find a solution to a complex situation or challenge.

While there is a clear overlap between the two, problem-solving generally presumes a defined challenge, whereas this is not a pre-requisite for creativity. In this way, creativity is an expansive process of widening the pool of potential opportunities or ideas, while problem-solving is about reducing the pool of potential approaches to the best one.

(7) Creativity

Creativity is about about the students' capacity to use their imagination and generate new ideas. This is underpinned by structures and frameworks to support an individual's thinking.

Being able to make conceptual leaps or bring together new ways of thinking or ideas is highly valued by employers and universities, and can often underpin entrepreneurial endeavours. And while we often think of creativity as a character trait, our experience shows it is buildable too.

In the classroom

It is telling that I didn't really notice that my class lacked creativity for quite a while. There was very little call for such skills initially – the outcomes the class were working towards were prescribed and I generated the task that would produce the evidence that they needed to tick off that outcome.

It wasn't until I was building the course that became Enabling Enterprise that I really noticed. They were starting their businesses and I wanted them to come up with some ideas. This seemed simple to me – there was a whole world of ideas out there that I felt my students could do. As a young person myself, I'd been used to doing a bit of tutoring, child care, car washing (or 'valeting' as I called it when I wanted to put my prices up), producing Christmas cards and a whole lot besides.

But the students struggled to generate ideas for themselves.

A big part of the challenge was that I had no idea how to teach creativity. Actually, by throwing wide the range of options I wasn't encouraging creativity but stifling it because creativity is fuelled by its constraints. Once there were some constraints, the ideas flowed a lot more easily – it had to be legal, had to be sold in school, it had to draw on the students' strengths, interests and available resources. In short time we had a staff car washing service, a laundry and ironing service for teachers, a customised clothing and trainers company, a tutoring service and a couple of rivals to the school canteen.

Beyond the classroom

Creativity is also more widely important and applied than might be implied from a normal classroom setting. We sometimes think of this as just something for the creative sectors – an important but narrow set of careers. However, when we look in more detail at exactly what the skill of creativity means it is clear that its application is much wider than this.

Employers are increasingly driven by innovation – both the development of incremental improvements and also new thinking that draws together ideas in new ways to create value. For entrepreneurs, trying to make a breakthrough against incumbent companies, the ability to approach things differently is absolutely essential.

Even in the academic arena, while university research stands 'on the shoulders of giants', breakthroughs need more than just existing knowledge.

How it is built

For the youngest students on Enabling Enterprise programmes, we talk about 'using imagination'. This is something that comes very naturally to these students – they live in parallel worlds where they test out ideas and build their own understanding of the world. Caroline Sharp in 2004 summarised lots of the research into creativity and how it develops in children. She found that 'most theories of child development view young children as highly creative, with a natural tendency to fantasise, experiment and explore their environment' but also added that 'this high level of creativity is not necessarily maintained through childhood and into adulthood'[79].

To overcome this frequent trap, we support the building of creativity through several stages. Firstly, at the start of primary school we want students to be able to generate ideas. Secondly, they start trying to articulate the process by which they are developing these ideas so they start to become repeatable strategies. As they continue to develop their creativity skills, they can start to apply their creative thinking to make connections and generate new ideas.

By the time they leave school, students have a range of creative strategies on hand – including mind mapping, word association or snow-balling ideas. They can also create their own parameters around situations to focus their creative processes, and then evaluate which approaches might be best suited to a particular problem or opportunity.

Teachability and impact

The teaching of creativity is a controversial area in some ways – it easily becomes one of those areas where we presume that some students are the creative ones – or not. Yet in almost all areas of work and, indeed, university or entrepreneurship, the creation of ideas is paramount.

These skills are most at risk of being pulled into the rolling battle of conservative versus progressive views on education. For example, Sir Ken Robinson, who is a flag bearer of the progressive side, is a strong advocate for teaching creativity in schools – claiming in his 2006 TED talk that 'creativity is as important as literacy and we should treat it with the same status'[80].

There is a distinctly different skill in being able to take existing knowledge and reconfiguring or rearranging its use into something entirely different – or being able to create hypotheses and new ways of thinking. These techniques include, at basic level, mind-mapping, seeking associations, or finding similarities between different silos of knowledge. This may run the risk of just encouraging mimicry of the creative process but only if there is no deeper building of the skills and underpinning creative models before students are let loose to be creative.

In the schools we partner with, we've seen that just building some of these basic techniques helps break down the barrier to all students being able to structure and capture their creative thinking.

(8) Problem-solving

Problem-solving, our eighth and final skill, is all about how we approach challenges and situations where the solution is not immediately clear – either because of complexity, or because there is no single correct 'answer'.

We accept as a given that you need to have a good grounding of knowledge to solve a problem, but what we focus on is the second part, which is as important: the ability to break down and structure a problem to solve it. This is where we instead draw on the tools of logic like deduction and induction, the creation and testing of hypotheses and the identification of gaps in knowledge. Without these tools, students will not be able to tackle more complex problems, or those where their knowledge is imperfect.

The challenge

In my classroom, the problems that my students had to solve were few and far between, because the path that they needed to take was so clearly marked.

Those problems that they had faced had been of the very simplest variety – generally finding a piece of information and replicating it into a space. The finding of the information was hardly a challenge either, since it was all in the textbook.

However, as they embarked on the Enabling Enterprise course that I developed for them and started their own small businesses, the deficit in this area emerged. Once they had to wrestle with questions that didn't have a single textbook answer, things got a little more challenging. For example, how to decide on the 'right' price for their products, how to refrigerate their cakes during the day, how to safely store money, how to account for their stock. These were all meatier problems and their problem-solving skills had to start to develop too.

Beyond the classroom

Of course, beyond school this sort of problem-solving is a basic expectation. In the real world, many problems do not have a clear answer. Many need to be approached by drawing out first principles and building on those to reach an answer. Even in the setting of a university, students are wrestling with problems that do not have one answer but require a greater level of nuance and evaluation.

Many roles that are well-paid are for those who can solve problems that others cannot. This can be based on an inherent set of knowledge or from being able to structure a problem-solving process – for example, through the work of management consultants. Deductive and inductive approaches to problem-solving crop up in the higher levels of many different jobs, and are highly valued by employers.

How it is built

For the youngest students, we are looking for students to be able to solve a simple problem with structuring and support from an adult to guide them through developing their ideas. Over time, this might not need to be an adult, but could also be another student or a peer.

As with creativity, articulation is the important next step – being able to explain how they approached a problem, broke it down and worked through each part of it in turn. Still focused on simple problems, which don't require extra information, they should then be able to identify a couple of different possible solutions, and be comfortable with the fact that multiple solutions might exist to any given problem.

Once they are able to do this, we can start introducing more complex problems which need extra information to complete. This will initially require quite a lot of support from an adult to provide the structure around finding the information – perhaps including where the students should be looking to try to find it.

The step beyond this, by the time they are 13 or 14 years old is that they can independently evaluate the solution they have come up with to a problem. More advanced still, they will be able to evaluate multiple potential solutions to choose the most effective one and to be able to justify their choices.

Ultimately, the most advanced students can move beyond clearly defined problems to look at more complex phenomena – for example, social problems. They will be able to dig into what the root causes might be, and think about longer-term solutions involving multiple steps. They might also be able to pre-empt risks and build mitigations into their ideas.

Teachability and impact

Problem-solving is sometimes seen as being much more grounded than creativity even though we have seen that many of the processes are quite similar. For some reason, we are just more comfortable thinking that solving a problem is more of an academic skill.

However, problem-solving as a generic skill is pretty contentious – arguably the most contentious of the whole eight that we've explored here. The critique here makes a lot of sense – that to solve a problem requires a great deal of knowledge and understanding of everything surrounding that problem. This is a point that Daisy Christodoulou makes strongly in her book 'Seven Myths about Education'[81] and I broadly agree.

Except that there is an element of being able to problem-solve that is distinct and valuable. Management consultants have built an industry on applying models of decision-making and logic to situations where they tend to have much less specialised knowledge than those they are working for.

Similarly the modern business phenomenon of the Lean Start-Up is about a methodology to create and test hypotheses to reach answers[82].

We can go back to the ancient Greeks for putting problem-solving on this higher footing – when *logos* or logic was seen as a critical part of learning[83]. There were different versions of logic too – whether you take Plato's view that there was one truth that questioning a logical deduction can eventually reach ('the one correct answer') or Aristotle's view that such a truth did not exist, and therefore that one should start with the real world and build from there. That was built on by Francis Bacon in the 17th century who saw an inductive approach to logic and problem-solving approach (that is, reasoning from the particular to the general) to be essential for scientific understanding and progress.

Today, we can support our students by helping them to understand deductive and inductive logic, decision trees and ways of forming testable hypotheses. While they won't solve any problems without being able to draw on a lot of knowledge and context, nor will they be able to solve complex problems without these skills either.

Conclusion

There will never be a perfect set of essential skills. At Enabling Enterprise we chose and refined these eight on the basis that they broke down the four areas that were consistently cited as vital employability skills, personal skills and study skills. We observed them to be part of the gap in what most schools are teaching.

We have seen in the last decade of Enabling Enterprise that if a student builds a high level of competence in these skills they become better set up to both engage during their time in school and thrive in whatever they wanted to do later.

Our eight essential skills are also meaningfully interlinked – both in their pairs and as a set. A deficit in one skill is likely to impede progress in the others, whilst an advantage in another can help boost them all. That is why they work as a set: they are both essential and interdependent.

I hope these chapters have helped to bring those skills to life – both why the skill is relevant to the gap, but also how that skill can be taught, and what the subsequent benefits of doing so are.

Next we will ask: If there's a gap, and these skills could be the missing piece, then why aren't we teaching them?

Chapter 7:
Why aren't we teaching them?

It has taken six chapters to pin down exactly what the gap really is, and to explore the essential skills that could form the missing piece. That is part of the challenge – but it doesn't really explain why we aren't teaching them.

If you're ready to dive into getting started, then feel free to jump ahead to Part 3 where we look at the practical principles for implementation.

When we looked at each of the skills individually, the case for building them is clear – so what is going on?

To answer that question we have to face the big barriers to teaching the skills – the practical, the ideological, and finally the pedagogical.

We pick up the story of Enabling Enterprise as we move beyond my classroom and see the response.

Enabling Enterprise: Getting Started

The early days of running Enabling Enterprise back in the autumn of 2009 were exhilarating, challenging, exhausting and chaotic. The start of any social enterprise is little more than survival: taking that flickering flame of an idea, and trying to protect it against the onslaught of the world. At the beginning there was just the course that I'd created for my students being shared across a handful of schools.

I'm not someone who likes to leave anything unchallenged, and so my constant question to myself was why, if this was such a great idea, was it not already being done?

After my years of teaching, I thought I couldn't be phased – but going into schools to try to persuade them to engage with our programmes was as daunting as three consecutive periods of IT with Year 9. I wanted each school to get involved so much that any rejection felt like a harsh personal disappointment.

As I started out, I realised that there were a set of possible objections that tended to emerge – and in turn I began to get better at pre-empting them. Some of the barriers were obvious and practical – money, time, resourcing and priorities. These were clear but also surmountable barriers. As we dug deeper it became clear that there were a few other sources of resistance – and some of these were actually why we never even got a foot in the door. These deeper roots were sometimes ideological – both about whether it was the place of schools to teach skills that seemed to be about employment, and whether this was just a 'trendy, progressive fad' as one headteacher queried. For balance, I also got asked whether 'all this measurement and rigour would take the fun out of enterprise'. But there was something that continued to come up – the question of whether these skills really were teachable.

I stuck at it because I knew the difference it had made for the students in my classroom. But what made the breakthrough for Enabling Enterprise were the schools who gave it a go and saw the impact on their students for themselves. Because in the end, no theoretical basis for our work could be as compelling as when we started to see the programmes really taking off in our schools – and it turns out nothing I could say is ever as convincing as a quick phone call with a fellow headteacher who is seeing the impact on their students.

Schools did start to sign up, mainly due to the efforts of 20 enthusiastic classroom teachers who pushed their schools to let them take part. Sometimes these were on a very small scale initially – just one teacher with one of their classes. But over time, many of our schools have become more ambitious.

The wider debate
Beyond my experience in Enabling Enterprise schools, the debate on how we should teach essential skills is far from the top of the agenda.

What is interesting, though, is that this is not because there is active dispute over whether having the skillset we discussed in the previous chapter would be a desirable thing. Not once has a teacher questioned me on whether having those skills would be useful.

It is not enough just to recognise that there is gap, or that there exists a set of skills that would fill it. We have to make the leap to actually teaching them.

This chapter takes on these barriers – first by demonstrating that they are real, then by showing their effects, and then how they can be overcome.

The Barriers to Building the Skills

(A) Ideological Barriers

Education in the English context is an ideological battleground. To an extent that is a healthy thing – after all, it avoids too cosy a consensus forming, allows space for innovation and new thinking, and acknowledges that in something as complex and important as education there are considerable nuances.

The danger, though, is that new ideas and approaches can be quickly judged through a polarising ideological lens. There are two main ideological battles that we have to force our way through: firstly, on the purpose of education; and secondly, on whether we have a progressive or traditional view of how we learn.

(i) The Purpose of School

Whose responsibility is it to teach the skills?

One perspective holds that the primary purpose of compulsory schooling is economic. Universal education was not driven, after all, by altruism but by the need for an increasingly educated and skilled labour force.

The other side of the argument focuses on building a love of learning and deepening and enhancing the cultural wealth of a nation as well as personal self-improvement and growth. In this view, economic considerations muddy the waters of learning.

If increasing the economic output of the nation is the priority of a school, then the argument for building these skills is easily made. Given that employers are calling out for these skills, then we can reasonably assume that they would increase economic productivity.

If we believe, and for the record I do, that boosting economic output is not the sole purpose of education then we need a slightly more nuanced argument. Only slightly more though: as we explored in Chapter 2, although I might call them essential skills, a very similar set of skills are also known as study skills at university or personal learning and thinking skills , or entrepreneurial skills in their field.

The question, then, is that even if we concede these skills are useful regardless of where you lie on the spectrum of prioritising economic outcomes from education or not, is school really the best place to build those skills?

The UKCES suggested that 'only employers really know what employability is'. All jobs have specific skills that are important – whether it is being attentive to customers in a retailer, or being able to communicate over the telephone in a call centre, or having developed a specific skill or trade in the construction industry. I would agree here that such skills are best taught by the relevant employers, or through focused courses alongside colleges or universities – as happens for professions like teaching, the law, accounting, or medicine. But if you think of employability like this, it is easy to lose the wood for the trees – there are still some skills that most roles need – or which are required if an individual is to progress further in their role.

Additionally, these essential skills help students to learn effectively during their time in school and they also build off foundations that are best built early – they are harder to teach properly later on. This is a point made by Anders Ericsson[84] – that there is some evidence that some skills are better learnt sooner than others, particularly those focused on emotional and social development. This is a principle that we will explore in a bit more depth in Chapter 10.

(ii) The Progressive vs. Conservative Battlefield

The second ideological battle is perhaps more vicious, because it focuses less on the purpose of education as the best means of delivering it. In the first chapter, I made explicit very quickly that I absolutely did not want what followed to be seen through the lens of the progressive versus conservative battlefield of education. For the uninitiated, this is the running battle of whether we should be primarily building the knowledge of our students with the expectation that skills follow, or that actually we should focus on transferable skills as knowledge can be picked up as required.

A knowledge-based approach

Advocates of the more conservative perspective see the building of knowledge as the principle bedrock for developing further skills, becoming autodidactic and living a full life. This requires strong conceptual understanding of the world. For example, learning the kings and queens of England as a fundamental part of bringing structure to the sweep of history. Within this framework, it is then possible to delve into the detail in greater depth. Similarly, English literature can be approached through the classical canon.

This means an early focus on spelling, grammar, times tables, and the other core building blocks and unifying frameworks. The logic here is sound – that given a limited working memory, we must commit a great deal to our long-term memories in order to be able to problem-solve, think critically, evaluate, comprehend through reading, or perform analysis.

Teaching methods will focus on building and retaining knowledge. Quite often this might mean a more didactic style of learning – listening to the teacher, reading or taking notes. Examinations are a strong way of assessing this type of learning, and seen therefore as the essential measure of educational success.

Champions of this position include Daisy Christodoulou who argues in her thought-provoking book *Seven Myths about Education* that we have sacrificed building a deep understanding to a preference for building skills and worrying too much about engaging activities[85].

Overall, this view holds that skills cannot be separated from the context in which they are used, so knowledge must come first.

A skills-focused approach

On the other side of the fence, a progressive advocate worries less about knowledge and more about skills. The simplest argument is this – in a world of Google and instantly available facts, what is more critical than any particular knowledge is the ability to find information and then to be able to use it.

In this view, to take the example of history again, learning the kings and queens of England is fairly meaningless. Such information, it could be argued, is just a few clicks away for students who can navigate Wikipedia with ease. Instead, what they would emphasise is that it is the skills of being a historian that should be the focus – and that the content is only a means to develop the skill. The skills of a historian would be things like being able to seek information or evaluate a source.

Champions of a more progressive education include Sir Ken Robinson who argues for schools to build creative young people, and who bemoans the factory approach of building a consistent set of knowledge and instead wants greater divergence and diversity in how young people develop[86].

Bringing the two together

Martin Robinson does a brilliant and somewhat reassuring job in capturing the ideological battlefield in his fascinating book *Trivium 21C*. Drawing on the approaches to education that he sees echoing from Ancient Greece and through the medieval period to the present day he sees two main schools of thought:

those he calls grammarians and the dialecticians. Grammarians, very briefly, want to teach the facts, or the truths that are known. Dialecticians want to question and probe and are sceptical about the existence of any real truths. In short, this is a long-running debate.

In the early days of Enabling Enterprise, we got together a great panel to discuss exactly that question – of whether we should be focusing on knowledge or skills. Of course, the basic answer came through strongly – that it is a false dichotomy to try to teach either knowledge or skills, but that there was an essential place for both, and indeed that the two reinforced each other.

So where do Essential Skills fall?

My experience is that neither extreme of the debate really works when it comes to how we think about essential skills. What we saw in the previous chapter is that for each of the skills they are best deployed in real life through having that rich knowledge and contextual understanding. That is not easily replaced by having access to Google or Wikipedia.

However, strong academic or contextual knowledge alone is not enough to automatically build these essential skills which draw off their own discrete set of knowledge and require separate practice.

Take the example of riding a bike. You can know your local geography, the route to your destination and the Highway Code – important contextual knowledge – but that won't be enough to reach your destination. You won't be able to do that successfully until you separately know what the handlebars, pedals, seat and all the rest do. And then you also need to practise the skill of balancing and riding. On the other hand, you might well get to the point of being able to cycle in loops around your garden without any of that contextual knowledge but that won't get you to your destination.

We cannot give a compelling presentation without a strong knowledge of the subject at hand, and skills of communication. We cannot learn through listening without a grip on the context and terminology and also the ability to sift for meaning and take notes.

We cannot solve complex problems without the best information put into decision-making structures or set against hypotheses that we are skilled in laying out.

The essential skills don't remove the need for knowledge and they don't make it less important. They are not so transferable that a skilled individual can lead a team to complete a task that they have no knowledge or experience of. But they are extractable from that knowledge and can be built on their own – whether it is presenting, leading, or the logical models that underpin problem-solving – before being combined with knowledge on deployment. They can also be built in parallel with knowledge – knowledge is essential but it is not sufficient.

(B) Practical Barriers

If we can get past the ideological traps on the path to teaching essential skills, our next stop is to unpick the practical reasons why these skills do not get taught. I will touch on these only lightly now, as they are more fully addressed in Part 3 when we look at the principles of what can be effective instead.

(i) Essential Skills and Business Studies

Firstly, there is a real challenge around how essential skills are viewed in school – when they are often referred to as enterprise or employability skills. Particularly at secondary school they are often either seen as being part of business studies, or employability which is only relevant to the very oldest students.

This is unsurprising when these skills are cast as part of enterprise education. The definition that Ofsted, the school inspection agency, use here is broad, drawing not just on enterprise capabilities, many of which are actually attitudes or character traits, but also a lot of economic, financial and consumer understanding. Ofsted looks for evidence that students have a decent level of financial literacy and are savvy consumers alongside having the traits for future success. With this blending of skills, character and knowledge it makes sense that this becomes seen as an extension of business studies or economics.

We will look at what should happen later on, but the danger with treating enterprise or the essential skills as nothing more than an extension of business studies is that it is put in a completely different silo from other learning – treated as a niche concern rather than something which has implications for all students' experiences of learning in school and their future opportunities.

The other obvious effect is that we overlook the skills of younger pupils. Business studies teachers, unlike almost all other subjects, are specialists in 14- to 19-year-old teaching. I remember as a teacher how difficult it was to make up ground with these students whose earlier education had certainly not equipped them with these skills.

For primary school students, business studies and employability are basically irrelevant – they may be more than a decade away. If we frame the essential skills in this way, then it is much harder for a primary school teacher or headteacher to justify focusing on them from a young age.

(ii) Crowding out

It happened quite often that a cloud would come across the face of a hitherto enthusiastic headteacher. There would be a pause, then a frown: 'So where are we going to find the time to do this?'

This is not just a reflection of a curriculum that can feel to teachers like it is already bursting at the seams. It is also a reflection on the tightness of school accountability frameworks – at both primary school and secondary school. Teachers and headteachers are tightly bound to pupil assessment measures – particularly formalised assessments like SATs, GCSEs or A levels. As one commentator at a recent conference remarked, 'schools are having to put an enormous amount of energy into *showing* student progress'.

Competing priorities also take up capacity – whether in the form of the English Baccalaureate, the Progress Eight measures or school improvement plans. Floor targets can be a particular worry for schools who serve the most disadvantaged cohort of students.

Schools are also bound to fulfil the targets and priorities of Ofsted. That is not to say that Ofsted completely ignores the development of essential skills. They do recognise their importance – for example, in 2016 they published a review of enterprise education across secondary schools[87], and were generally unimpressed by what they saw. In just four of the 40 schools they inspected were they comfortable that the characteristics for effective enterprise education, including development of enterprise skills, were being fulfilled. The report acknowledged that school leaders did not have the resources to focus on these skills, and they saw their remit solely as being a particular set of exam grade outcomes.

(iii) Enterprise education fatigue

I am often struck by a sense of enterprise education fatigue in the schools I visit. This is important because, as already noted, our essential skills are often termed enterprise skills.

Successive initiatives, policies and implementation criteria have, as I've argued, led to enterprise education being seen as a catch-all category.

What we have ended up with is therefore not an intellectually robust or consistent approach, but rather a set of approaches that have become standard and acceptable.

- Schools try to distil the building of essential skills into one-off enterprise days, externally provided workshops, or outside the school context.

- Schools try to embed the development of essential skills into the whole curriculum, by making their development an additional expected outcome of each lesson.

- Schools allow the development of all learning skills, including essential skills, to dictate the activities and approach in all learning, particularly through cross-curricular learning – for example, by breaking down subject barriers to create 'topic' learning.

Because we have muddied aims, we have not been sufficiently rigorous in assessing which approaches have the most impact.

(C) Pedagogical Barriers

The final set of barriers are pedagogical. Whether acknowledged or not, there is a presumption that essential skills are not teachable.

Our experience at Enabling Enterprise has shown that before we start working with schools, teachers lack confidence in their own ability to teach these skills. This lack of confidence can be reinforced by pedagogical beliefs or assumptions, which tend to fall into three categories:

- That essential skills are basically innate.
- That essential skills can only be developed by experiences outside the classroom.
- That essential skills lie dormant, but are ignitable with a spark of inspiration.

As we looked at the eight essential skills, we started chipping away at the challenge of teachability for each skill individually. For what comes next, though, it is essential to dissemble the misconceptions that attach themselves to the whole group of skills.

(i) Essential skills are innate

I have lost track of the classrooms where teachers proudly indicate their natural leaders, natural team players, and natural presenters. They seem surprised when I highlight their implicit assumption that the majority of their students will therefore be unable to build those skills.

This is unsurprising as we are so often encouraged to categorise our children and young people, whether as teachers or parents – including identifying those of 'high or low ability', those who are sporting, or clever, or like reading.

The implications for teacher practice

If essential skills are innate, then there is little that the teacher can do beyond nurturing those with the inherent ability, and avoiding harming those without.

We see this behaviour all the time – the child who repeatedly gets picked to present in assembly, or who gets the leading role in the school play. Or the students who get picked to be team leader or captain at every opportunity. And conversely the students who are overlooked despite their waving arms, until eventually they don't even try to put their hands up any more.

The effects

Malcolm Gladwell, in his thought-provoking book *Outliers*, highlights how small advantages early on are often compounded once opportunities are directed at particular students[88]. An often-cited example is that of how cut-off dates for eligibility for selective junior sports teams like hockey leads to a disproportionate concentration of team members who are born in the same months. Their small physical advantages from being the oldest in their cohorts are compounded over time by the fact that once they are chosen for these teams, they then get extra training and support. This turns small advantages into significant differences in performance by the time they are young adults.

Similarly, it is small wonder that those 'innately' skilled students may eventually surpass their peers in those essential skills. This is a perfect example of a self-fulfilling prophecy.

There is also a strong effect on student self-perception. We are not very good at objectively analysing ourselves. Instead we build up our own narrative which tells the story of where our strengths and weaknesses lie, and then seek opportunities to reinforce those strengths and avoid any situations that might highlight our weaknesses.

Where this comes from

One driver of this is a confusion between the essential skills and personality traits. The 'big five' traits are extraversion, agreeableness, openness, conscientiousness and neuroticism.

So we might presume the extrovert child to be better at presenting because, in the words of one teacher, 'they are talking all the time anyway'. Similarly, an extrovert might appear to be more of a leader because they put their ideas forward more willingly and forcefully.

We might presume that the conscientious student will be better at aiming high, while the neurotic student will struggle at staying positive.

However, there is growing evidence in management academia that introversion is more likely to be a hallmark of an effective leader than extroversion[89]. Similarly, there is little link between neuroticism and the ability to stick at goals.

Moreover, we are even currently seeing a shift in thinking around whether academic ability is innate. This has also been highlighted as the 'Flynn Effect' – drawn out from a combination of studies that showed that average IQ test scores have risen over time[90].

The reality

Personally, I have no doubt at all that essential skills are teachable. I have seen first-hand that if you work with children from a young age, it is perfectly possible for all of them to become confident and competent presenters, unless they have related special educational needs. It is even possible to build a basic level of presenting skills in students, even if you leave it until they are a bit older. That, of course, is not the same as a high level of proficiency or mastery – that requires a long lead-in and continued development into adulthood, but it is certainly better than the alternative.

Another way of thinking about the skills is to think about each component that builds up to a high level of competence. One to start with is taking turns – we all believe that it is possible for a child to take it in turns. They may not be automatically driven to want to share but the mechanics of taking it in turns is fairly elementary.

What about contributing to a team? Now, we may not initially or ever enjoy being part of a team. We might lack confidence in building those relationships. But we can learn to ask others what contribution would be most helpful. We can learn tactics to contribute in meetings and discussions. We can divide off our piece of work, perhaps complete it individually and then bring it back to the whole. If we can learn to do each element and then practise it in different settings then of course we can do it.

So to me, arguments that these skills are innate and unteachable are as unfounded as to claim that some people are just natural car drivers, or natural readers. Yes, some people might have natural advantages (the evidence on this is limited) and may start in different places (often due to past practice or learning that is not clear to the instructor), but all can benefit from focused learning and practice.

(ii) Essential skills are built in the environment

Another idea that some people hold is that essential skills are built in the wider environment. This has an intellectually comforting 'nurture and nature' feel about it – that those skills are the sum of all the experiences, interactions and learning of a lifetime.

We see those who have mastered them at work, or are put into situations where they are cultivated and built through experiences perhaps.

This is reinforced by the sense that many extracurricular opportunities are also about nurturing these skills. Some do this explicitly – for example, the Duke of Edinburgh awards explicitly talk about 'skills and attributes such as resilience, commitment, self-motivation and team working'[91]. Similarly, the National Citizen Service (NCS) 'encourages personal and social development by working on skills like leadership, teamwork and communication'.[92]

The implications for teacher practice
If we see essential skills as being formed by the surrounding environment then the prescription for the teacher is different. This is more of a model of osmosis – we can little control what happens beyond putting the students in an intuitively more promising environment to absorb skills from.

In this way, much enterprise education leaps straight into activities – the chance for students to work in teams, to present things, to do a Dragons' Den-style challenge. The very presence of activities should help to develop skills.

The effects
We do not take the building of essential skills in the classroom seriously if we do not really feel that we cannot have much of an impact on the outcomes. Instead we look to external providers, or employers or parents to make up the gap that we see in our students.

The other effect is that if we just see skill development as a process of osmosis, we might well think that repetition of activities is a way of making progress. Anders Ericson describes this as 'naïve practice' rather than 'deliberate practice'.[93]

Where this comes from
Much of this reasoning comes from the confusion of tangible skills like being able to set goals and have tactics to stay on track with deeper character or personality traits.

There is evidence that in building character traits they as much 'caught' as they are taught – that values and ways of thinking are often formed through experience and through the modelling of others. That is why the Jubilee Centre emphasises the role of extracurricular opportunities as ways of building those attributes – something that is repeated when you think back to the winners of the government's Character Awards.

It is also the case that extracurricular activities can be helpful in building essential skills. Indeed, I would go further than that and say that I would want every child to have those opportunities. In some cases, the wealth of extracurricular opportunities that students have access to alongside parental networks are sufficient for them to build the level of skills required to thrive.

The problem, though, is that many students do not have access to these same privileged opportunities. While there is a place for ensuring greater access to these chances, I would strongly argue that this will continue to be insufficient in the absence of a systematic solution for all children. We would simply not accept relying on *ad hoc* extracurricular opportunities for any other essential learning.

The reality

The evidence is very much against the idea of building essential skills by osmosis. If we believed that 'doing more' would naturally lead to better skills or greater performance then we would expect that more years in a particular profession would lead to higher performance. This has been repeatedly disproved though – for example, in 2005 a group of researchers at Harvard Medical School reviewed how the quality of care that doctors were providing changed with experience. Having reviewed 60 studies, they found that doctors' performance stayed the same only in the best cases – in most, performance declined over time[94].

While multiple experiences can be useful for practising, school still plays a unique role as a 'spine' which can bring coherence to multiple experiences in different settings. In the same way that effective maths or English tuition, library classes, STEM workshops or whatever else are linked back to the classroom, there is a real advantage to those extracurricular activities also having a common link. This is unifying framework is more than just an administrative advantage – it is important as a way of achieving a higher level of competency in our skills.

We can use this combination of a common link and diverse practice to ensure students can replicate patterns of action that lead to high performance and the deployment of skills in different settings[95].

(iii) Essential skills are ignitable

Too often schools buy into the idea of the 'quick-fix' – that a single insight, or speech, or competition will unleash skills that have been previously dormant. After all, in a packed curriculum that would be truly helpful.

It's also a view that is helpfully promoted by external providers who can sell a workshop or event that will 'tick the boxes' for a school and achieve incredible outcomes in a short period of time.

The implications for teacher practice

If we think that essential skills are just waiting to be turned on, we could merely point students to opportunities that exist. In a more extreme view, we would expect students to seek them out themselves. In this case, there is really no role for the teacher or for the education system as a whole to do anything. We expect that students will do this for themselves.

Where this comes from

This final view, that these skills lie latently like desert grasses, waiting for the rains to bring them to life, is something of a hangover from the confusion over definitions – particularly the difference between essential skills (particularly when called enterprise or employability skills) and entrepreneurial attributes. In this view, the sole purpose of enterprise education is to provide inspiration – to inspire people to use their skills.

In many classrooms, teachers cite entrepreneurs who struggled in school but had inherent gifts which activated outside the school environment.

The reality

There is growing scepticism that there are any skills that lie latent in this fashion. In his review of what drives performance, Anders Ericsson argues that 'there is no evidence that any otherwise normal people are born with the innate talent to sing or do math or perform any other skill'[96].

Summary

We started this chapter with a critical question: if we believe there is a gap in education and that the gap could be filled by teaching eight critical essential skills then why don't we teach them?

What this chapter has shown, I hope, is that there are several barriers to why we have not yet made the breakthrough to consistently teaching these skills in our classrooms. Some of the resistance is ideological – both on what we see the purpose of education as being, and what the most effective pedagogical approach is. Some of it is practical – like finding time in the timetable, or from the fatigue that arises from some of the confusion that we highlighted before.

The experience of myself and my team, who have now cumulatively trained and supported over 10,000 teachers, suggests that the biggest barriers are often pedagogical. There is a pre-existing set of beliefs about the skills that stop teachers investing energy in building them – that they are innate, built in the environment or ignitable.

To really overcome these barriers, though, we have to take a conceptual leap. Are you ready?

Chapter 8:
Reconceptualising Essential Skills

We know what the essential skills are. We can see that if our students are able to achieve a high level of competence in them, then this could make a great difference to their chances for future success.

We have also seen why they do not often get taught – a combination of ideological, practical and pedagogical drawbacks. But these ideological barriers can be navigated, the practical barriers have already been overcome by hundreds of our schools, and the pedagogical barriers are based on misunderstanding.

But it is insufficient just to see these skills as something to tag onto lessons, or as a discrete subject, or as a set of school mantras or values. If we're serious about filling the gap, we have to see them as the essential underpinning skill set they are.

And that means placing them alongside literacy and numeracy.

What works in building the skills

By 2012, three years in, we had nailed down the essential skills, albeit that we were calling them enterprise skills, and we had committed to an ambitious mission: to ensure that one day, all students leave school equipped with the essential skills, experiences of the working world and aspirations to succeed.

Our programmes had ballooned by this point – driven by a desire to see what worked. Our core programme for 14- to 16-year-olds had been complemented by a more advanced programme for 16- to 18-year-olds. Meanwhile our initial pilots with younger students had continued to expand.

Alongside what was happening in the regular enterprise classes some of our schools were now running, we also had a series of after-school clubs, we did some intervention work for students falling behind and we ran summer schools. We worked alongside other partners to create short projects, we delivered our programmes in special schools and alternative provision schools alongside mainstream schools. We ran big one-off challenges and events – including a 2000-student extravaganza for Global Entrepreneurship Week.

Some of this was working well. Some of it was not. But the overwhelming sensation was that we were trying to apply a sticking plaster to massive wound.

We stopped, and took a long, hard look at what was actually working. We realised that there were several schools where the programme was highly effective – where we could see a tangible difference in the students, and whose teachers were increasingly engaged and excited. Schools like Curwen Primary School.

At Curwen, the school had really embraced the programme. The essential skills were clear on entering the school, as was a book of their highlights from the programme. The students could immediately explain what the skills were and what they actually meant – and what they were individually working on. The buzz of their enterprise lessons was palpable – not just from the students but from the teachers comparing notes in the staffroom.

The students and their teachers were taking the programmes seriously, taking pride in the work that the students were producing through their weekly projects – whether prototype toys, plans for school improvements or a fundraising campaign. They were making the most of the opportunity to visit businesses in the centre of London – only a handful of stops on the train into town but somewhere many of the children had never gone with their families.

They were achieving a brilliant combination of focused time on the skills, application in different contexts, and continual reinforcement.

We also saw that there were other schools where the programmes were giving the students an enjoyable and useful experience but were not having the transformative impact that they needed to have if we were actually going to achieve our mission.

It was an exciting time – we could see the flickering of something special in the midst of everything that was going on. At the same time that we were spending days in the 147 schools that we were working with at that point, we were also looking closely at the evidence that was coming back from the schools in the form of the student skills progress – which at that point was principally self-assessment. We could see that our hunch was right – some students were making much greater progress than others.

In parallel, we started to unpick the approach that we were using, to re-examine its academic and pedagogical underpinnings, and we realised we were thinking about it all wrong.

We knew that rigour was important – and felt strongly that one of the main failings of enterprise education to that point had been to put too much emphasis on fun or engaging experiences and activities and not enough on drawing out the learning that came from that. Indeed, at the risk of sounding like a complete killjoy, we know that the process of building skills in a deliberate way is not always that fun. Just ask the pianist who practises their scales and arpeggios over and over again. The joy comes in the performance, but we cannot skip the vital step of practice.

To build this rigour and focused practice, though, we were using the conceptual framework of trying to rebuild Enterprise Education as a *subject* alongside any other academic learning – whether history, English literature or science.

The problem of course is that these are essentially knowledge-rich subjects that develop some skills through the application of that knowledge.

Instead, we realised we needed to think of essential skills as an essential component of learning alongside numeracy and literacy, which are themselves identified as the basic skills that underpin others.

Different ways of conceptualising essential skills

There are basically four different ways that you could think about essential skills:

- As values
- As an embedded subject
- As a discrete subject
- As basic skills

Values

Schools certainly do sometimes think of them as values – enshrined as part of the school motto or as an acrostic which conveniently spells out some inspiring word. If they are values they are important for building a pattern of behaviour and reinforcing norms and attitudes. The problem is that values are about behaviours and therefore about character – they are about informing the choices that we make, not our abilities.

Embedded subject

Another approach is to embed the skills in other learning. The simplest way of doing this is to make the development of a skill part of every lesson. To an extent this can work – what Professor Bill Lucas refers to as 'split screen teaching' – where we are both teaching subject knowledge on one hand, and then in turn are also building the skills through the design of activities[97]. This can work if a teacher has a high level of confidence and experience in building both knowledge and skills.

The challenge is that 'embedded' is often a code word in schools for not-really-done. It requires a particularly high level of teacher expertise to be combining knowledge teaching with the building of embedded skills. By adding a box on a lesson plan to highlight which skill was a focus we just get a simple tick-box exercise. When I was teaching, I would tick the 'teamwork' box if there was any group exercise, or 'communication' box if students shared their work. They were using these skills, potentially, but they were not deliberately building them.

Discrete subject

The third approach is to make essential skills a discrete subject – perhaps by calling it enterprise – which is where we started, having seen that simply valuing the skills was not enough, and embedding was rarely successful.

This makes some sense – there is a body of knowledge associated with building these skills – otherwise the executive education market would be less saturated with leadership, teamwork, presenting or self-management books. Our experience of going down the road of building Enabling Enterprise as a strong, rigorous subject was that it was incredibly helpful for building teachers' understanding of how essential skills are built, and giving the space to build students' understanding of the skills and to practise them in a controlled, focused environment.

However, it is not enough by itself because in the main we are not trying to build an academic appreciation of the skills. We know that, to be useful, we also need students to be able to apply them consistently in different settings.

What we were finding, as many critics of the concept of 'transferable skills' will recognise, is that things that they could do in their enterprise lessons were not being transferred to other areas of learning or beyond the school walls.

Basic Skills

So, what we came to realise at Enabling Enterprise is that none of the other ways of 'placing' essential skills really works. Instead, we need to look to the curriculum core of literacy, numeracy and, to an extent, IT as better reflecting how we really need to be thinking about essential skills.

I understand that this is not an unprecedented comparison. It is easy to claim that whatever one personally believes to be important in education to be central – and since literacy and numeracy are almost universally acknowledged to be important, they are frequently drawn in as comparison.

However, that is certainly not where we started – it would be wonderful if essential skills could really just be embedded or taught as a discrete subject. Unfortunately, as we have seen, both of these approaches have already been tried and found wanting. What we need is *both* – taught discretely, and then practised by being embedded elsewhere too.

So, putting aside any initial scepticism, it is useful to think about the hallmarks that mean that numeracy, literacy and IT are seen as being the basic skills. I would argue that there are four critical characteristics:

(i) They are primarily about the ability to do something

This might seem like an obvious starting point and it is important not to get too simplistic. What is different about numeracy or literacy, particularly when contrasted with mathematics or English literature is that they focus on application.

Literacy is widely defined as the ability to read and write. If that seems rather too basic, then UNESCO have a much bigger definition which is the 'ability to identify, understand, interpret, create, communicate and compute, using printed and written materials associated with varying contexts. Literacy involves a continuum of learning in enabling individuals to achieve their goals, to develop their knowledge and potential, and to participate fully in their community and wider society'[98].

Numeracy is defined by National Numeracy as 'being able to reason with numbers and other mathematical concepts and to apply these in a range of contexts and to solve a variety of problems'[99].

That is not to say that they do not include knowledge – of course they do. Being literate is underpinned by identifying letters, being able to reproduce sounds, having a wider vocabulary, understanding of grammar and much more. Being numerate equally requires concepts of counting, arithmetic, multiplication tables and many other concepts. But the real test is that they can be applied.

Essential skills are absolutely about the ability to do things too: being able to work with others, self-manage, creatively solve problems, and communicate effectively.

Earlier, we established that whatever the arguments from a conservative or progressive view of education, all subjects have a combination of knowledge and skill. The knowledge of the kings and queens of England give the ability to place an event in historical context. Knowledge of rock types and their characteristics gives the ability to identify specimens. Medics have to learn huge amounts of information in order to be able to treat patients.

Really, there is a spectrum for subjects from pure knowledge or theoretical understanding through to practical application. And while it is not black and white, essential skills are definitely on the practical application end alongside literacy and numeracy.

(ii) Useful throughout life
While it is possible to frame many parts of the curriculum as being about 'the ability to do something' – particularly if you take a more progressive view of the purpose of education – it is harder to argue about the universal importance of these essential skills.

Casting back to Chapter 1, we saw that in order to learn effectively in school and then excel in whatever you do in life, literacy, numeracy, and increasingly IT are seen as being vital. It seems almost farcical to point out how little it is possible to do now without a basic level of literacy or numeracy in modern life. Those people who miss out on developing a basic level of those skills will never achieve a minimum standard of qualifications and their opportunities and choices in life will be greatly curtailed.

This is in contrast to much of the curriculum. I think that in order to live a full and satisfying life which achieves its potential, understanding how the world works from scientific, economic, cultural and historical contexts matters. But it is telling that employers are much less worried about the specific knowledge of school leavers (just 23% cited this as a priority) than they are about the skills of those school leavers, where 89% cited them as a priority[100].

(iii) Unlock other learning

Sometimes what a government really cares about can be found in the measures that it wants to put in place. It gives a lot of curriculum flexibility in some areas but literacy and numeracy are always key. They are also meant to be reinforced elsewhere in teaching.

Beyond absolute basics, there is little that can be taught in the formal education system if students do not also grasp literacy and numeracy.

What is clear is that we often see that students are being held back in their learning through shortages in their essential skills too. Whether that is the ability to listen to and process information, communicating their own thoughts and ideas, or self-management to take control of their own learning.

As students progress and build up a strong framework of knowledge and understanding, they will find that many areas touch on other areas. There is, indeed, a whole movement against putting educational learning into 'subject-specific silos' on the grounds that the sciences and the arts suffer from being artificially separated. However, building a deep knowledge of history, for example, is not a pre-requisite for being a successful scientist.

Essential skills are up there with literacy, numeracy and IT as being essential for deeper learning across different subject disciplines – whether you consider any separation between those disciplines as artificial or not.

(iv) Transferability

What essential skills do is to focus on a small number of basic skills that can be transferred. They have their own theoretical base, in the same way that literacy and numeracy do and can similarly be used in many different settings. For example, if you want to evaluate a hypothesis, you can't do that effectively without an understanding of the scientific context.

What essential skills do is to focus on a small number of basic skills that can be transferred. They have their own knowledge base, in the same way that literacy and numeracy do but they can be used in many different settings.

This transferability isn't fully automatic – Chapter 14 makes clear that they must be practised in different settings to increase their transferability – but if built effectively they are not tightly bound to any specific setting or subject context either.

Of course, when applied, as with literacy and numeracy, contextual understanding is critical too[101] . Students read better when they understand the topic. Similarly, a team will perform better on a task they are familiar with.

But while having the skill doesn't reduce the importance of the knowledge, having the knowledge is insufficient without also bringing the skill to bear.

Summary

At the end of this chapter, we can see that recognising the value of having essential skills is not enough. It is not even sufficient to isolate them.

We cannot just approach them as values, although it is great if they are prioritised. We cannot just teach them as a discrete subject, because that loses the transferability that makes them fundamentally important. Nor can we just embed them, because we lose the ability to provide focused opportunities for mastery.

They fulfil four key principles that set them apart: they are primarily about the ability to do something, they are universally important throughout life, they unlock other learning, and they are transferable to different settings.

They should sit alongside literacy and numeracy as the basic skills. This is the vital lens to make sense of how we should build them for all our children and young people.

The question now is how to turn that aspiration into a reality.

Part 3:
Filling the Gap

Realising that we had been thinking about essential skills the wrong way for four years at Enabling Enterprise could have been a heart-breaking moment for us. But I remember a slight wave of euphoria – as we could suddenly start to make sense of what we had been seeing in the schools where I could see the transformation in the students that I had dreamed of for my own.

We started to draw out the parallels between literacy and numeracy and what was going on in these schools. That's when things started to get really exciting – because what we saw was that the same principles that drove improvements in literacy and numeracy could also drive our work to make a high level of competence in essential skills achievable for all children and young people.

We didn't stop questioning though: we worked through the literature ourselves – looking at the principles over the course of 2014 and 2015 to produce what we internally called 'the Little Book of Enterprise'. We then went back over the skills and our skills framework, and pushed ourselves to improve their alignment and calibration, and the clarity of language. Over the course of 2015-16 we produced a series of booklets on each of the skills to dig into their basis, how they are developed and why they can be so powerful. We pushed ourselves to ensure that they really were teachable and to create resources for teachers that they could see would make a real difference.

In 2016-17 we commissioned education think tank LKMco to look into the hypotheses that we were developing independently, to stress-test the principles and the evidence base for what we were seeing, learning and experiencing in Enabling Enterprise schools.

The following six chapters explore the six principles that we have found successful in building essential skills in our children and young people. While we have looked at them primarily from the perspective of schools and teachers, there is no reason why they cannot be picked up by parents or other organisations as well.

Briefly, schools who are developing the essential skills effectively are following six principles to:

- *Keep it simple:* Focus on a simple, consistent set of essential skills that cover interpersonal skills, self-management, communication, and creative problem-solving.
- *Start early and keep going:* Don't see these skills as a last-minute quick fix – they need be developed from the outset of education to give students every chance to develop their skills as fully as possible and access other learning.
- *Measure it:* Measure essential skills by using a comparable approach to maths levels or reading ages through the Skills Builder framework.
- *Focus tightly:* Use this understanding of students' essential skills to teach them deliberately and directly.
- *Keep practising:* Like literacy and numeracy, dedicated learning time matters, but so do opportunities to reinforce those skills throughout school life and beyond it.
- *Bring it to life:* Essential skills are most valuable when they can be applied in different settings – which is why linking to the wider world, including employers, universities and entrepreneurs is vital.

We've seen the scale of the problem, where we're going wrong, and how we can re-focus if we think about essential skills completely differently. Now let's look at how to fill the gap.

Chapter 9:
Keep it simple

We have already identified our set of essential skills. But to make the most of them we must be consistent, understandable and memorable in how we use them. We need a shared understanding, as we do for literacy and numeracy.

We must also avoid abstraction: that is, we should avoid trying to work on, or too readily claim progress against, broad student dispositions like 'being confident' or 'being a charismatic communicator'. Instead, we need to be disciplined in sticking to the same specific skills that can be broken down into manageable and teachable chunks.

We must keep it simple.

The challenge today
In too many schools essential skills are lost somewhere in the midst of:

- *Knowledge:* Including career routes and industries, how to apply to college, what qualifications are important for different job roles, financial literacy, basic economics, how to manage a budget, and even how to legally incorporate a company.
- *Virtues or character strengths:* Including honesty, integrity, risk-taking, dedication, hard work and a lot more besides.
- *Skills:* Include communication, self-management, goal-setting, working with others, problem-solving and creativity.

If we fail to separate these out, it becomes impossible to focus on any of them properly. As a result schools often fall back on an untargeted array of generic 'enterprise activities'.

Before Enabling Enterprise, I witnessed students spend a day designing an entirely hypothetical music show, based on paper worksheets. It was unsurprising to see most students playing on their phones as some poor business volunteers, brought into the school for the occasion, gamely tried to keep them engaged.

I saw more than a few competitions too – students being given a sum of money and told to invest it in some entrepreneurial activity to earn a return, for example. At the end of the day, students dutifully filled in a feedback form on how their confidence had soared, as if a few diverting hours had set them up for life.

This seems a long way from a focused, coherent approach to equipping young people with the skills they need.

Why this has come about

Our essential skills are most often cast as enterprise skills, and therefore part of enterprise education. The Department for Education have a working definition of enterprise education that covers:

- Enterprise capability – enterprise skills and a can-do attitude
- Financial capability – understanding and managing basic finances
- Economic & business understanding – understanding the business context[102]

It is also interesting to see why Ofsted see these skills as being important: for example, 'young people, as a target for highly persuasive advertising and marketing, need to develop a critical awareness as consumers. In secondary schools, many have part-time jobs and almost [all] will need to develop a range of employability skills for when they enter the labour market. Many have bank accounts while at school, and from the age of 18 will have access to credit and a huge range of other financial services – and thus need to develop sound financial capability. All will need to understand something about the economy in order to function as well-informed citizens'[103].

As you can see, essential skills can easily get lost in the midst of all of that.

An approach that works

Part 2 made clear that we can cover the essential skills in four pairs:

- Interpersonal skills: Teamwork and Leadership
- Self-management: Aiming High and Staying Positive
- Communication skills: Presenting and Listening
- Creativity and Problem-solving

These skills have already been discussed at length, and the critical point in this chapter is that they cannot just be thrown into the mix. They have to be consistent, simple and reinforced.

The schools who are effective are disciplined. They are disciplined in the language that they use and maintaining a steady focus on these eight skills. They are also disciplined about avoiding abstraction.

Avoiding abstraction

We need to avoid abstraction in how we think about these skills. One of the ways in which these things get confused is by trying to work on something that is far too big and expansive. For example, imagine that the goal of science lessons was to get to the point where a student was a 'dedicated scientist'. That would be hard to effect, might be influenced by parental attitudes, and lacks specificity to the extent that working on it would be very difficult.

We run into exactly the same problem if we think in terms of abstract constructs such as conscientiousness or agreeableness. Similarly abstract dispositions include individuals being cooperative, assertive, responsible, empathetic, or persistent[104]. These dispositions merge character and skill in a way that makes them very difficult to teach.

Instead of setting too big a goal in terms of working on students' dispositions, we do much better by focusing on skills which are, in the words of the same Brookings Institute article, 'specific, contextual, socially observable, [and] easily malleable within the environment of classrooms and schools'[105]. Hence, at a classroom level the disposition of 'resilience' becomes the more teachable skill of 'staying positive'.

This requires discipline because it is easier to communicate the idea of building resilience, or confidence or collaboration. But if we over-claim what we can directly teach then we are doing ourselves and our students a disservice.

The power of simplicity

This simplicity is beautiful. Indeed, as Leonardo da Vinci purportedly said, albeit probably not in English, 'simplicity is the ultimate sophistication'.

This level of simplicity is vital because schools are complex organisations, with many competing priorities, and trying to get sufficient airtime for any single area is difficult. This is particularly the case in an environment where academic attainment is schools' most pressing concern.

It is also important that students and parents understand the language that is being used. It matters that the skills can actually be remembered. It is important that each skill is broken down in a way that gives credibility to the notion that it can actually be taught. Finally, the skills must make sense in the world beyond our classroom – to be understood by employers, colleges and universities.

For everything that follows, this simplicity is critical: to measure progress we need a stable, clear set of skills we are building; to build them from an early age and across school transition points we need a consistent language; to engage employers the skills need to be understandable; and to be reinforced across school life, they need to fit on a poster.

Of course, in targeting simplicity we miss out on some of the detail or the nuance. I can see that time management is a good skill, as is providing great customer service. Differences in definition can be meaningful and reflect deeper assumptions or underlying beliefs.

But to achieve the change we want to see requires a substantial shift in what we teach and prioritise. To do so, we need to focus on that simple core set of essential skills that bear up to the tests of transferability and measurability, so that they unlock further learning and are built in a cumulative way.

By aiming for simplicity and consistency, we move away from essential skills as a set of promising-sounding attributes to being something that we can all understand and jointly focus on – in the same way as we can numeracy or literacy. What we lose is, I believe, greatly outweighed by what we stand to gain.

The principle
The principle is that schools who are excelling here are focusing on a limited number of teachable essential skills – the ability to communicate effectively, to creatively problem-solve, to work with others, and to set goals and achieve them. They are disciplined and consistent in their use.

What it looks like in action
It is not hard to spot an Enabling Enterprise school that has embraced the idea of keeping it simple and making the skills an area of focus.

At Heartlands Academy in Birmingham, the set of eight skills meets visitors in reception as a statement of their importance to the school.

Meanwhile at Malmesbury Primary School in London, every classroom reminds the students of the same set of essential skills. Displays in the hall and reception area share the highlights of how the students have been building their skills that term.

In Cambridge, Isle of Ely and Chesterton Primary Schools both have a skill of the month to keep the profile of the essential skills high. In Yorkshire, Crossley Street Primary School went even further by launching their commitment to the skills with the students producing a podcast to explain them.

You can see the same set of skills reflected on websites across the Enabling Enterprise partner schools – a visible commitment that this is something that matters to them.

Putting it into practice in your classroom

If you are introducing the essential skills in your own classroom for the first time, it's worth investing a little time up front to build your own confidence and familiarity with the skills. We've put some free guides together at www. theessentialskills.org which help to dig into each of the skills and suggest some simple activities or approaches that can be used.

Visual displays are a great reminder to yourself and the students about what they are aiming for. They will be a good hint to you too when you want to reference them in other learning. Some teachers go beyond this – for example, by having a skill of the month for the students to focus on, or celebrating successes.

It's also essential that students know exactly what these skills mean – again, there are posters with age-appropriate definitions that you can access at www.theessentialskills.org and it is worth taking time to ensure a strong understanding of these, and to revisit and reinforce them in other settings.

We'll come on to build them as we look at the other principles.

Putting it into practice as a school leader

If this is your first attempt at introducing a focus on essential skills in your school, remember that you can't do it alone. Starting this journey towards building your students' essential skills requires a few things:

- Leadership: In every school where we have seen these skills really being built, we have seen a high level of personal investment from senior leaders across the school. Although there will always be competing priorities, it doesn't require a huge time commitment – more the willingness to champion the value of the skills consistently over a period of time, and highlight their value to teachers, students and their parents.
- Allies: Critically, if you're looking for a wider school impact there need to be champions from within the teaching staff too. Perhaps these are individual teachers who are particularly interested in this aspect of learning, or who already have some experience of it.

- Longer-term commitment: This is something that needs to become a core part of what a school values and prioritises and that means thinking of it not as something as a short focus, or a special project but a shift that will be supported and encouraged over the long-term.

On this basis, there are a few things to get started:

- Introduce staff to the language, the goals and the definitions.
- Use visual cues around the school to raise awareness, and use assemblies to reinforce the skills and how they are useful.
- Ensure that the same language is being used across interventions or at least that students can see the link between other extracurricular activities and how they directly link to supporting essential skills.
- If there is competing language or inconsistency the potential power of a simple approach will be lost.

Putting it into practice as a parent

If your child is at an Enabling Enterprise school then the chances are that they will already be very familiar with the language of the skills and able to reel them off on demand! There's a fascinating conversation to be had around what your child perceives the skills to mean – and when do they feel they show them? Where do they feel their strengths lie? Where would they like to improve? What could they do to do just that?

For other parents, I hope you now feel comfortable enough with the skills to begin to introduce them to your child – perhaps alongside reading or homework, or reward charts if they are younger.

There is also something compelling for children about their parents' own reflections – perhaps you could open up the conversation about where you feel your strengths and challenges lie against these skills? What about when you were younger, or the age of your child? What helped you to make progress?

When you are with your child you could highlight when you are having to use the skills to help them see how they are really used.

An important note, though, is that when introducing the skills or talking about them, it is important to keep remembering that they are teachable and learnable. Be careful not to put off your child by using the language 'I'm rubbish at...' or 'I could never...' or 'I'm just not someone who...'. Instead, build their sense, as everything that I have learnt over the last ten years has borne out, that with focused energies almost every child or young person can improve their skills, and accomplish a lot whatever their starting point.

Of course, the question is when to start – and that's what we turn to next.

Summary

If we want to set our children and young people up for success, we need to put essential skills at the heart of learning, as a core, basic expectation alongside literacy and numeracy.

Currently, we are a long way from that: schools are pulled by frequent emphasis on financial and economic knowledge and understanding over that core, transferable set of skills that we have already seen is vital for our students.

There is great beauty in simplicity. So, at Enabling Enterprise we have worked to hone a neat set of eight skills that we have covered in Chapter 3. But beyond that, what makes the difference is schools who embrace those skills with consistency and make them as tangible as possible.

This simplicity is vital to building a common understanding of what we are aiming for among teachers, parents and employers and, most importantly, for the students themselves. It also underpins all the more sophisticated things that we need to do in the following principles to really build the skills in all our students.

Chapter 10:
Start early and keep going

Too often, essential skills are seen as something for the oldest students and only begin to be a focus when students are preparing for the world beyond school. This is odd because at the outset of the school journey, we are comfortable that the youngest children need to master some basic social and emotional skills before they can access learning. But in the intervening years of their lives, these skills are largely overlooked.

In the same way that numeracy and literacy take continual application and effort throughout education, we need to take the same approach with essential skills. Building these skills is a continued journey – not a quick fix.

We need to start early – and then keep going.

What's going on

As a school system we tend to worry about essential skills only when life beyond the school gates starts to loom. Even then, as teachers, we sometimes only reference them in a slightly grudging acknowledgment that other people want to see them – whether in a college or university application or on a CV. We sometimes see success in this context as honing a strong answer to an interview question – 'Can you give me an example of when you've worked effectively in a team?'

I fell into exactly the same trap when I started teaching. Particularly as a sixth form tutor with the unenviable responsibility for my students' university applications I was preoccupied with evidencing skills rather than building them. I was sure that somewhere my students must have an example they could dig up. Over time, I realised that they couldn't find any such examples because they didn't have the skills. In that context, it was as valuable to try to find examples as it would be to get them to pretend they had read Dostoevsky to evidence strong literacy or to claim a supporting role in solving Fermat's last theorem.

When I realised they didn't have examples, I still fell into the second trap of focusing on those 15- and 16-year-old students on the cusp of leaving school to cram for these skills. But, as we found, you can replicate a behaviour in a setting, but you simply cannot build breadth, depth and transferability of essential skills quickly.

What we've seen at Enabling Enterprise

As Enabling Enterprise grew, it became clear to the team that we were never going to achieve our mission by focusing just on the oldest students. Over time we started working with children from the age of 5, and now we work with children as young as 3 years old.

This was driven by demand from the teachers of the oldest primary students who thought that this could be beneficial for their students – and then increasingly the younger classes in their schools. And then the reception classes and nurseries wanted to know why they were being left out.

Where we have been less eagerly received by primary school teachers, it often goes back to the central problem of confusing or merging essential skills, enterprise and employability. If you substitute employability for essential skills, it is perfectly reasonable that this should not be a priority at primary school – but if you instead talk about understanding the emotions of others, being able to overcome setbacks or social skills, then it seems much harder to argue that those things are only useful when you are 14.

If we make the comparison with literacy and numeracy, as teachers we're not at all squeamish about building those from a young age because we see them as vitally underpinning other learning too. Given how we have seen this is equally the case with essential skills, the fact that they are also useful in the future should not make them unpalatable now.

However, it is not just that we don't consistently build these skills at primary school, but that even at secondary school we tend to do little until the students are on the very cusp of leaving school.

What drives this?

There are a few structural reasons why this is the case: firstly, there is the pressure of time. For younger students, employment is such a long way away that it can be hard for some school leaders to see building these skills as a priority. There is, completely understandably, no accountability mechanism that links primary school with future employability. But it is less explicable that there is no accountability for the development of essential skills.

With credit to Ofsted, they recommend a 'well-planned provision for enterprise education at all key stages'. When they evaluated 28 primary schools as part of their enterprise education review in 2011, they highlighted that the best schools had integrated enterprise as an essential element of the whole school curriculum. The challenge, they acknowledge, is that there is no statutory requirement to provide it in Key Stages 1-3[106].

Secondly, when resources are tight, it is understandable that we would intuitively focus them on those students closest to leaving school. The government-initiated Careers and Enterprise Company has a remit to build the enterprise skills and capabilities of students, and support the consistent provision of careers information and guidance. However, their scope only runs from the age of 12[107]. This was also reflected in Lord Young's review, Enterprise for All, which limited recommendations on primary school to the 'Fiver' programme – where students are given £5 to grow through entrepreneurial activity[108].

Thirdly, external organisations are often more comfortable working with older students. The National Citizen Service (NCS) is one such example. The two- to four-week scheme explicitly talks about building skills and meeting new people. Students take part in an adventurous experience. They then return to a 'uni-style' experience where they build their confidence, leadership and communication skills. Finally, they apply and build these skills further through undertaking a short youth social action project[109].

While this sounds like a wonderful experience, the communication around NCS highlights building skills for a CV and UCAS, and is exclusively targeted at 15- to 17-year-olds.

Another national campaign, the #iwill campaign aims to boost youth social action. Again, we can admire the bold vision and drive of the campaign to substantially increase the number of students taking part in this sort of action – with a goal of 60% of young people taking part by 2020. It won't be a surprise at this point that the age group targeted is 10- to 20-year-olds.

Similarly, great programmes from the Duke of Edinburgh Award, the Prince's Trust, Career Ready and many others all focus on those older students.

Finally, we see a similar challenge for employers. Paul Drechsler, the President of the CBI, has repeatedly highlighted primary school support and engagement as a 'business blind spot'[110]. Again, this is unsurprising: employer engagement in education is considerable, generally done for the right reasons and hugely valuable for many young people. However, it also relies on employers to take the initiative. Where businesses see their engagement with education as part of building a pipeline of future employees or apprentices, then it does make sense to focus on those students who are at that point in their educational journey.

Research from the CBI shows that while 70% of businesses surveyed had links with secondary schools, only 35% of businesses had links with primary schools[111]. There are around 20,000 primary schools in England against 3000 secondary schools so this leaves a lot of primary schools without any links to businesses.

What should happen

If we shift our focus back to the essential skills that we highlighted earlier on, we realise that most of the challenge here comes from the intersection of enterprise and employability.

Literacy and numeracy skills start early on, because they are so essential for other learning. The skills are constantly built and exercised throughout a child's time in school.

Indeed, we know that one of the greatest challenges in closing the gap in attainment between students from relatively disadvantaged backgrounds and their wealthier peers is the differences in literacy and numeracy when they start school[112]. As teachers, we have long recognised the huge imbalance between those children who enter the classroom for the first time at the age of 4 already able to read and perhaps even write a little, and those who have had minimal interaction with written text.

Similarly, we recognise the difference between students who, when they hang up their coats and bags for the first time, can already count and recognise numbers, and maybe even do some basic addition, and those who cannot. The Early Intervention Review led by Graham Allen highlighted that a child's development score at just 22 months can serve as an accurate predictor of education outcomes at 26 years old[113].

What is also clear to teachers in a primary classroom is the sometimes-staggering difference in the students' broader skills – which we are calling essential skills. The tell-tale signs are there: students who don't want to let go of their parents; students who are unable to articulate their ideas to their teachers or their peers; those who struggle to engage with imaginative play; those who disengage when asked to work with others; those who give up when faced with difficulties – whether that frustration is sullen or angry and aggressive.

Even when we recognise these challenges exist, we too often slip into the trap of assuming that these are traits – that is, just the reflection of an underlying character. Or we make the same mistakes of assuming that this is about familial nurture, and beyond our ability to influence.

Now, I absolutely recognise that parental influence is huge, but no child is responsible for the advantages or disadvantages of their background. We focus on trying to fix the imbalance in students' literacy and numeracy as a priority. We should care just as much about catching up students' essential skills too.

Essential skills as a bedrock

From the outset, building a balanced set of essential skills is critical. To work with others, you need to have the ability to understand different perspectives and experiences. That is just as much the case for leadership, which often proceeds from building an early understanding of the emotions of others.

This comprehension of others then underpins effective communication, as much as being literate does: without accurately gauging an audience's reaction, we run the risk of talking without being understood. We are unable to predict how a communication will be received, and so we cannot plan effectively. So both presenting and listening need these early foundations firmly in place.

The skill of staying positive builds off strategies and tactics to bounce back from setbacks. Without this, another of the eight skills, aiming high, would equally be redundant: setting goals and stretching aspirations are almost pointless without the ability to work towards them through thick and thin.

The final focus of essential skills, on problem-solving and creativity, requires both an understanding of others and the ability to stay positive together. The understanding of issues, challenges, and alternative experiences and views are essential for creative thinking. And to be an effective problem-solver requires sticking at a problem for as long as it takes to work it through.

Building core skills early has a positive impact on other learning too. For example, Kwok has found that starting earlier with these skills can have a knock-on effect on achievement in other curriculum areas. He gives an example of a study of first-grade students with low literacy skills, and found that those who were better able to react to change subsequently performed better on Woodcock-Johnson reading and maths assessments[114].

Finally, we know that it is easier to build some of the skills from a young age when attitudes are still forming. This is part of a broader phenomenon known as the 'bent-twig effect'[115] – that small tweaks to the direction of the twig at an early stage will lead to much larger changes as the twig grows into a branch. This is because the brain in children and young people is more malleable and adaptable earlier than it becomes later on.

Not just starting young, but keeping going

So, there is a huge value in starting early but there is also a value in keeping going. This is an important point, because I've seen many examples of schools where at early years, teachers are thinking about the students' wider skills and abilities. They do talk about imagination, managing emotions, listening to others, and paying attention.

For example, the *Development Matters* toolkit which is widely used with 3- to 5-year-olds highlights key outcomes like making relationships, self-confidence and self-awareness and managing feelings and behaviour. It also emphasises the importance of particular attributes to effective learning – like 'being willing to have a go', 'keep trying', and 'having their own ideas'.[116]

However, there can then be a shift between this and 'real' school which kicks in from the age of 5 or 6 and goes on from there, when expectations around literacy and numeracy really start to ramp up and some of those 'basics' are seen to have been ticked off insofar as the children can navigate their way adequately through the school day. As one of our headteachers reflected, 'We seem to imagine that in Year 1, students suddenly snap into being able to just learn didactically'.

The parallel with literacy and numeracy is instructive here again. You can be ahead or on track in your literacy or numeracy when you are young. You might have greatly benefited from parental support or other experiences. But it is not a box to be ticked – you can be highly literate as a 5-year-old – but only against the expectations of a 5-year-old. You can be exceptionally numerate – but even the record-breaking 6-year-old with a maths GCSE only got a C. They certainly have not mastered the field of mathematics. Students continue to build their literacy and numeracy throughout their whole education – and we should equally be building the essential skills too.

That is because, as with mastering literacy and numeracy, it takes time to build a high level of competence in these skills. If we don't allow this time for mastery, then we just end up with mimicry. We only have enough time to work all the way through the scale of essential skills to high competence if we start young and then keep going.

Finally it is worth noting that with all skills, the level of competence fades when the skill is not being actively built. This should not be surprising – and reflects the widely cited finding that years of activity does not lead to improved performance without deliberate practice. Sadly, even if our 6-year-olds were on track or even ahead at that early stage they will not progress simply by continuing to get older.

If it is vital to build essential skills consistently for their own sake, it is particularly important not to drop the ball during the transition from primary school into secondary school. When we look at the skills assessments that our schools carried out in 2015-16 of students who had never completed an Enabling Enterprise programme, we saw that on average students in Year 7 actually performed worse than their peers who were a year younger.

For teachers, this will be a familiar story – students leaving primary school apparently confident, articulate and enthusiastic who then become increasingly withdrawn and disengaged from their learning. My view on this is that this transition point is one of multiple shocks: the change of location, a completely new set of teachers and school staff, often a very different culture, often a different set of peers. Add to this the hormonal changes that characterise becoming a young person and it unsurprising that there are headwinds in this year.

What is exciting, though, is how possible it is to maintain essential skills through this difficult period, and how effective an enabler they can be to making a success of it too.

The principle

Schools who are excelling in this area are introducing the essential skills from early years, and then consistently building them through education to support our children and young people to learn in school and set them up to be successful thereafter.

What it can look like

Enabling Enterprise students are as young as 3 years old, and just attending nursery. Curwen Primary School in East London serves a diverse but disadvantaged intake. The children joining the school will have had a variety of experiences depending on whether English is the primary language spoken at home, whether there are siblings around and whether parents are around. The result is quite differing starting points in terms of essential skills – as there are often stark differences in the students' literacy and numeracy.

Curwen works with children from nursery, involving them in the Enabling Enterprise programme along with their older peers. At this stage, they are building their social and emotional skills. Using the same language, though, means that they, their parents and their teachers are able to make links between these basics, and the opportunities and projects that the children will take part in later on.

At the other end of the scale, up in Lancashire, Nelson and Colne College is one of the country's top tertiary colleges. They have made the development of their students' essential skills a key part of their wider pastoral offer. That has included an extended social enterprise challenge which has seen students having to develop and apply their skills in the context of solving some of the challenges in their local area. These projects are valuable in their own right – for example, 'YoUniform' provides a place to buy, sell and exchange school uniform and equipment.

Putting it into practice in your classroom

If you're thinking about building the essential skills, the biggest challenge that this chapter is probably posing is which students to focus on.

If you're a primary school teacher, you might have one class who are your particular focus. Take some time to reflect on your initial sense of which students are relatively strong or weak in different skills – an interesting exercise to come back to in the next chapter.

At secondary school, you are likely to have a variety of classes. Perhaps start by picking a couple to focus on – or a tutor group if you have one – and don't just assume that the oldest ones are the ones to start with. It might be that you have particular concerns about the engagement or attitudes of one of your classes and that might be the best place to start, regardless of age.

Putting it into practice as a school leader

When discussing the importance of starting young with students in your school, there are two important ways of framing this: firstly, to start with the long-term picture – what is it that we want our students to be able to do by the end of our time with them? This might mean the point at which students are moving on to college, university, employment or entrepreneurship. For a primary school, it might be about an earlier transition point like the move to secondary school.

However, the second framing is just as important: what do we need our students to be able to do *now* in order to make the most of their time in school?

It is worth addressing head-on some of the resistance that might naturally emerge from teachers and others who to date have seen enterprise and employability skills through the lens we explored in this chapter.

There are a series of tools and videos to help with this at www.theessentialskills. org.

Putting it into practice as a parent

The thing to take away from this chapter as a parent, I hope, is a more joined-up sense of the continuity between the basic social skills and empathy and resilience that we focus on with our children when they are young and how that must continue to be reinforced and encouraged right through to when they are young people going into the world themselves.

What this looks like is explored in a bit more depth in the next chapters.

Summary

In this chapter, we've seen how essential it is to ensure that we start building essential skills from a young age, and then keep going.

Schools don't do this at the moment for a number of reasons – largely because we tend to see these skills as something for beyond the school gates, chiefly employment. Even in the latter part of secondary school, we see our roles as teachers as simply evidencing these skills for college or university applications, which is understandable given how difficult it is to build these skills quickly.

This is driven by several things: firstly, there is no statutory obligation to teach skills, with enterprise education not being compulsory. Secondly, with limited resources it can seem intuitive to target most energies at those closest to leaving school. Thirdly, we can too often believe that essential skills are best developed in an extracurricular setting, and those settings often best lend themselves to older students. Finally, employers see their input as most valuable to the oldest students.

However, there are compelling reasons to refocus on the youngest students: the differences in students' essential skills on starting school are as stark as differences in reading, writing and numeracy to their teachers. We work hard to close gaps in literacy and numeracy – and we should not write off differences in essential skills as simply nature or the sole preserve of parental nurture.

Even more importantly, all these skills are evidenced as being able to support learning in the classroom (including supporting numeracy and literacy). Building them sooner allows students to make the most of their learning throughout their time in school. Most pressingly, understanding others has been shown to be best developed early – it becomes much harder to build a high level of competence later on.

Starting early is insufficient, though, if we don't then keep going: essential skills are rich and complex and mastery takes time. The transition to secondary school can be eased by continuing to build the skills.

By starting young and keeping going, we give our children and young people the best chance of mastering and then capitalising on their essential skills.

The next question is, how do we make sense of that long path from 3 years old to 18?

Chapter 11:
Measure it

In an education system where measurement is often overdone, we seem strangely averse to any measurement around essential skills. We behave as though the skills are immeasurable, or that measurement itself undermines them.

What passes for measurement and assessment in the skills is often little more than counting activities or self-assessment which bears little relation to whether our students are actually making the progress they need to.

We should be working towards rigorous, quantifiable measures of essential skills. By breaking each skill down into its component blocks, we can assess when each of these is mastered and therefore gauge students' overall progress, against age-related expectations.

Once we can do this, all the effort that goes into these skills becomes meaningful and rewarded – as well as allowing us to learn the most effective ways of building them.

Minimal measurability

At the moment there is minimal measurability around essential skills. I've heard it said by teachers, enterprise coordinators and others that such skills are unmeasurable, or that the very process of measuring them somehow makes enterprise activities ineffective. I will always remember with despair the Enterprise coordinator who told me that 'we don't need to measure it, because we can see when they're enjoying themselves'. As Ofsted remarked, 'even where schools were delivering enterprise education, it was often unclear whether this was having any impact on pupils' knowledge, understanding and skills'[117].

As a result, if things are measured they tend to be experiences rather than the skills themselves – essentially the equivalent of assessing whether a child can read by tallying up the number of books they have borrowed from the library, or assessing numeracy by how many worksheets a student has completed.

Alternatively, we ask the students – generally for their perception of how confident they feel using a particular skill or whether they feel they have improved. This is often a pleasant and rewarding experience – students are smart enough to know that they are meant to make progress. It's telling, though, that we don't rely on students' confidence in reading – we assess whether they can routinely do specific things.

What drives this?
It is unsurprising that schools have this laid-back approach to measuring essential skills. I've already highlighted the challenge with definition – and where this confusion exists I can completely understand why schools get stuck. This is particularly the case if we confuse character attributes like honesty and extroversion with skills like staying positive and communicating effectively. It is very hard to measure character traits beyond self-assessment. For example, in her excellent book, *Grit*, Angela Duckworth presents a self-assessed Grit scale, which is a proxy for elements of resilience, whilst acknowledging how difficult it is to make reliable assessments[118].

But even if we just focus on skills, confusion persists. For example, the National Foundation for Education Research in 2008 put together guidance for schools on measurability[119]. In doing so, it explored six exemplar approaches for schools to use in putting together their own preferred approach:

- *The Enterprise Passport:* This is a paper document where students capture what they have done in different sections. They 'log' the activities that they have completed and then potentially get these 'signed off' by a teacher to authenticate.
- *Performance Radar:* Although it sounds a lot more high-tech, the performance radar is surprisingly like an enterprise passport on closer inspection. There are a number of capabilities (12 in the example they gave) and students add detail to what they have done for these. For an activity, students were asked to assess whether this had helped them to achieve a particular outcome.
- *Benchmarking of enterprise capability:* This starts to sound a bit more promising. Students are asked to give themselves a score of 0-8 against

25 capabilities. The relative strengths and weaknesses can then be picked out and focused on by teacher and students.

- *Personal Effectiveness Tool:* This tool allows teachers to upload information about the enterprise activity, and then provides a structured self-reflection against the outcomes the activity might be expected to develop (for example, 'I supported others in carrying out their roles' – with choices of 'strongly agree' through to 'strongly disagree'). These scores were then aggregated to move students through different stages from 'Enterprise Beginner' to 'Enterprise Guru'.

- *Award scheme:* This approach sees the students gather evidence of using their skills, in this case for 15 capabilities. They gathered examples and evidence and were able to move up through the different levels of Bronze, Silver and Gold.

- *In-lesson assessment of enterprise capabilities:* This is a more interesting approach, with an emphasis on teacher assessment. In the example they looked at, the school would focus on one of six possible enterprise capabilities each term and then try to draw out this learning across multiple subject areas. The students assessed themselves too against a series of more specific descriptors – for example, 'I/we had good eye contact with the audience'.

What's going wrong here?

The challenge inherent in all of these approaches is that they depend on recording activities rather than outcomes, and student self-assessment of abilities.

We'll address the recording of activities first. As with literacy and numeracy, what matters is not what has gone in but what the *result* is, in terms of what students are then able to do. It is irrelevant how many words a child has read. Nor does it matter how many maths problems a child has solved – they might have quickly mastered a concept and moved on to long division, or they might still be struggling with basic addition.

We should care a lot less about whether a child has taken part in a dozen or a hundred team activities. It may well be that the child who has worked in a team a hundred times might be more adept at teamwork than her lonelier peer, but that is just an assumption. That former child may have just been playing on her phone or napping. The activities she has taken part in may have been pitched so poorly that she has been put off teamwork for life. By merely counting them, we have no idea.

While it can be helpful to record activities, this is only ever an interim step. For example, when learning to read, it would not be unusual for children to log how long they have read for, or the occasions they read aloud to a parent. Equally, keeping a score of how many maths problems have been solved and awarding stars or merits or house points can be a motivating thing. It can also be useful to record activities for the simple reason of remembering them. As a sometime sixth form tutor who had to write my tutor group's university references, this could have saved on time spent hunting for examples.

But these measures can only ever be a small part of how we track progress. They measure quantity, not quality.

The limitations of student self-assessment

When it comes to making a real judgement about quality of experience and essential skills progress, another tendency is to rely too heavily on students' own self-assessment.

It's an understandable choice because there is a value in self-assessment – namely, that it encourages students to reflect and understand their skill set. Without an external 'grading' to compare students with, it can feel more straightforward to believe that students have a much greater level of insight into their own strengths and weaknesses than any external observer can. For time-pressed teachers, it just seems easier.

Where there are no clear descriptors to measure against, we tend to fall back on assessing reactions to statements like 'I feel confident working in a team' or 'I can organise myself to get things done'. The challenge is that not only are you relying on the student to assess themselves, but you are also relying on them to know what 'good' looks like.

Imagine instead that we were asking students to respond to the statement, 'I am a good reader'. Now, there is some value in whether a student is a confident reader or self-identifies in that way, but the answer to this question is very unlikely to really illuminate whether a child can read effectively. Children are likely to construct an answer based on whether they feel they are behind or ahead of their peers (which they are often a poor judge of) or whether they feel they have improved. Even more likely, though, it will depend on their mood and the most recent events. If they've struggled with a new book they are likely to mark themselves down, or if they are tired, or if they have just had a fight with their friends or parents.

For a time, we did attempt to use self-assessment measures at Enabling Enterprise. But the inherent challenge in this approach was evident when we looked at these assessments over time – and the apparent dip in their skills over time. Students are often more confident before they realise what 'good performance' really looks like, or before they have had to put their skills to the test. What we saw was that students' confidence would often dip at the end of their first term of having to work with others, or organise themselves. The scores would then often recover as they saw the progress they were making, but they had no idea if they should really have been a 4 or a 6 or a 9 on the scale.

Beyond confidence measures

When we moved away from confidence measures, we started to use much more precise descriptors of skills and then asked students to assess whether they agreed with the statement. For example, 'I can take turns with others'. This seemed more promising – we could change what the descriptors were according to the age of the students. There was also a real learning value in students thinking clearly about their own skills and what the next step for development would be – and this was much more valuable than just asking about confidence in skills in a vacuum.

However, ultimately this was insufficient. For the youngest students, they can't even read the descriptors let alone self-evaluate against them. For the older students, the language can still be confusing and it can be hard for them to get a good perspective on their own performance.

Beyond that, it's well-known that any self-assessment will have a high degree of subjectivity about it. Our confidence and self-perception is quite an emotional judgement, even when there is a clear matrix of outcomes to plot against. I know that perfectly well for myself – when I was taking an extended programme at the School for Social Entrepreneurs the 'distance travelled' measures (similar to confidence measures) fluctuated far more according to my day-to-day highs and lows of running a new organisation than according to my developing skill set as a social entrepreneur.

What should we be aspiring to?

In 2014, the Department for Education put together some broad guidelines for what an effective assessment system should look like[120]. The principles, in summary, were that assessment should:

- Allow meaningful tracking towards end of Key Stage expectations
- Provide information which is transferable and easily understood to cover both quantitative and qualitative assessment
- Differentiate attainment between students of different abilities, to identify those who are falling behind or who are excelling
- Be reliable and free from bias

- Help provide information to improve the quality of teaching
- Give students feedback to improve their own learning, and be specific enough to be helpful
- Produce recordable measurements that can demonstrate comparison against expected standards and reflect progress over time
- Be created with those delivering best practice locally
- Be mindful of best practice internationally

If you've made it to the end of these nine, it will be clear that none of the six suggestions that NFER looked at before really makes the grade in terms of those principles.

If we're serious about making the development of essential skills as rigorous and grounded as building literacy or numeracy this matters a great deal.

Skills Builder framework

The good news is that we can create such a system. We have to start by building off the first principle we saw in the previous chapter – that of keeping it simple. In the six examples that NFER looked at we saw a varying number of competencies being assessed – up to 41 in the case of the enterprise passport. This is an impossibly high number – whereas looking at the eight that we've identified means that we can look at each in much greater depth – and crucially as teachers, parents or employers we can get a handle on eight.

At Enabling Enterprise, we have developed a framework and set of assessment tools called Skills Builder. The framework provides a set of age-related expectations for what students can do from the age of 3 years old through to the highest performers at 18 for each of the eight essential skills.

For each of the eight skills, we started with the end in mind. The end that we are looking for is not simply 'good teamwork' or 'good at staying positive'. For example, at the point of leaving school an employer might be looking to see that students can:

- Contribute to the decision-making process and be willing to compromise on their own ideas to reach a group decision
- See the importance of involving all team members in discussions
- Demonstrate an awareness of team dynamics and work to avoid or overcome conflict
- Accurately analyse the performance of the team and suggest improvements

At Enabling Enterprise, we built Skills Builder by talking to employers and looking at the ways that they not only assessed performance at interview, but also how they then evaluated the performance of their employees once they were inside the organisations. We had some great support from PwC with funding from the Social Investment Business at this point too, who stress-tested these 'final skills outcomes' with colleges and employers to check that they were consistent with their expectations. By doing this, it was clear that in many cases our expectations for where students could get to were bold, and that if we could get them to these levels then we should be confident that they would be set apart by their level of competency in these areas.

Now, this is all very well but as we've already seen, we knew we needed to start young – and at the age of 4 or 5, these outcomes were unlikely to be relevant. They would likely be 'working towards' these outcomes for over a decade.

So, we worked backwards to identify what the expectation for each child should be at each age in order for them to be on track for success at the point they left school, right back to the age of 3. This gave a series of indicators right back to, in the children's language, 'I can take turns when an adult tells me to' and 'I can include others in my play'. Along the way, continuing with the example of teamwork, students learn to 'explain why teams can be more effective than individuals on some tasks'. These were cross-referenced with mentions or suggestions of the skills elsewhere in the curriculum to check that the expectations at different ages were consistent (for example, speaking and listening is referenced elsewhere, as is problem-solving).

The result of all of this will look familiar to any teacher. It is essentially a levelling framework of one level for each year from Years 1-13, along with two more stretching levels. For early years, we have a separate set of six mini-levels for 3- to 5-year-olds where development tends to be in rapid increments. The familiarity is deliberate, because it should be comfortable for a teacher to take up and use.

So what is different?
This approach is a complete shift in the rigour with which essential skills can be measured. If we look back at the principles that the government outlined in 2014, we see that hits them.

It enables us to not just collect activities or see progress, but to compare the outcomes that the students are achieving – that is, the skills they demonstrate – with what we would expect from them at that age. This in turn helps us to ensure that they are on the right trajectory to be successful, and to quickly identify those who are exceeding their age-related expectations and those who are falling behind.

What's more, because the framework flows from 3 years old to 18 years old (and indeed it can be taken well beyond that outside of schools) it can be picked up and used each year, and help teachers to understand the pattern of how a students' skills have built over time. The information can also be transferred between schools to help avoid the reset that might otherwise happen between primary and secondary school.

Most of the students who are assessed using Skills Builder are assessed at least twice a year by their teachers – which in turn allows for a sense of progression from the students, and to re-focus on the next step in each of the skills in a timely way. A simple overview of the Skills Builder framework can be found in the Appendix – and the fuller framework is available at www.theessentialskills.org.

What could be controversial?
As we started to build this skills assessment framework ourselves, I kept wondering why it was that this did not already exist.

Partly, this is a result of the confusion of definitions surrounding these skills. Where the skills are blurred with knowledge and character then measurement *is* difficult and *should* be based on self-reporting or activity-counting. But if we achieve the clarity of essential skills from our first principle in Chapter 9 then this need not hold us back any more.

There is a challenge around objectivity too – and the principle that assessments should be reliable and free from bias. The approach we use depends on teacher assessment and I'll address one concern head-on – that teachers might just cook the assessment to see the progress that they target. Now, this could well be a possibility – but I would argue that it is no more likely for essential skills than it is for numeracy or literacy or any of the other things that teachers assess along the way in the absence of examinations. That is particularly the case as schools use the Skills Builder framework over multiple years, meaning that one teacher's end of year assessments gets passed on to the following teacher. Additionally, the results of the assessments are not required to be reported on externally by the school – lowering the stakes significantly.

So, if we minimise our fears about bias, then how do we feel about reliability? For a start, we have to put some guidelines in place. Skills can be tested, but that is not always easy – the driving test is an obvious example. Instead we encourage teachers to observe their classes over a period of up to four weeks before completing the first skills assessment. This is important to see a pattern in the use of skills – which will not always be applied consistently either over time or in different situations.

We also know that because no child or young person (or indeed adult) will ever behave in exactly the same way, there has to be an element of subjectivity about the judgements and a decision about 'best fit'. We encourage teachers to think about whether a student 'mostly' shows the skill when deciding if they have achieved that level, rather than seeking it every time.

The next line of challenge is often around whether skills development is cumulative. By this, I mean 'Do you need to know one thing in order to learn the next thing?' – which is of course the basis of any levelling framework which sets a level as the 'highest' thing that a student can do. Again, I would argue that the underpinning logic is sound. The biggest test here is when teachers use it. If there was no logical progression, then we would not expect there to be any clear pattern of progress over the year. The reality, though, is that we see a pattern which is highly consistent with a cumulative levelling framework:

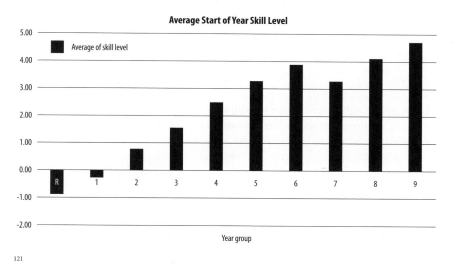

121

Finally, the challenge is whether teachers are able to make consistent judgements. This is difficult – particularly because teachers have minimal training at the moment around the pedagogy of essential skills and how they are taught. We have found that training is essential, and some of our partners including Ark academies have been experimenting with clever ways of supplementing this with internal moderation, including videoing some students completing activities that would draw on the skills and assessing their levels together.

The vital thing to remember through all of this is that we are assessing essential *skills* not character attributes. We are observing actions, not trying to divine the traits or attitudes that sit beneath those actions.

The principle
The leading schools bring rigour to the essential skills through consistent measurement and formative assessment, as they do literacy or numeracy.

What it looks like in action
I love a good cliché, and 'what's measured is what gets done' is a classic. Measurability changes everything because it means that progress becomes tangible. It ceases to be something that we just hope for, and becomes something that we can influence and change – and so becomes a rewarding thing for teachers and students alike to work on.

In his work on Action Research, Richard Sagor put it nicely when he said 'Teachers who elect to integrate the use of data into their work start exhibiting the compulsive behaviour of fitness enthusiasts who regularly weigh themselves, check their heart rate, and graph data on their improving physical development. For both teachers and athletes, the continuous presence of compelling data that their hard work is paying off becomes, in itself, a vitally energizing force'[122].

This is certainly the experience of William Tyndale Primary School in London who have been using the skills assessment to help inform how best to support individual students – as well as the priorities of each class as a whole. As one of their teachers reflected, having to assess their classes really helps to challenge their own perceptions of their students. Understanding what age-related expectations look like gives a better gauge of how the students are really doing rather than just comparing them to their peers. This means that the priority skills for the class can be identified and nurtured.

The school uses these assessments internally to help to focus their efforts as teachers, and they also report on students' progress to parents. This includes giving examples of how parents can best support their children to develop their skills further.

At the secondary level, we have been working with Ark academies who have been using the same skills assessment framework, Skills Builder, with a group of sixth form students. Their programme has particularly focused on getting these students ready for employment or the next stage of their education and so essential skills have played a large part. Teachers have assessed the students at the start of the year and then at the end of each term to track their progress.

In doing so, they have found that the measurement helps to make the progress the students are making in their skills much more tangible – and that it is much more rewarding for the teachers to see their efforts in this area pay off. It also raises expectations around this 'softer' set of outcomes closer to a par with traditionally 'harder' academic outcomes.

A note of caution

It is important to note at this point that the last thing I would want to see in schools are league tables of essential skills. We are at an early stage in understanding how best to nurture, build and measure these skills. If school or government were to twist the outcomes to achieve a 'target' level of progress their usefulness to support learning and teacher effectiveness would melt away.

As Daisy Christodoulou points out, these sorts of measures are really meant to be formative rather than summative[123] – otherwise they can far too easily be warped to achieve some externally mandated line of progress. We want teachers to be mindful of the trajectory that students should be on towards future success, and to direct their efforts to achieving this for their students – not expending those efforts on just trying to 'prove' this.

I am thrilled that we are starting to build a real coalition around using a shared framework for building these skills including leading charities and education bodies Business in the Community, Teach First, Ark and Career Ready – a breakthrough opportunity that I will come back to later.

Putting it into practice in your classroom

Looking around your classroom, you might well already have a hunch about which of your students seem to be thriving in regards to their essential skills, and which students seem to be struggling. You might well have a strong sense of which students seem to do their best work when working with others, and which groan at any attempt to engage them with their peers. You are likely to know which students are happy to be called on for answers, or to share their work in front of the class.

Some of these insights might well turn out to be assumptions though – which have morphed into patterns of behaviour. In a packed lesson, with 30 students to keep engaged it can be difficult to keep mixing up which students get called on or who presents their work. There is a phenomenon that we often hear about from our teachers where the most outgoing students are presumed to have the most developed essential skills – when they are just deploying them more loudly. Teachers have also admitted to presuming that those students who are more able in their literacy or numeracy are also more able at their essential skills.

That is why it is so important to try to take a dispassionate look at your class over a longer period of time, seeking evidence for where your students are using their essential skills and to what level they are being used. The tools at www. skillsbuilder.org make that possible.

You might well be surprised by what you see when you give students similar opportunities to use their skills. Some essential skills are also likely to be less obviously manifested – for example, which of your students are able to set themselves goals, or which are able to be creative when faced with problems?

Having this view is likely to give some insights into the other dynamics in your classroom too – and to what seems to work or not with your class. It's an essential starting point.

Putting it into practice as a school leader

At a whole-school level, the idea of introducing a new type of assessment is unlikely to be immediately appealing. Speaking to our headteachers and enterprise leaders in schools there are a couple of essential balancing acts to making the assessments useful at a whole-school level:

- *Useful, not a burden:* Our senior leaders say, unsurprisingly, that engagement from teachers is highest when the value of the information is seen by teachers. This is likely to mean training beforehand so they can see a demonstration of how it works and why it is making a difference for teachers like those described in this chapter.

- *Reducing the stakes:* Whilst making timelines and expectations for completion really clear, it's important that this is a low-stakes, formative tool. This will reduce the stress around the assessments and probably increase accuracy too (which makes it much more useful as a teaching tool). Starting with just one or two classes, especially at secondary, makes it manageable.

- *Do it twice:* It can be motivating for teachers to know that they will be coming back to it again at the end of the year. This is motivating when it enables teachers to quantifiably see the impact of their work on their students.

If you're following the principles through here, you might want to allow some time for the initial language to permeate across the school before introducing Skills Builder as the next stage.

The frameworks and assessment tools can be found at www.skillsbuilder.org.

Putting it into practice as a parent

Finally, as a parent I wouldn't recommend formally assessing your child – but it might be helpful to have a look at the simple version of the skills framework in the Appendix of this book, just to get a rough gauge of what age-related expectations look like.

Summary

It would be infeasible to build essential skills with the same rigour as literacy or numeracy if we had no way of measuring them. Indeed, it is impossible in the current culture of schools to justify spending much time in the curriculum without seeing tangible results.

To date, it has seemed that when it comes to essential skills, measurability is weak – reliant on capturing activities, or leaning heavily on student self-assessment which can be inconsistent and based on fluctuating confidence. These measures certainly don't fulfil the principles that the Department for Education set out in 2014 for what a robust assessment system should look like.

What is exciting, though, is that when we focus on our tight set of essential skills we see that it is possible to build a cumulative levelling system. Once we have this, not only can we gauge where students are against age-related expectations, we can also see what their next steps are to progress, and track their progress over multiple years.

This has exciting implications for how we teach essential skills – and that's what we turn to next.

Chapter 12:
Focus tightly

Essential skills are not mysterious. They are not just to be hoped or willed into existence.

The teaching approach must be about how to build each incremental step in the skills as effectively as possible. That means moving beyond the idea that great enterprise learning is just doing as many activities as possible. Nor should we be satisfied with the idea that the students can simply discover the skills for themselves in their own way.

Building essential skills should be part of a strategic plan for progression. The outcomes for the students need to come first – and measuring and understanding their strengths and next development steps are critical to that.

In a crammed curriculum and with limited time, we have to squeeze every drop of value out of the time we can focus on these skills. That means being comfortable with direct teaching from the front of the room, and then carefully pitched, deliberate practice.

The current situation

I remember one school presenting me with a glossy booklet of all of the different work that they did to build the skills of their students. I was blown away by the sheer size of this booklet, the number of logos on every page, and the complete incoherence of this mass of activities.

When I first talk to a school about Enabling Enterprise, I always start by framing our work in the context that we focus first and foremost on building essential skills. After all, there's nothing like a bit of definitional debate to build rapport.

Then there are a few questions to ask to get a handle on whether our work is really a good fit for them, and the stage they're at. What do you already do? What do you find is working well? How do you know it's working well? What are the outcomes that you are looking to achieve for your students? Do you have a strategy for how to do this?

I want to ensure that our work really does enhance the skills of their students – and that is only possible if it is pitched right.

The other challenge is that I often see a 'discovery learning' approach to building essential skills. While I will come on to the importance of practising in different settings in the next chapter, it is not efficient for students to try to discover these skills by themselves.

Why is this the current state of play?
When the government focused on enterprise education in 2002 it suggested that every student should 'have the opportunity to experience enterprise activity at some time during their school career'[124]. The expectation of what students should get out of enterprise learning was set as a quantity of activity – five taught days over their time in secondary school – rather than as any particular set of outcomes.

So it is unsurprising that by the time that Ofsted reviewed enterprise education in 2011, they found that the huge menu of activities being offered were often leading to a 'lack of coherence' in enterprise provision[125]. This was at least partly driven by a 'failure to identify and assess learning outcomes' which was blamed for difficulties in effectively developing enterprise capability in students.

More recently, in 2016, Ofsted's latest review of education highlighted that 'the biggest weakness across the schools visited was a lack of coherence in planning enterprise education' and further that 'pupils who spoke to inspectors during the visits frequently said that their experience tended to be a series of one-off events that lacked any sense of progression'[126].

Tangentially, work from Anthony Mann and others showed a link between the number of interactions with employers that a young person had and a significant reduction in the likelihood that they would fall into the category of being 'not in education, employment or training'[127] (NEET). This effect was summarised in many places as being that if a young person had four or more interactions with employers they were five times less likely to be NEET[128]. It should be noted that the study was slightly more nuanced than that – not least because it was about those young adults who could *recall* four interactions and that only 7% of young adults could make this recollection.

However, the point stuck that 'more is more' and a renewed emphasis to achieve the apparently golden standard of four employer and workplace engagements. There was little to say about what would make one of those employer engagements a meaningful or memorable one and so it gave a boost to counting activities.

What should happen?

As with literacy and numeracy, essential skills development has to be part of a strategic plan for progression. This builds straight off the previous chapter, where we saw that the eight skills that we focus on are cumulative, in that steps of progress build off the previous steps – in much the same way that counting is a foundation for all more complex mathematical concepts.

If this is the case, then it is obvious that activities should be chosen and tailored to support progression towards an outcome. Indeed, as the CBI pointed out in their 2014 report 'A Better-Off Britain', the best education systems start off with the outcomes in mind and work back from there[129].

We must be led by the outcomes that we are working towards at each age group and then we can focus the activities appropriately.

This is not just for neatness. Anders Ericsson draws together the principles that research has shown sits behind the concept of 'deliberate practice' – a concept that we have already mentioned here[130]. As the man behind the concept of '10,000 hours of practice', he writes to emphasise that just practising for 10,000 hours is *not* enough. Effective practice must instead have four key hall-marks.

Firstly, purposeful practice must have well-defined, specific goals for that session – not just practising working well in a team, for example, but ensuring on three occasions that you are able to articulate an idea that builds upon someone else's contribution.

Secondly, that purposeful practice requires focus – it needs to be thought about and to be the focus of that session. That is why, as I have already discussed, essential skills cannot *only* be embedded in other lessons as a way of being developed. They can be reinforced elsewhere, but have to be central to learning somewhere too.

Thirdly, that it also involves feedback – feedback that can be given in the context of embedded skill development or as a standalone focus on essential skills, but it must be expert and specific to be helpful. For example, celebrating 'Great use of your essential skills' is basically useless to a student. 'Great use of your teamwork skills' is marginally more useful, but think about the equivalent to a piano lesson and the comment 'Great use of your piano skills' is hardly useful feedback. Rather more useful would be something like 'What you did well there was to allow Jacob to finish his point and take time to reflect on it, before offering a counter-argument. That time allowed you to come up with a better idea, and also helped Jacob to appreciate that you had listened to his ideas too'. Even better if then followed up with, 'To do even better, could you think about how to link what was good about Jacob's idea to the idea that you proposed?'

Finally, purposeful practice requires getting out of one's comfort zone; this is why careful pitching is so important – over time, we want our students to be actively seeking out challenges (indeed, that is a key part of building the skill of aiming high). But for students earlier on that requires careful planning of activities to take them just beyond what they can already comfortably do. Activities that are too broad or lack structure will simply not allow that to happen.

The principle
When building essential skills, leading schools are making focused time available to directly build the skills, and to allow for deliberate practice. This means ensuring that teaching is stage- and age-appropriate, building on prior learning and expertise to achieve maximum progress.

Putting the skills framework into action
The exciting thing here is that the essential skills framework, Skills Builder, allows for exactly that sort of careful pitching. Not only does it help to uncover what the students can already do but it also helps to think about the next thing that they need to master in order to move forward.

This is important, because the first step towards meaningful progress in any skill or field is a sense of what the next step is.

If we know, for example when focusing on the essential skill of aiming high, that a student can consistently set their own goals and aims, the next step would be to introduce them to SMART targets – that is, those that are time-bound and have a quantifiable success measure. By focusing tightly on this, it is possible to make rapid progress. Perhaps this means introducing the theory of SMART targets – why they can be helpful, what their limitations are, and what they need to include to be useful. The students might then practise creating these for themselves – through a series of short activities or a longer project.

In any case, the concept of a SMART target is not overly complex, although it can take a while to fully grasp – particularly the question of attaching the target to a tangible measure to judge success or failure. The point is that by focusing on it at the right time, students can actually learn it pretty quickly – and then move on to the next step.

However, imagine that we just introduced SMART targets randomly one form period. If students have never set their own targets or goals before, it will seem overwhelming. If they have never had to logically work through creating a plan to reach a goal then making a target a 'SMART' target won't make it any more likely to be achieved.

We normally introduce SMART targets around the time the students are 14 or 15 years old. It is hard for them to make further plans for their lives if they don't have the ability to set time-bound, relevant and measurable goals so it is vital they 'get' this first.

This is just one example. The complement to aiming high in our approach is staying positive. These two together make up our work on self-management – the ability to set goals and ambitions, and then to form the strategies to stick at those plans and achieve them.

For our 8- or 9-year-olds, our staying positive goal is that they can keep trying when something goes wrong, and reflect on what happened. This requires them having already built the ability to stay calm when something goes wrong, which needs students to have previously internalised that getting angry or giving up when something goes wrong is not helpful. Of course, to know that, it's vital that they've built an understanding of what emotions are, and an expectation that different situations might initially create an emotional response.

Looking forward, if students can keep trying when something goes wrong and reflect on what happened, they are well positioned for some of the next steps in staying positive. That will include being able to support and encourage others, being able to describe the positive side of a situation, and coming up with ideas to make more of that positive situation.

If they can do this, we have set up these students to progress to be comfortable taking calculated risks, to seek out new challenges and ultimately to bring others along with them too.

Moving beyond osmosis

Once we are building off this framework, it becomes obvious that we don't just acquire these skills by osmosis. Back in Chapter 7 we referenced that common perception, often because the skills are confused with character attributes or virtues, that essential skills are 'caught, not taught'.

If we can see the increments, though, we can be comfortable that each step is perfectly teachable. For example, to continue with staying positive, some of the earliest activities might be as simple as recognising emotions in different pictures and having a circle discussion where the children can discuss when they've felt the different emotions. Another one that I've seen work well with these 5- or 6-year-olds is the 'falling tower game' – something like Jenga works well. As the teacher removes pieces of the tower one by one there is an increasing likelihood that the tower will fall. As the teacher models this, they verbalise the emotions they are feeling – the nervousness of picking a piece, the excitement or relief when the tower doesn't fall, or the disappointment when it does. The students can then repeat this process, identifying their own feelings.

This is all about being deliberate in building the skills. Once we are deliberate, we can achieve a great deal more in a concentrated amount of time – something that as a teacher I know will always be a constraint. With a few activities like this, reinforced through references elsewhere in teaching (something we will look at in more depth in the next chapter) it is possible to achieve the first two steps of building the skills of staying positive: to recognise basic emotions, and then to see that when things go wrong people can react with anger or sadness.

Why we must be discrete

There are some real advantages to teaching essential skills in a discrete subject. At Enabling Enterprise, our primary schools all teach a series of 'lesson-time projects' which are discrete enterprise lessons, normally delivered for one hour each week. One of our teachers at Longlands Primary School reflected on the importance of 'taking time away to have that chance to build [students'] confidence and these core skills, because they get lost in education at times. It really helps them to achieve other things across the curriculum'.

At secondary school, we offer a range of lesson-time projects of up to six hours, but also, through a new initiative called Teach Enterprise, a set of punchy 10-15 minute activities that focus on building the next learning step in a selected skill. We also use the Challenge Day format as a catalyst of dedicated time to raise awareness among the students of essential skills, and set a challenge that can then be followed up and reinforced elsewhere in learning.

We've seen that one of the advantages of using a discrete approach is that it allows students to focus on those skills, rather than also trying to focus on the other knowledge that might otherwise be the primary goal of the lesson – it can be hard to balance outcomes. The feedback from our teachers too is that by focusing just on building essential skills for a period of time helps them to deepen their confidence and understanding of those skills too, rather than it being another box to fill in on a lesson plan.

On the other hand, I've already been making the argument that essential skills are as essential as literacy and numeracy to underpin other learning. Literacy and numeracy are constantly applied in other lessons, and these skills should be too. This is a point that we will come back to in the next chapter.

Putting it into practice in your classroom

Depending on whether you are a primary or secondary school teacher you might feel that you have differing levels of flexibility with how you use your teaching time.

At primary, you might well be able to carve off time for discrete essential skills development and use a project-based learning approach to building the skills over a period of time. This is generally the approach that our partner primary schools take with the Enabling Enterprise programme. The increased flexibility is reflected in the diversity of approaches that our primary teachers take to delivering the discrete enterprise sessions.

At secondary, it can be more difficult to find this dedicated time. Instead, teachers might draw from the short, punchy learning activities that we have developed and made available at www.teachenterprise.org. These were specifically designed for exactly that problem and allow complete focus on the next building block of that skill in an amount of time that might fit as part of a lesson or be used effectively during form time.

This will be a valuable use of time.

Putting it into practice as a school leader

At the level of a school, I fully appreciate that finding time for discrete essential skills development can be challenging. We saw back in Chapter 7 that one of the duller reasons why enterprise is often not covered in much depth in schools is the sense of pressure on the timetable.

At Enabling Enterprise, we have several approaches to fitting in this discrete, focused learning time. Our dream scenario, and what seems to be most effective, is to have a regular enterprise lesson each week which uses a project to hold together a term's learning – whether creating a cookbook exploring recipes from around the world, or running a campaign. The project is just the vehicle – a way for students to learn more about the skills and then immediately apply them to put what they have learnt into practice.

Where that's not possible, though, we have found some schools who are able to find a couple of days each term to dedicate to teaching essential skills. This approach relies a lot more on the wider reinforcement of those skills in between the focused sessions, but can still work.

At secondary school, where schools struggle to make 'Enterprise' a discrete subject, there is still scope to build the skills in a focused, tightly pitched way. For example, we are seeing some secondary schools doing brilliant work by combining skills-focused sessions in form period with quick reinforcements of those skills before they are used in the context of another lesson.

The key thing is not that 'Enterprise' or 'Essential Skills' must exist as a separate timetable slot, but that regular time is allowed to focus solely on these skills and that this time is used effectively by being pitched just right – to the appropriate learning outcome, not just to offer an entertaining activity.

Once that focused time is there, teachers can draw on the Skills Builder frameworks or the free resources that are available at Teach Enterprise (www. teachenterprise.org) to bring punchy opportunities for progress into the timetable.

Putting it into practice as a parent

As a parent, pitching activities to support our children's skill development will look a bit different. The huge advantage that we have over a teacher, of course, is a much deeper understanding of our children.

For the youngest children, building empathy and resilience is the most critical thing that we can do as parents – and this continues to be important as they grow up into a young person and your relationship with them naturally changes.

One of the most powerful tools is modelling. This demonstration of your own empathy for your child is often best demonstrated through active listening – really listening, and rephrasing and repeating what they are telling you to demonstrate a real understanding. Similarly, vocalising your own feelings and explaining them can be very powerful.

At the same time, modelling resilience is important. When facing a challenge or a setback it is important to acknowledge the challenge and then to articulate what strategies you will try to make further progress. That might be to try a different approach, to wait for a chance in circumstances and then try again, or to seek expertise. When success comes about, celebrate that and highlight the effort that went in, and any adversity that had to be overcome on the way.

When your children are younger, you have more scope to find them activities that will support them to build these skills. Sports clubs, drama, music, or volunteering can help to support that skills development. But it isn't necessary to spend a lot of money on these activities. We can also apply these skills to whatever activities we're doing around the home or about our daily lives.

As your children get older and turn into young adults, you can continue to model to them, to ask them questions about their skills and to explore the activities that they do through that lens. Being open, but crucially not defeatist, about the challenges you have found or currently find in the skills can be reassuring and encouraging for them too.

Summary

This chapter has introduced the fourth principle for building essential skills – that we have to focus tightly. As helpful as it would be, essential skills cannot just be built up by osmosis or by doing things that use the skills in a broad sense.

Instead, we need to be thinking about direct teaching and deliberate practice. This is made possible by the skills framework that we introduced in the previous chapter because it allows us to understand both what a student is capable of doing now and also what the next step is on their road to mastering the essential skills.

We've seen a real value in finding time to focus solely on building those skills. Ideally, this will be through a regular, discrete lesson. Even if this is not possible we have seen many examples where finding smaller chunks of time can work. The key thing is that this time is focused tightly on a particular skill, and making a clear step of progress, rather than just choosing activities at random.

The next principle addresses the debate around how essential skills should be linked to the rest of life – both in and out of school.

Chapter 13:
Keep practising

We need time tightly focused on the essential skills. But that is not to say that they should be completely separated from the wider business of learning in schools.

All too often, though, this sort of learning is completely isolated – either by only building those skills on one-off days, or by outsourcing its teaching to external providers. This makes it much less likely that those skills will really be mastered.

The reality is that while we need discrete time to focus on building the skills, they also need to be reinforced elsewhere in learning and beyond it.

The current situation

I remember with some trepidation the 'enterprise days' that were run in my school when I was a teacher. A bunch of terrified business volunteers sent into a hostile class of 14- or 15-year-olds, to guide them through a simulated 'enterprise challenge'. As teachers, we were allocated to cover classes for a chunk of the day when we would normally be teaching that year group.

I used to brace myself with an extra-large cup of coffee for those sessions. The students would invariably be off-task. Those who disengaged easily anyway would need little excuse, and would certainly not be brought back onto the topic by the poor volunteers. Even those students who were more self-motivated would generally be underwhelmed – either because the task was a dull simulation, or they were fed up with their team mates, or they could see no link between this day and anything that mattered.

As teachers, our role was to sit at the back of the room and try to keep a semblance of order – better characterised as dampening down the flickers of anarchy as they emerged.

Now, I am quite aware that the problem is not about the use of the Challenge Day format in its own right. Indeed, Enabling Enterprise use Challenge Days as a core part of our programmes, alongside the regular enterprise lessons that I highlighted previously.

Literacy and numeracy need constant nourishment and reinforcement throughout school life – they are not isolated in this way. We do not try to compact them solely into discrete, one-off occasions or completely surrender responsibility for their development to external agencies.

Why does this happen?

The latest view from Ofsted in their 2016 review was that 'secondary schools should ensure that there is a coherent programme'[131] and a fear that students 'found it difficult to link different experiences and inputs whether from expert visitors, assemblies, tutor activities, or days when the normal timetable was collapsed'.

A large part of this comes back to a lack of teacher training and professional support around building essential skills – a point referenced in conversations I've had time and again – whether with teachers on our programmes or with teacher training providers like Newman University. David Weston, CEO of the Teacher Development Trust, points out that most schools instead focus their Continued Professional Development (CPD) on literacy and numeracy and issues that directly come out of inspections.

Interestingly, in their latest funding round, the Careers and Enterprise Company made clear that they wanted to fund interventions or programmes for schools – and explicitly not teacher training[132]. They also decided not to fund anything that involved co-delivery by teachers and employers. This reflects the Company's expressed view that it should act as 'the Uber' of its sector, helping to link schools to the best careers and enterprise providers[133]. The risk this runs is not really engaging teachers with the enterprise activity that is going on.

Why this is a problem

I've already referenced the fact that we have to think about skills in terms of their breadth, depth and transferability. If we compartmentalise essential skills too much, then we lose transferability.

Psychologist Daniel Willingham talks about deep versus shallow learning, arguing that learning and understanding will remain shallow unless students are able to make connections and understand how the different parts of what they are learning actually link together[134].

When Ofsted carried out their review of enterprise teaching in 2011, they found that there was far too much of this shallow learning. It is worth quoting from them at length, as they found that 'where schools depend solely on "suspended timetable" days, students developed only a partial understanding of the whole programme. The days became very isolated and fragmented experiences when not supported by the rest of the curriculum'.

What should happen

When we look at the example of literacy, Ofsted in 2012 found good evidence that 'strengthening whole school literacy work across all departments' raises standards in English. This is reflected in popular 'Drop Everything and Read' strategies, as well as George Sampson's famous declaration in 1922 that 'every teacher is a teacher of English'.

In *The Literacy Leader's Toolkit*, the authors Graham Tyrer and Patrick Taylor reflected on their experience of embedding literacy across their secondary school[135]. They talk compellingly of the shift that occurred when all teachers started 'sensing themselves as teachers of words' – and the shift as their GCSE English results were transformed from 65% of students achieving grade C or higher in English, to over 92% achieving at this level.

Some of the cited benefits from embedding essential skills into school life include giving opportunities for pupils to think about them in different subject contexts, increasing learner enjoyment and engagement and contextualising skills in relation to academic content[136]. This is particularly relevant when we remember that in Chapter 2 we saw that there is not much difference between our 'Essential Skills' and, for example, the University of Cambridge's 'study skills'.

The principle

The best schools are supplementing focused time on the essential skills with wider reinforcement and practice across the curriculum and beyond it.

Building teacher expertise and confidence

At Enabling Enterprise, we took an approach of creating a complete curriculum for schools to build essential skills. For students, our programmes combine regular enterprise lesson-time projects with trips to employers and a Challenge Day each year to bring the whole school together and raise the profile of what's going on – and hopefully involve parents too.

What we've found, though, is how vital it is for teachers to take ownership. We provide plenty of training and support, and the lesson resources that model effective essential skills development, but it is ultimately about enabling existing classroom teachers to deliver the programmes themselves. After they've become comfortable with teaching these pre-made resources, it's fantastic when you see them really taking charge and creating their own resources and new ideas for projects too. This allows the reinforcement and practice across the curriculum that we have seen makes a real difference.

Obviously, one of the reasons why enterprise tends to be compartmentalised is logistical: it's no longer a compulsory part of the curriculum and there are few specialist teachers. The lack of specialist teachers is compounded by the fact that there is no widespread generalist training either – whereas most teachers will have touched on literacy and numeracy as part of their teacher training, they will have had no similar training on essential skills.

There is a real value in working *with* other organisations or employers. Indeed, in the next chapter we will explore the role of other providers and employers in ensuring that these skills our students are developing are also linked to the wider world.

It is a false choice between the tightly focused teaching and deliberate practice illustrated in the previous chapter, and the need for wider reinforcement and practice that a whole-school, embedded approach can afford. We need to do both.

The essential role of parents

Parents can have a crucial part to play here too. The importance of parents supporting their children's numeracy and literacy at an early stage is well-known. Often they do a lot to encourage their children's social and emotional development from an early stage too.

This support can fall away as students get older. However, when schools continue to engage parents with the essential skill development of their children the results are excellent. This can be as simple as inviting parents in to see the work that the students have produced and hear them present.

This is what happens at Curwen Primary School, when for a day before the Christmas break normal lessons are suspended. Instead, the whole school shares and celebrates the work they have done on building their essential skills that year.

The corridors are lined with the students' work, as they keenly compete for attention to share what they have learnt and to show the outputs of their projects. In the school hall, students demonstrate their presenting skills with a performance. Meanwhile, groups of parents are welcomed in reception and briefed on what the students have been doing and what they have learnt from the experience.

Later on in the year, the school engages parents again with the opportunity for them to come into school to work with their children on some of the activities that Enabling Enterprise uses during regular enterprise lessons. The parents think about the skills in a new way, and the day gets great uptake and strong feedback.

William Tyndale Primary School use an 'enterprise skill of the month' as a way to provide focus, but also to engage their parents. The monthly skill is shared through the school website and at the top of the weekly newsletter home.

This exposure to the language of essential skills and what the students are working on can really help parents to support them to take the next step.

Using the skills across the school

It makes a huge difference to use a consistent language across the whole school, and to ensure that common standards are shared. I will never forget the first time I walked into the reception area of one of our schools and saw the eight skills up on the wall. It was such an obvious and simple way of highlighting how important they would be across school life.

Now it is quite usual. Most of our partner schools have the essential skills up around the school, along with reminders of what the students might be working on in that classroom. For example, for the 5- and 6-year-olds of Year 1, they might be reminded that they should be trying to listen to others, and to ask questions if they don't understand in order to bolster their listening skills. In other classrooms, you will see that they have put up evidence of what they have been doing in their Enabling Enterprise lessons as a visual reminder that they do have these skills and can use them elsewhere.

When the team sit waiting in school receptions, we sometimes leaf through a school's scrapbook of what they have done with Enabling Enterprise that year. Together these efforts add up to a constant drumbeat that reinforces the students' development.

Putting it into action

Just one example of a school bringing all these elements together is Our Lady's Catholic Primary School, a one-form entry school in the Tile Cross area of Birmingham. Their headteacher was left 'flabbergasted' by the number of parents who turned up one afternoon to find out all about the Enabling

Enterprise programme that their children were taking part in – necessitating a change of venue and a lot more chairs to accommodate the sheer numbers.

The opportunity to get involved in their children's skill development transformed parental engagement. As one parent said, 'It was so fantastic to be able to see first-hand the work Archie and his classmates produced – it is obvious that they have enjoyed every part of the project; they were brimming with pride'. By seeing the building of essential skills not as a sideshow but as a core part of school life, they brought the wider community together too.

Summary

In the last chapter, we started turning to the question of how essential skills should be taught. We knew that they had to be pitched right, but would that be best achieved by spending dedicated time focusing on them discretely? Or should it be the reverse – that actually there is a need to ensure that the development of these skills is completely embedded across learning?

This chapter has reflected what we've learnt at Enabling Enterprise – that you need both. Drawing on the parallel of how we build literacy and numeracy, this shouldn't be a surprise – we are comfortable with having regular English or Maths lessons and then complementing this with a consistent focus and application across other subjects too.

To achieve this, essential skills need to be a school priority, alongside all of the other principles that we have brought out so far.

What is the role of those beyond the school, though – particularly employers? This brings us to our final principle – to bring the teaching of essential skills to life.

Chapter 14:
Bring it to life

There is huge variation in how we engage our students with the working world – and what drives that engagement. Schools often struggle to engage with employers, and where that happens these opportunities are prioritised for those students closest to leaving school.

However, these links are critical for making the most of essential skills. We need to bring the wider world into the classroom, and take our students out of the classroom too. In this way we can enhance the motivation and drive of students to master these skills, and by deploying them in different settings they become much more transferable in the future.

To make essential skills really fly, we have to bring them to life.

The challenges
There are really three main challenges that are worth exploring when we think about how we bring learning about these skills to life.

The first is that too many schools still have only very limited links to employers. This is a challenge that Ofsted flagged in their latest review of enterprise education in secondary schools[137]. All too often, schools' links to employers are really based on the personal relationships of the teachers and their personal drive to make the most of those links. This is a big contribution on the part of those teachers but it is not a sustainable and systematic approach to linking schools and employers.

The second is that, where those links do exist, often they are prioritised only for the oldest students who are closest to employment. Even then, these links are almost always used for the purposes of inspiring students. As a result, these links are not about improving students' skills or even about linking their skill sets to future opportunities. They often leave the students to try to draw out any sense from the interactions that they have had with those employers.

In the previous chapter we saw the oft-cited work from Anthony Mann[138] which highlighted the link between recalled interactions with employers and an increase in the likelihood that students would make a successful transition beyond formal education. Of course, this insight gives little detail on what those interactions should involve.

Finally, schools seem to be becoming more nervous about bringing real-world links into the classroom. In the conservative versus progressive education debate, there are strongly held opinions that any sort of blending of the real world with classroom learning is a distraction from a tight focus on building students' knowledge. Project-based learning (PBL) methodologies are often conflated with 'discovery learning' and seen as inefficient.

What should happen

If we want to ensure the transferability of essential skills, and we surely do, then it is essential that from the outset we are trying to demonstrate how these skills can be used in a variety of contexts. Partly this can be achieved by following the principle expanded upon in the previous chapter – of reinforcing the importance of the skills in many aspects of school life, and even better by involving parents too in building and supporting these skills.

But we still run a risk of creating a barrier between what is being developed in school and the application of those skills in the rest of our children and young people's lives. We need to engage with the real world in two ways: by bringing it in to lesson-time, and by taking the students out into it.

The principle

Schools who are transforming their students' essential skills are using links to the working world to increase the depth and transferability of those skills. They give students opportunities to apply these skills in a much wider range of settings.

Bringing the real world into the classroom

One teaching method that Enabling Enterprise uses quite a lot in building the skills is a project-based learning methodology. Now, as I've already mentioned, this can sometimes produce a knee-jerk reaction from teachers who see it as too progressive or insubstantial. And it can be exactly that if it is done badly.

At Enabling Enterprise, we've run hundreds of workshops with teachers on building essential skills, and when we get on to project-based learning, I've always found it helpful to start with a short confessional. It turns out that most teachers have a handful of horror stories about disastrous attempts that have variously ended in anarchy, boredom or – and these were the majority – a nagging sense of having not achieved the intended learning outcome at the end of a lot of activity.

On the other hand, though, I have also witnessed some of the most brilliant examples of project-based learning. When focused and carefully planned, using a project for exploring or consolidating an area of knowledge is pretty compelling – and it works particularly well as a vehicle for building essential skills.

One great example I've seen was the creation of a radio show by a group of 8- and 9-year-olds in an Enabling Enterprise school. The project was introduced at a stage when it made sense to consolidate some of the creative writing techniques that the students had been working on. The students were given the freedom to ultimately choose the style and content of their show, having considered the different alternatives. The project was pitched at the right level to then also develop the students' communication skills. They had opportunities in the build-up to refine their ability to listen to one another. They had to be creative and generate their own ideas, making connections between other shows they had heard and learning and implementing a range of creative tactics. Finally, they learnt and applied techniques for how to share information.

In reflecting on the project, their teacher highlighted a couple of critical things that had made the difference. Firstly, that they were really making a radio podcast that would be shared across the school – with their peers and their parents. Secondly, that the project was introduced at the right time – building off knowledge they had already touched on, allowing it to be consolidated and for a focus on essential skills learning and development.

Before exploring further the principles of what we've seen make for effective project-based learning, there are a couple of things to get out of the way: Firstly, please don't extrapolate my informed enthusiasm for PBL in some contexts for the idea that project-based learning is always best. Students best explore and develop ideas off a strong foundation and in my experience PBL is rarely an effective way of introducing students to concepts and frameworks or underlying factual basics they need.

Secondly, teacher-led instruction still matters. For example, why spend ages getting students to guess or discover what a SMART target is when it can be taught so quickly, brought to life with a few examples, and then applied by the students to cement their own understanding? Why not just introduce students to three useful roles that people can play in group meetings (chairperson, timekeeper, note taker) rather than let them run ineffective meetings for weeks? This has all been touched on when thinking about the principle of focusing tightly.

Using project-based learning effectively

With those provisos, there are several stages that we see as vital for effective PBL: firstly, that students are presented with a real-world problem. That might mean that it is a problem that would be faced by an employer or a business, but even better if it is a real problem with a range of real possible solutions.

Another great project that I've seen run in some of our schools brings this to life. It builds off a partnership with King's Health Partners (part of the NHS) which sees secondary students running a public health campaign relevant to their school and local community. To provide context, the students start with a virtual tour of a hospital, understanding the different departments and how their work could be reduced by preventative measures at a local level. Then they decided as a group which public issues to target and how to get their campaign off the ground. This project not only gave students an understanding of the NHS and the roles within it, but also focused on them developing their communication and persuasive skills alongside having to make team decisions, and each having the turn to lead.

The stages of any effective project are also vital:

- Starting by pooling existing relevant knowledge and experience among the team.
- Using that to draw out the unanswered questions and what the students need to know in order to fulfil the challenge they have been set.
- Researching and seeking out that information – either by looking it up, asking others, or conducting their own research.
- Applying their knowledge to complete the task to the best of their abilities.
- Re-drafting and improving their work.
- Sharing what they have achieved, with a final product.
- Celebrating their successes and reflecting on what they have learnt in order to consolidate their progress.

We can introduce simple projects to support primary education too. Our youngest students, who are aged only 4 years old might just be organising and running a cake sale. Our 5-year-olds run an in-school postal service delivering letters around the school in the run-up to Christmas.

The key learning is not that they improve their baking skills, or their understanding of the postal system. This project is a vehicle for building and practising students' skills and demonstrating clearly along the way that the essential skills they are developing can be used for many different challenges in many settings.

To take the postal service example, the project is built around making tangible progress in three skills: creativity, listening, and presenting. Through direct teaching and then applied practice, by the end of the project we want students to be able to come up with multiple ideas to solve a problem, to be able to listen to other people and to clarify and follow simple instructions, and also to be able to talk in front of a small group of people they know.

Some of the activities they do towards these outcomes include having to arrange rotas for how and when to pool and sort post, having to run team meetings and reach decisions, and then for a rotating 'manager' to allocate roles each time they run the service.

This clarity about outcomes is vital to ensure that the project isn't *solely* about having an enjoyable experience – although we hope it does that too. The real life problem and context, and the way this changes in each project, helps demonstrate the skills' transferability to the students too.

Engaging employers

Alongside giving students learning experiences in the classroom that draw on real life examples, many schools opt to work directly with external partners. Generally, this means either bringing volunteers from an employer into the classroom or taking the students out.

Both of these approaches can be very helpful. At Enabling Enterprise, ever since my first foray in marching my Year 10 students through central London to visit a business, we've focused on taking students into those organisations. There are a few reasons why we've chosen this approach. Firstly, we think that the students get a much more immersive experience if they're actually in the organisations – taking in the space, seeing people at work, and being able to ask questions as they come up. We also do it because it makes it easier for us to facilitate the interaction – which, you might have guessed by now, means that we can more tightly tie together what the students will have been doing in the classroom with the lessons that we want them to draw out from seeing it in the wider world.

Every day now, hundreds of our students stream out to employer partners across the country, across all sectors – including law firms, airports, hospitals, manufacturers, retailers, construction sites and a lot more besides.

At a bank, students might be taking part in a game to simulate global trade as well as developing their ability to negotiate, to reach a team consensus and to problem-solve. At one of our law firm partners, students are likely to take part in a simulated legal case. They will get expert instruction from volunteers who are themselves legal professionals and they will need to use their ability to understand and digest information, and be creative in developing and responding to lines of argument – whilst also using their communication skills to deploy their arguments and counter-arguments effectively. At an engineering firm, the students get to work with engineers to create their own design – combining creativity and problem-solving and setting project goals.

Our programmes enable thousands of these experiences every year – where students take the essential skills they have been honing in the classroom and deploy them in the working world alongside the professionals who use those skills every day.

There is lots of good work from other organisations in bringing employees into the classroom. Business in the Community (BITC) and Career Ready, for example, both run masterclasses that bring volunteers from their partner businesses into the classroom to share their experiences with the students. Future First does something similar but draws on the alumni of the school to do so, which is particularly powerful. Founders4Schools helps schools to find individuals who are willing to share their experiences with the students. When effectively deployed as part of a broader strategy and with the other principles, these can be a valuable addition to a student's experience of education.

Seeing it in action

There is nothing as thrilling as seeing students enjoying a business context. When I see our students marching through the hallways of a professional services firm between suited bankers, accountants and lawyers, or lounging in the pods at a tech start-up, I'm heartened that we have the opportunity to make them feel comfortable in these settings. When they have the chance to interview the generous employees at those firms who volunteer to work with the students, I am excited to see them broadening their horizons and their sense of possibility before my eyes.

As Sally Lamb, the headteacher of Old Moat School near Manchester, reflected, 'The children need to see that the skills they are learning in the classroom are transferrable. They will be the same skills used by adults in the work place. This is something that the children commented on during their trips. They asked questions such as "Do you have to work with people you don't like and agree on things?" or "What happens if you're late for work?" and "What happens if you don't get something done in work time?" Making these links changes everything.'

When coupled with essential skills development in the classroom, something very exciting starts to happen.

Putting it into practice in your classroom

The most critical thing if you're looking at this for your classroom is to think about what you want to achieve through engaging outside partners. Bringing in a real-life link can be helpful for illustrating the wider value to students of what they are learning, but sadly these interactions are often not particularly valuable in their own right without context, follow-up, or direct learning. If you're designing a project for your students, do think about the principles that I outlined at the start of the chapter.

Some of our teachers have found real success, though, when they've brought employee volunteers into the classroom – and some of the organisations that I've mentioned in this chapter can be invaluable for setting up these occasional links and experiences.

Putting it into practice as a school leader

If you're looking at building up these links in your school, the key thing is to be proactive in planning out what you want, and who you want. Random assemblies because someone has got in touch aren't likely to have any meaningful impact – whereas a closely planned series with context for the students and follow-up afterwards is likely to be a lot more powerful.

If you're looking at using project-based learning to complement skills development, it's important to strike the right balance between using local labour-market information to make projects locally relevant, and also to widen horizons too. Don't underestimate the time that will need to go into developing really effective projects or the support that your teachers will need to do this well.

Finally, you can use this engagement with the wider world as a powerful boost for adding impetus and relevance to the skills learning and helping bring it all to life. It's well worth the effort.

Putting it into practice as a parent

As a parent, you might want to think about how you can help your child to broaden their understanding of the working world. Sharing your own experiences of working can be helpful – perhaps discussing the different jobs you have held but also talking about your day-to-day work – what you've been doing, what's going well, and what is challenging? There might be occasions when you can bring your child into the workplace to see it for themselves.

Some are blessed with great professional networks which can help secure work experience, but just chatting with our friends and colleagues in different roles or stages of life can be invaluable for widening our children's understanding of the world. Particularly as children get older and become young adults, it can be helpful to get them to prepare for these conversations by helping them think through what they really want to know.

But it is increasingly recognised that these advantages need to be put in reach of all children. When it comes to careers, there are more and more free online tools available to help explore different careers. This may be something that you can work on together.

Finally, there are opportunities for work experience out there – My Kinda Future, for example, posts lots of opportunities of different lengths to help young people build up their CVs.

Summary

This chapter explored our sixth and final principle for effectively building essential skills – by bringing that learning to life. This could happen a lot more, and is generally held back by a shortage of school links with employers, but also a nervousness about bringing the working world into the classroom.

We explored two of the key ways that the real world can help to enhance how students build their skills. Firstly, by using real projects with a clear focus and outcomes to bring the real world into the classroom. These can provide a meaningful opportunity for practice and application of essential skills. Secondly, by taking students out of the classroom into the working world to apply their skills in context.

When this works well, these links help to provide real drive and energy to building essential skills, as well as helping students build the transferability of those skills.

This section has explored the principles which together characterise schools who are leading the way. These six principles are, we believe, they key to ensuring that all children and young people build high levels of competence in their essential skills that will set them up for life. The best schools:

- *Keep it simple:* Focusing consistently on the same core set of essential skills.

- *Start early and keep going:* Starting with children as young as 3 years old and maintaining that skills development until students are leaving school.

- *Measure it:* Quantifying students' skills to ensure a balanced understanding of strengths and weaknesses relative to age expectations and to help understand progress.

- *Focus tightly:* Using an understanding of the students to pitch activities in students' stretch zone, and allowing time just to focus on those skills.

- *Keep practising:* Using appropriate opportunities to apply and reinforce essential skills in other areas of teaching and beyond the curriculum too.

- *Bring it to life:* Using real-life links to bring the skills to life – both by taking students out of the classroom and by bringing real-life problems and challenges into the classroom.

At Enabling Enterprise we have seen hundreds of schools and thousands of teachers embrace these principles. In doing so, they improve the life trajectory of tens of thousands of students.

The final part of this book looks to the future. What is the outlook for essential skills? What questions do we still need to answer? And what will it take to ensure that one day *all* students are building the essential skills to succeed?

Part 4:
For all children and young people

Eight years in, Enabling Enterprise was an established national organisation. We were working with children and young people across the whole country, from Newcastle down to the South Coast. We had offices in London, Birmingham and Manchester from which our team fanned out every week to schools across the country.

On any given day, we might be at our smallest school of 33 students, perched on a hill at the end of a long and winding lane in rural Shropshire, or in a bustling secondary school in Liverpool. We could spend a day working with a group of 3- or 4-year-olds who were just beginning to realise that their peers had emotions too, or working with 17-year-olds who were weighing up their next steps.

That year, 2016-17, we were delivering our programmes with over 85,000 students. This was no quick-fix either: most of those students were receiving regular Enterprise lessons that used direct teaching and project-based learning methodologies to systematically build the essential skills for education, employment and enterprise. These were complemented by occasional Challenge Days to bring the whole school together. Then we also gave students the chance to link their learning to the 'real world' through trips to employer partners.

On any given day, hundreds of children and young people arrived at the doors of our employer partners for a day of challenge and insight – and a chance to apply those essential skills in different settings. These 130 employer partners are an exciting group – including airports, engineering companies, law firms, construction, public sector bodies and hospitals across the country.

This was being made possible through the hard work of thousands of teachers – over 3500 that year. Our team at Enabling Enterprise were out and about to train and support those teachers and their students – both in school and as we took them out to visit employers.

And most importantly, our model, built off the six principles, was working. Through our skills assessment approach we were able to see the change that teachers of Enabling Enterprise were seeing in their students. The previous year, we had seen that students on our programmes were making over a third more progress in their essential skills than their peers. This changes everything – taking students from a trajectory where every year they fell further behind to putting them ahead of that curve.

Only a start
All of this was very exciting. But there was also something very sobering too: at that point, we were working with just over 260 schools. This was a little more than 1% of schools in the country.

Of course our energies were a bit more focused than that – we knew our programmes had more impact where students didn't already have the same access to professional networks through their parents, or extracurricular opportunities. So, that year, over two-thirds of our schools were serving the 20% most deprived communities in the country, with 86% serving the 40% most deprived.

But even if we really thought this was solely an issue for those communities, and I do not, then we would still be only working with about 1 in 25 of those schools.

I walked the long way back to the office one day from a meeting in the gleaming centre of the City of London back up past Liverpool Street and then out through Shoreditch and on past the pawn brokers, betting shops and pubs of Bethnal Green Road to our office. As I walked, I was aware that I had timed my walk to the end of the school day and the pavement was filled with students from one of the local secondary schools.

I thought of our mission – to ensure that one day, *all* students leave school equipped with the essential skills, experiences of work and aspirations to succeed.

Enabling Enterprise had always been a partnership – of schools, teachers, employers, students and of parents. But this partnership alone would not achieve our mission.

What will it take?

The final part of this book looks at what it will really take to ensure that *every* child and young person builds their essential skills and fills that gap in their education. There is a crucial part for all of us to play – whether we are parents, policy makers, students ourselves, employers, teachers, or school leaders.

What's more, this is a young field and there is a lot more to learn. If we can align the work in this area, we should be able to start achieving some real breakthroughs in how we build essential skills.

Finally, it has become a cliché to point out that we live in a period of unparalleled change – but that doesn't make it untrue. I look at some of the changes that will affect the children and young people we educate today and how those changes will only make essential skills more critical in the future.

176

Chapter 15:
The roles we all have to play

There is an alternative to where we are today. Where we don't simply accept that some children and young people are endowed with a much fuller, deeper basic skill set than others. Where we don't presume that some students have a very limited capacity to work with others, lead, set their own goals or communicate effectively. Where instead we recognise that while not every child will be a transcendent orator or historic leader, each should grasp essential skills. After all, these skills sit alongside literacy, numeracy, and a rich foundation of knowledge to set our students up for the rest of their lives.

To reach that, we must shift to a world where we collectively believe three things, with the same determination that we believe in the importance of all children becoming literate and numerate today.

Firstly, to have a shared belief that these essential skills are vital. It is not enough for a few of us, or even the thousands who have been through our programmes, to see why these skills are fundamental. To make the leap from where we are today to a world where all children are building these skills, we need to shift attitudes to the point where these skills are seen through the same lens as literacy and numeracy: fundamental to unlocking learning and success in life beyond school.

Secondly, to know that it is possible for every child and young person to build a strong level of competence in those skills. Seeing their Enabling Enterprise programmes in action, and the transformation in their students, is often enough to shift teachers' expectations and preconceptions. But that is only part of the picture. We need to go well beyond the 3500 teachers that we trained last year as 35,000 new teachers start training to become a qualified teacher every year in England[139]. And obviously there are many more teachers in schools who have long before become qualified.

Teachers aren't the only part of that equation – the role of parents, as already highlighted, is absolutely critical. These high expectations are powerful – whether a student is getting work experience, or taking part in a club outside or an intervention within the school environment. Expectations really drive what subsequently happens in reality.

Thirdly, to establish a shared language and common standards around those skills. This is the only way to ensure that our combined efforts add up to at least the sum of their parts. Otherwise, not only is there no link between the different experiences that students have in building those skills, but there is little way for teachers or parents to reinforce those experiences. It will also be impossible to achieve the principles around measurement, focusing tightly or reinforcing their development.

If we can achieve these three changes, then we can ensure that all of our children and young people are able to build the essential skills to unlock their potential.

To do this, though, we all have to work together.

It's not all about schools

So far, I've focused a great deal on the central role that I believe teachers and schools can play, while also trying to provide some useful pointers for fellow parents.

Perhaps because essential skills have been neglected in the core curriculum for so long, there is even more focus on building those skills elsewhere – sometimes at home, often from other charities or social enterprises, provision beyond school or extracurricular offers.

Essential skills are fundamental and should have a central role in what happens in schools – but that doesn't make everything else less valuable. Building a shared core will multiply all of our efforts.

Setting up every child and young person for success

The six principles are central to making this happen. As we cast our eyes towards making this a reality for *all* students, we need to think about how to take these principles from exceptional schools to being commonplace. There are four big things that we can do, to give every child and young person the best possible chance to build their essential skills:

- Better training and supporting teachers and teaching assistants
- Creating and maintaining a shared language and expectations
- Ensuring that value is placed on essential skills throughout the education system
- Properly engaging parents

It's worth digging into each of these in turn.

(1) Training and supporting teachers and teaching assistants

Enabling Enterprise is built on the brilliant work of thousands of teachers and teaching assistants. Our team is primarily made up of experienced teachers, but we have always known that the programmes we have designed are most effective when delivered by classroom teachers who really understand the needs and priorities of their students.

Anders Ericsson makes a very similar point: that anyone who has achieved a high degree of success in any field has done so through expert teaching and coaching[140].

What is interesting, though, is just how lacking in confidence even some of the most experienced, effective teachers are when it comes to building essential skills. This should really not be a surprise – many teacher training courses make no mention at all about developing these broader skills. This is a point that many of our teachers came back to as I chatted to them in staff rooms across the country – the closest training any of them could recall was 'that stuff about growth mind-set'.

We've already seen that building these skills is not always intuitive. It is not the case that you build leadership skills by putting one student in charge, or that just doing activities in teams will necessarily build teamwork skills. I remember some of the early training sessions that I delivered when I was just setting out at Enabling Enterprise – asking the gathered teachers to define teamwork, leadership, and the rest only to find an awkward silence. One teacher broke the silence by declaring that 'I don't exactly know how I'd define teamwork…but I know there is no "I" in "team"'.

If we cannot even define these skills consistently, then we cannot possibly teach them effectively – let alone build in the sort of sophisticated progression that our students actually need.

Creating expert teachers

Some schools have got around this challenge through one dedicated member of staff being the school's Enterprise Coordinator. This individual becomes the source of expertise for the school and takes on responsibility for its enterprise provision. At secondary school, this is often a business studies teacher (although this subject specialism is unnecessary) or an advanced skills teacher. At primary school, it is often a senior teacher or a stretch opportunity for a confident classroom teacher.

There is a real value to having specialists for essential skills in a school. They develop a deeper understanding of the pedagogical foundations to successfully build the skills – including how skills are built, how to track and measure them and how to use project-based learning effectively to practise the skills. Fully implementing the six principles will need real leadership.

Indeed, our experience at Enabling Enterprise has been that schools that are doing this well have all had leads or champions on the ground. These senior leaders and teachers act as the conduit for sharing best practice and then actively support their colleagues to put their programmes into practice on the ground. This might include modelling enterprise teaching, or learning walks to help identify and promote best practice around the school, as well as running training sessions.

We should be looking to accredit teachers who build this particular specialism around essential skills, in a similar vein to other teacher accreditations like Chartered Maths Teachers, or leading geography teachers who are recognised by the Royal Geographical Society.

The depth of this field is such that there would be real value in recognising expertise – and then finding ways to draw in more knowledge and learning from the front line of teaching too, and sharing it more widely.

Giving all teachers a good grounding in essential skills

Having a champion doesn't negate the need for all teachers to have a grounding in building essential skills in their students. We are comfortable with having literacy and numeracy coordinators at primary school – but that doesn't mean that other teachers aren't proficient at building those skills. Similarly, there is increasing focus at secondary school on ensuring that all teachers can reinforce their students' literacy and numeracy. Talking to our teachers suggests that this is patchier than would be ideal, but certainly that is the aspiration.

At Enabling Enterprise, we put a lot of energy into ensuring a strong training programme for all of our teachers. For our partner schools, this means up to six sessions of support over the year. This starts with the basics of introducing the goal that we are all working together to achieve, and the skills we are working on and why, and the basic language. We also introduce the tools for skills assessment and then set them on their way to observe their classes over the next four weeks.

After that time, teachers can complete their first skills assessment of their class using the Skills Builder framework. The second training session then focuses on using this assessment to draw out the strengths and weaknesses of their classes relative to age-related expectations. With this knowledge, teachers can start to fine-tune their approach.

Thereafter, sessions become more flexible – and might include learning walks to capture best practice across the school, modelling ways of emphasising skills progress or supporting individual teachers. For schools who have been involved with Enabling Enterprise for a number of years, they are likely to be looking at more advanced topics – like focusing on particular student needs like those with English as an additional language, those with special educational needs, a tighter focus on one particular skill, or formative assessment and differentiation practices when teaching essential skills.

At the end of the year, the final training session captures some of the achievements of the year, and a review of where the students have made more or less progress – and what we can do in the following year to build on this.

The Department for Education's Standard for Teachers' Professional Development shares some goals which are critical for any successful programme of training[141]. These are helpful for how we should approach building teacher confidence and expertise in the essential skills:

- A clear focus on improving and evaluating pupil outcomes
- Underpinned by robust evidence and expertise
- Include collaboration and expert challenge
- Sustained over time
- Prioritised by school leadership

These are sound goals and emphasise the point that there can be no quick solution to the challenge of ensuring all teachers are trained and confident. As we saw earlier, our six principles chime significantly with these – with the need for measurability, implementation discretely and in combination with others, a long-term commitment, reinforcement across the school, and the use of real life links to bring that external challenge.

Our most effective schools, like William Tyndale Primary School, make regular training time available to support the on-going development and refinement of the skills. Others give their Enterprise lead teacher time to support other members of staff too.

Building essential skills into Initial Teacher Training and other training offers

Beyond training in school, there is a lot that can be done to increase the introductory training on these skills for trainee teachers. I completed my teacher training a decade ago now, and there was certainly not much focus on enterprise or the associated skills then – even though I was training as a Business Studies teacher.

Of course, one of the big challenges with teacher training in England now is that the model is so fragmented with many different routes and training providers – whether universities, Teach First, School Direct, a multi-academy trust offer, or one of the other hybrid routes.

At Enabling Enterprise, we have had some experience of being involved in this initial training – for example, through Teach First and at universities including Newman University. The challenge is that we often only get a couple of hours in their schedule which is enough to introduce the skills as something to be mindful of but hardly provides a solid grounding. The energy and enthusiasm of the response, though, re-doubled our commitment to better supporting these new teachers.

As a result, we've followed this up ourselves by creating a set of online tools for primary and secondary teachers. These provide a much deeper understanding of each of the essential skills, their theoretical and pedagogical grounding and practical ways to embed building these skills through other learning too. These can be found at www.theessentialskills.org. For secondary teachers, alongside these training materials we've also created dozens of focused short activities that can be used to build the skills, helping teachers to see what it looks like in practice. All of these can be found at www.teachenterprise.org.

In the future, we are looking forward to working more with providers of Initial Teacher Training, as well as other providers of Continued Professional Development to help build more of this thinking into the training that teachers receive. Having a joined-up approach and clear language will obviously be a big help here.

Sharing what works through peer networks

Ultimately, the call for essential skills will have to become a movement led by teachers for it to reach students in every classroom.

That's why it's exciting to also see the surge of teacher-organised events and peer sharing, like Teach Meets. These have tremendous potential as a way of sharing best practice and learning from what works – we have already found these a brilliant route for our teachers to share their insights around the skills, whilst also being in a position to learn from others too.

Elsewhere, online communities, Twitter and blogs have become invaluable sources of insight, ideas and challenge for teachers across the country. As momentum builds behind essential skills, peer learning and sharing will be an essential part of the next wave of progress.

(2) Creating and maintaining a shared language

A shared language would be an absolute game-changer for how we build essential skills.

Imagine being taught how to drive a car by a dozen different people in different ways over a number of years. It could just about work if they all took a slightly different tack – one focusing more on theory, another using a bicycle to navigate the roads, another using simulators. It would obviously work considerably better if this was done in a logical order – starting with the basics of how a car functioned, say, and the theory of how the road system works, what the signs mean and all the rest.

It would be catastrophic if each new instructor paid no heed to anything that had happened before, and just jumped in at the point that interested them most. And then imagine too that there is no shared language for either – one instructor's bonnet is another's hood which is another's ECD (or engine covering device), but another refers to it as the lid. One instructor's car looks surprisingly like a hovercraft, and another is quite clearly an articulated lorry. And you should hear what they call left and right.

In earlier chapters we saw that one of the biggest reasons why all of this activity hasn't achieved its potential in the past was that there was no coherence in what we called a fairly stable and consistent set of skills.

One joined-up approach

Imagine instead that there was one set of eight skills, uniformly known as the Essential Skills. These skills were consistently described from when a child first entered a nursery classroom, and followed them throughout their time in primary school, through the transition into secondary and right up to when they left at the age of 16 or 18. Perhaps they would even be picked up and built on by colleges, universities or employers.

The students themselves would have a very clear idea of what those eight skills were, and would know where their relative strengths and weaknesses lay. They would know what their next steps were to get better and be able to connect the skills they were developing in an after-school club with their enterprise lesson. They would be able to deploy their teamwork, presenting or listening skills to other lessons.

Their parents would be able to follow what was going on too – able to reinforce and celebrate progress in these areas in the same way they can in literacy or numeracy progression at the moment. They would be able to provide encouragement or help their children make a connection between new situations they faced and the skill set that they had already mastered so far – building confidence and the virtuous circle of pushing themselves in a new situation. Perhaps they would seek out opportunities to build the skills that were lacking.

There would be a huge benefit for their teachers too. It would make it much easier to have a joined-up conversation with their students' previous teachers about the strengths and weaknesses in their students' skills. It would mean that when there were suitable opportunities in class that the skills could be referred to, activities could be designed at a level that was age- and stage-appropriate. When a student came back to school raving about their experience with the Scouts, the Duke of Edinburgh Award or National Citizen Service programme, they could see the connections between those experiences and classroom learning too.

Not just a pipe dream

Now, it might feel far-fetched to imagine that we can get there. Except that it is already starting to happen – Enabling Enterprise, along with Franklin Scholars, Ark Academies, Teach First, Business in the Community and Career Ready, have already come together to refine the Skills Builder framework into just such a common language. This is not an easy process – language and nuance gets easily baked into a programme and an approach, and often takes on a much greater symbolic meaning than might be initially obvious. We are joined in this endeavour by a dozen other organisations who are piloting the framework in their setting, and benefitting from the expertise of more than 50 others – including academics, practitioners, and employers.

Through Skills Builder (at www.skillsbuilder.org), it is now possible for any school or other organisation to start using the same framework and tools for measurement.

We have already seen the impact: that schools who are using multiple interventions are better able to target and tailor those approaches to the right students; that their teachers are able to reinforce their learning by having essential skills up in every classroom too.

Bringing this change to a systemic level will need a lot more though.

A unified approach: the other players

Other schools

Firstly, we need to reach well beyond those already teaching in Enabling Enterprise partner schools. We would, of course, love more schools to become Enabling Enterprise partners but I am realistic that will not reach all 24,000 of them in England.

That has been the motivation behind making more of our training materials and teaching resources available in formats that work for individual teachers where there is no whole-school approach to building essential skills.

External providers

Secondly, there are many providers out there whose work can support achieving the principles – some provide competitions, opportunities to engage with employees, or skills programmes. A few examples are Career Ready, Future First, and My Kinda Future.

Matching outcomes to that unified framework should be possible over a period of time. For more established programmes, that would sometimes need revisions but we know that most programmes are regularly refined. For newer programmes or organisations, we have often found a real enthusiasm for being able to adopt something rather than trying to create it from scratch. Organisations like the Careers and Enterprise Company could play a vital convening role here as it funds and brings together different providers working in this space and encourages outcomes to fit into that common framework, whilst also sharing learning about what works.

Employers

Our third group, employers, have a big role to play when they support the transition from the world of education into employment.

Some of the larger employers provide their own schemes to support the development of skills and experiences, such as Barclays Life Skills. Where employers are doing this, they could maximise impact by using the common framework and language that we are developing. That can also extend to using the existing frameworks to help ensure that activities are pitched at the right level so that students are getting the most out of activities.

Where they don't have established schemes in place, I would strongly encourage firms to get involved. There are lots of things that can be done, according to capacity. Work experience and careers talks are the perennial favourites, but alongside building understanding of the working world, there is also a role that employers can play in building the essential skills too.

Employers are obviously crucial in what happens to most young people as they end their formal education. One trend is that employers are increasingly moving their focus away from academic measures, and instead to the skills and attitudes of their recruits. This makes sense in the context where these are more highly valued by employers than just the raw academic achievement. PwC and EY are two leading accounting and audit firms that have moved away from always requiring degrees, for example.

When it comes to interviewing candidates, we are some way from a stage where a student will present their 'essential skills certificate'. Unless we could provide a robust external assessment of their skills, then we would be making teacher assessments much higher stakes than they currently are. My feeling is that that would lead to all the wrong incentives around the assessment and development of those skills – the assessment would become something to be gamed and the risk of subjectivity would be hugely exacerbated by rewarding higher grading.

Nevertheless, there would be some value in similar language being used by employers at the interview stage. This would help students better articulate how they have built and demonstrated those skills before – which would be invaluable, particularly for less experienced candidates who might otherwise struggle to find examples that should be at their fingertips.

Influencers in education and employment

Finally, one of the most powerful ways of influencing this change among educators would be for the Department for Education and Ofsted to explicitly start using the same consistent set of skills in their communications. At the moment, there is recognition of the value of a stable definition within a school[142], but a reluctance to impose a central definition. The Careers and Enterprise Company have similarly shied away from a clear definition of enterprise activity to date.

One of the often-cited reasons for this is that it doesn't allow enough adaptability to local context or to the values of the school. I think that makes sense in some ways, but actually the skills are such a basic and universal foundation I don't think we should be so anxious about this. Language and dialects vary across England but we don't feel the need to have different terminology around literacy in different parts of the country.

Indeed, Lucy Ashman, who is Director of Social Innovation at Teach For All across more than forty countries, emphasises that where this challenge is talked about internationally, it is the same skills that come up time and again.

Similarly, employers are more likely to take up a common language if key influencers like BITC, the CBI and the Institute of Directors start using the same language. I was thrilled when BITC announced that they would get behind the Skills Builder framework, and encourage their members to do so too.

This alone is not going to make the full difference, but it would certainly help to align employers with schools and build a greater continuity of students' experience along the way.

(3) Ensuring value is placed on essential skills in the education system

Together, a confident and trained teaching force and a common language and set of age-related expectations will achieve a great deal. However, engaging schools across the country will require a shift in the value that is placed on essential skills in the education system.

The role of government

Some of the greatest levers for systematic change obviously come from government – at the simplest level, the curriculum, what is measured, what is funded, and what is inspected.

What is interesting is that on one level, schools do have the flexibility to make space to build essential skills – the curriculum is much less prescriptive than in many other countries and academies need not follow it at all. We've seen, of course, that it is possible for the hundreds of schools who are already partners of Enabling Enterprise to fit their programmes into a busy timetable.

There is also recognition from Ofsted that this matters too. In their common inspection framework they explicitly highlight an expectation that 'English, mathematics and other skills necessary to function as an economically active member of British society and globally are promoted through teaching and learning' [143]. Surely, essential skills have to be at least a chunk of those 'other skills necessary'? This is backed up by the clear call, a couple of pages later, that provision should support learners' 'employability skills so that they are well prepared for the next stage of their education, employment, self-employment or training'. Which, again, sounds not a far stretch from what we've been setting out so far. Several of our school's Enabling Enterprise programmes have been positively mentioned in their Ofsted inspection reports.

Ofsted's focused review of enterprise education in 2016 helped to demonstrate why this mention was insufficient though[144]. At its heart, it found that 'the extent to which schools used their curriculum to prepare pupils for the world of work was largely dependent on whether school leaders considered it to be a priority'. Very few of the 40 secondary schools that it reviewed were effectively building their students' enterprise skills. Another segment of the report found that 'in some cases, school leaders simply told inspectors that [enterprise education] was not a feature of their curriculum and that they saw themselves as accountable only for achieving a narrow set of outcomes focused around examinations'[145].

Ultimately, in English education currently, school accountability frameworks encourage schools to put a great deal of emphasis and energy into examination results and other interim measures of academic progress.

To move beyond this, the Department for Education, Ofsted, and other agencies such as the Careers and Enterprise Company will require a stronger and more explicit focus on whether there are structured, age-appropriate opportunities for students to build their essential skills at all levels in the curriculum.

Firstly, there would be clear value in reinstating enterprise as a core requirement and an expectation of the level of dedicated learning time that students could expect. Given the importance of these skills for social mobility this would seem to chime with the thinking and drive of the current government.

Secondly, promoting clear, up-to-date guidance that gives much greater clarity on language and age-related expectations would be valuable. A common set of essential skills (incorporating enterprise and employability expectations) would enable schools to compare what is working, and to avoid the need for each school to 'reinvent the wheel' by developing its own bespoke approach.

Thirdly, dedicated funding originally drove a lot of enterprise education work, and there was certainly an uptick in activity. We've already explored why much of this activity missed the mark, but with a clearer focus we could take much greater advantage of this – particularly if the spending had to be on programmes that could demonstrably support students meeting those age-related expectations.

Finally, stronger destination data – that is, data on where students end up a small number of years after their time in school has ended – could do a lot to justify to schools making this wider investment beyond students' academic attainment.

(4) Properly engaging parents

As a fairly new parent, it's sobering to see first-hand what I've felt as a teacher for the past decade: that the influence and role of parents and carers is undoubtedly the greatest in a child's life, particularly in those early years.

Parents are critically important in modelling to their children how to behave in different situations. This comes from both the verbal and non-verbal cues that we give. Part of it is how we interact with them – at an early stage, are we giving space for them to talk without interruptions, and using questioning to help them expand their ideas?

We are also increasingly aware of the way that language shapes the way our children see the world: for example, do we use the language of 'trying their best', and emphasise effort not just achievement? This is an idea that Carol Dweck explores extensively through her work on the growth mindset[146].

We've also seen that one of the greatest determinants of whether a child keeps trying at something or gives up is the behaviour that they see from their parents. If something is hard, do we model trying to find an alternative way of doing it, or do we express frustration and then move on? Do we show that we set longer term goals and then take the steps towards achieving them, even though it will take time and concerted effort?

As a new parent, I think there's a lot of space for more explicit guidance on how we can help build these skills in our children – not because it will make them employable two decades hence, but because it will enable them to get the most out of their precious childhoods and time in school. We do this through the health visitor developmental checks in the early years, so parents are unlikely to be fazed by informative leaflets or similar materials. It could make a real difference.

Giving opportunities to build the skills

As our children and young people get older, we often seek out opportunities to help them build their skills. For example, giving children the chance to build skills through taking part in a sport or a drama team. We all have different means – and some of the more expensive options will be out of reach. But thinking about the skills and strengths of our children and recognising and encouraging their efforts, even in everyday activities, can help to build them.

Being able to have conversations with schools around these skills and how they are being developed in school is already a possibility for many parents whose students attend Enabling Enterprise partner schools. The schools report that this additional insight into their children's development is invaluable.

A final point here is that I know that parents have a lot on their plates. Whatever support or guidance we offer must be a complement to busy lives: simple tips that can boost a child's basic social skills, resilience and empathy from a young age.

Summary

Through the work of Enabling Enterprise and others we have seen that it is possible to fill the gap in basic essential skills for individual students, for classes, and across whole schools. The challenge is that this is a fundamental gap in the whole education system. Many students do build these skills through parental networks and extracurricular opportunities – but many do not.

To make the difference for all students, we need to make three profound shifts:

- Firstly, to a shared recognition that essential skills are essential.
- Secondly, to a shared understanding that these skills can be built and that all children and young people can achieve a high level of competence in those skills.
- Thirdly, towards a common language and set of standards that will help us to focus our combined efforts most powerfully.

To do this, we can all make a contribution – whether as parents ourselves, students, policy makers or employers. There are four big steps to take:

- Training and supporting teachers and teaching assistants
- Creating and maintaining a shared language and expectations
- Ensuring that value is placed on essential skills in the education system
- Properly engaging parents

There are already some exciting signs of progress here – from other organisations who develop these skills coming together around shared language to parents seeking out opportunities to build them in their children.

There is still a long way to go. The final two chapters make clear what we must still discover, and what we still have to do – and why building essential skills is only going to become more urgent.

Chapter 16:
The next leg of the journey

This is both an old and a young field.

It is old because this is a fundamental, timeless set of skills.

Indeed, opponents of '21st century skills' like nothing more than to point out that Roman infantry needed teamwork skills or that Machiavelli quite clearly had the planning skills and foresight that forms a part of aiming high. We saw earlier that rhetoric was one of the earliest things to be taught – what we at Enabling Enterprise would term listening and presenting – alongside logic which touches on problem-solving.

But despite these antecedents, the building of essential skills is in many ways a new field. When seen in the same context as literacy or numeracy, it is clearly not as established, and has not yet benefited from the same focused waves of innovation and intellectual development.

Building a new discipline: Sources of optimism
The patterns of how literacy and numeracy have developed are encouraging though.

To take literacy first, the concept of the written word was about utility, not the capture of artistic or deep cultural importance. Indeed, Martin Robinson cites that it was Phoenician traders who first introduced the Greeks to the written language as a means of supporting trade[147]. There was a genuine fear that writing would undermine the skill of memorisation which was how poetry was communicated. This is an interesting point for those who worry that essential skills lack the academic purity of other learning: perhaps we have not yet considered that they could in fact be the key to helping many more children to succeed in their academic studies as well.

The idea of universal literacy in England did not catch on until the 1870s. Up to that point, there had been little call for it. Most people worked in manual jobs where their managers were all-powerful and allocated simple, repetitive tasks that could be taught without any requirement for a greater level of education. It was the military ascendency of Prussia and the US who had made similar investments in education and which seemed to be paying off militarily that encouraged the government in the UK to introduce a universal basic expectation of education.

Indeed, when the idea of universal literacy was introduced there was resistance. Was it was even possible for the general population to be literate? Would it be a desirable outcome if so? Would it be a good use of limited resources?

Now, it had always been possible to teach some people to read as far back as the hieroglyphics of ancient Egypt – through expert tuition, and a large input of resources for each student. The challenge was how to take this to scale.

In broad terms, in 1475 the literacy rate in Great Britain was approximately 5%[148]. There was simply not the call for literacy beyond the religious orders or the extremely wealthy. The introduction of the printing press led to a much wider value being placed on literacy and by the mid-17th century the literacy rates in Great Britain had risen to about 55%. And here they stagnated for the following two centuries until the introduction of compulsory schooling.

Literacy rates in England have subsequently increased over time to an assumed basic literacy rate of 99% now. Sustenance of that improvement saw multiple waves of innovation. These have included the introduction of reading ages, standardised language around literacy, the national strategies of the Labour government from 1997 and a more recent emphasis on phonics.

Technology is also being mobilised to support the development of literacy. Just one example is Accelerated Reader, which supports students to read more age- and stage-appropriate books. The programme works by encouraging students to select and read books that put them in their 'stretch zone' and then using short quizzes to verify that those books have been read. As students make progress, they accumulate points, which can be translated into prizes, recognition or just the satisfaction of making quantifiable progress.

Patterns in building numeracy

The story of numeracy follows a similar early pattern although counting and the ability to manage money have been important as universal skills from an earlier stage. Once again, the acceptable standard of numeracy has of course increased over time.

In the past, basic arithmetic was generally seen as adequate whereas today the definition of being numerate deployed by National Numeracy is 'being able to reason with numbers and other mathematical concepts and to apply these in a range of contexts and to solve a variety of problems'[149]. This might include being able to interpret data, charts and diagrams, being able to process information, to solve problems, to check answers, and to understand and explain solutions, and then to make decisions based on logical thinking and reasoning.

Technology is also coming into play more here too. One example of this is Khan Academy, which uses a series of carefully curated and organised short videos to help people of all ages master and practise key mathematical concepts through simple YouTube videos and quizzes. Again, this ensures that students are able to work in their stretch zone.

Other classroom-based approaches include Maths Mastery which revisits approaches to mathematics teaching to break them down into distinct elements which can then be mastered one at a time. In Australia, an approach called Maths Pathway combines these two elements of Khan Academy and Maths Mastery by ensuring that students are working at their own pace, and allowing teachers to ensure students have really grasped a concept before moving on – but not being held back once something is mastered.

While these innovations are at an early stage, they provide encouragement that we too can grow our expectations for building essential skills.

The future for building Essential Skills

Both examples of how literacy and numeracy have developed as fields give grounds for optimism, and an interesting parallel. As they've been seen as increasingly important, changes in teaching, resources, and standards have driven levels in numeracy and literacy higher and higher. My greatest hope for the work of Enabling Enterprise – and this book – is that it helps to kick start a new wave of innovation and progress in building essential skills.

We all build on the work of others. The work of our schools and employer partners at Enabling Enterprise has added to this by moving the thinking a bit further along through the six principles, and developing some of the tools to help bring those to life – things like the Skills Builder frameworks and assessment tools, the lesson-time projects that help model skills, our guides and resources for teachers, the employer engagement and so on.

But there is still a lot more to do. These areas are ripe for development:

- Learning internationally
- Further research on the essential skills, including longitudinal tracking
- Innovating in how we teach the skills
- Wider application of technology

Learning from overseas

Over the last few years, I've been fortunate enough to have a few opportunities to share our work overseas – in Hong Kong, the USA, China, Mexico, Estonia and Poland, among others. What has struck me time and again is that the essential skills translate universally, even if the language we use differs. In French, direct translation has proved quite convoluted – but there is the same recognition that these are important skills to have.

That point was made particularly starkly when I was in China, sat in the back of a remarkably disciplined classroom in rural Yunnan province as a guest of Teach For China. I watched as 7- and 8-year-olds sat with remarkable poise and focus through a Chinese language lesson – the often-envied discipline that our students are supposedly competing against in a great global race. But what was fascinating was that outside of the lesson the administrator of the school district was openly sharing his concerns that the students weren't able to work together, or be creative or come up with original ideas to tricky problems. Evidence, perhaps, that knowledge alone is insufficient to use these skills.

I heard the same things in Poland and Estonia. In those countries, the point was made a few times that cultural norms, for example an often-mentioned 'shyness', would make the activities that would support building the skills more difficult. But the same individuals emphasised that that only made it even more essential that the skills were taught and reinforced as a core part of students' learning.

I saw quite a different contrast during my time in Uganda, when I had the enormous privilege to share our work with a number of organisations focused on young people in the country and to see others' work in this very different context. Where the formal economy of regular pay checks is limited and with less consistent social safety nets, people have to be entrepreneurial with micro-businesses instead of formal job roles in order to survive.

But what was also clear was that the attitudes of entrepreneurship or 'being enterprising' are insufficient. The bigger gap here was business knowledge, and

194

also communication skills, interpersonal skills, and self-management through planning and goal-setting.

Finally, on a couple of trips to the USA I saw how different Charter Schools were trying to grapple with a problem even more acute than I've already described in England around university drop-out and disengagement from school. They saw that a highly structured knowledge-focused approach to working with some of their most disadvantaged communities was getting students into college – but was insufficient to get them to stay. In response, some of the leading Charter School networks like KIPP schools were focusing much more explicitly on building the character and the skills for individual students to thrive.

Alongside the privilege of touching down in unfamiliar countries, we've also been pleased to welcome interest in Enabling Enterprise's approach from other parts of the world. Over the last few years, we've crammed into our small offices delegations from Thailand, Lithuania, Morocco, Germany and many others. Equipping young people with essential skills is not just a challenge that we are grappling with in England or the UK, but a much bigger global concern.

Over the next few years, I would love to see a lot more opportunities to learn internationally from what works in building essential skills in different countries and different settings. Enabling Enterprise programmes have now been run in Italy, Spain, Uganda and the United Arab Emirates but I know of home-grown programmes in Colombia and many other parts of the world.

In her fascinating book, *Cleverlands*, Lucy Crehan explores how some of the countries that are acing the traditionally academic PISA tests are now working to build these broader skills too[150] – and she cites Japan and Canada as particularly interesting examples[151]. The challenge so far seems to be a perceived trade-off between investing in PISA success or wider skills development but I suspect that application of our six principles might change this equation.

Recently, the OECD announced a renewed interest in those wider skills. Having looked at collaborative problem-solving in 2016, the Director Andreas Schleicher announced that in 2019 the tests would also consider how to assess these 'global competencies'[152]. This may well encourage greater innovation in this area internationally.

I am sure that there will be lessons that we can draw on in the future as we build a global community around the need to ensure that all students build essential skills to navigate successful lives – wherever in the world that is.

Further research, including longitudinal tracking

Another area where we must continue to focus over the next few years will be to build up the strongest possible longitudinal picture of the links between essential skills and the future outcomes that we care about for our students.

When we asked LKMco to review the evidence base[153], they found that teachers and others in the field believed there were strong positive benefits to building these skills as well as evidence of the efficacy of individual essential skills. They also made a key recommendation that researchers should investigate potential qualitative relationships between these skills and other academic and non-academic outcomes.

These outcomes are likely to include an increased probability of making a good transition from formal education into further or higher education, employment or training. It may include higher long-term pay, or access and success at university, or the realisation of entrepreneurial ambitions. It might extend to differences in attainment, and support the closing of the achievement gap between students from disadvantaged backgrounds and their wealthier peers. Through this book, I've sought to highlight what we already know but there is still more to learn and to understand.

As we move to a more standardised and agreed set of essential skills, and expectations of outcomes at different ages, we can combine resources more effectively to refine the model and understand how the different elements interact in greater depth. For example, we might discover that rather than seeing the eight skills as linear in their own right, there might be much more important interactions – say, that one cannot progress in leadership without having mastered particular elements of teamwork, or other such interdependencies. Or we might find that particular combinations or timings of activities make them more effective.

So, while we have confidence in a framework that has been successfully used by thousands of teachers and tens of thousands of students, there would be huge value in continuing to build and refine that model and to understand and perhaps revise some of its nuances over time.

Innovating in how we teach the skills

While the six principles should be stable, they allow for considerable innovation in how we actually build the skills around them.

At Enabling Enterprise, we've got to a point where pretty consistently we can get students to be progressing in their skills at the rate that they need to in order to be on that trajectory for success. That translates into at least a level per year on the Skills Builder framework – and we are now seeing that our students make an average progress of 20% above that.

Through that framework, we've been driven to improve how we teach the skills and to prune out approaches that don't work. I look forward to the day where students are making twice the progress we currently see.

At Enabling Enterprise we're certainly not resting on our laurels. For example, we're trialling a new approach to building skills at secondary level which we're calling Teach Enterprise. Aimed at individual secondary school teachers, we're using a model of highly focused 10-minute video-based activities which tightly target making one level of progress in a single essential skill. This will still have to fit into a broader programme to fulfil the six principles, but is an alternative way of providing a focused experience.

We're also keen to learn from others who are doing brilliant work in this space. One example is Career Ready which takes a much more intensive model of working with smaller groups of students over an entire year with regular mentoring, skills workshops and an internship.

We have already seen that there are plenty of approaches that don't work. With a joined up set of outcomes, I hope that we will be able to work more quickly and in a more focused way to make progress in the techniques that best build the skills.

Use of technology

Finally, the continued development of technology, and particularly elements like artificial intelligence might hold some interesting keys for the future.

For example, at the moment we see an important part of our programmes as the opportunity to take students out of the classroom to visit employers. The challenge is that this is the most expensive element of the programmes we run. Of course, the reason we continue to see these trips as core is the value of meeting the volunteers at those employers, seeing the workplace first hand and getting a real taste of what that organisation does. It is an essential element of achieving the principle of 'bringing it to life'. The opportunity for simulations or virtual reality might well be a way to make those real-life engagements much more widely available – and to increase the multitude of opportunities that are available.

Beyond those experiences, simulations might also give students more focused opportunities to build those skills. In the same way that Khan Academy have used individualised pathways, we might be able to help each individual student to chart their most direct journey to building a really high level of effectiveness in essential skills.

There is already interest in how to capture and share the experiences and achievements of students – for example, Lord Young's report on Enterprise For All proposed the development of an 'Enterprise Passport' to create a digital record in this way[154]. As a former sixth form teacher who wrestled with trying to extract from my students the details of what they had achieved, this is an attractive offer. Even better if this could help students to track their skills outcomes – with the proviso that it must avoid creating tick boxes or incentives to game the system.

Technology also offers some interesting opportunities around how we might assess essential skills. At the moment, we primarily use teacher observation and assessment, combined with online tools to help teachers to structure and record their assessments. We've seen some interesting extensions of this too, though – for example, some schools have used video of activities to help model to teachers what performing the skills at different levels looks like and to help them to moderate their own assessments.

The principles are likely to continue to hold true – but technology might well help us find increasingly focused ways to deploy them in a busy timetable and with limited financial resources, whilst also broadening students' experiences and rates of progress.

Summary

While essential skills have a pedigree that stretches back to ancient history, they have not had the rigorous focus that more established basic skills of literacy and numeracy have received in recent decades.

As such, this is still a young field and there is a lot to learn. We can learn by seeking to explore the international context further – both to share what works and to understand how the principles play out globally.

We must test how the essential skills quantifiably affect the gap that we are seeking to fill – and the nuances of how they interact, what activities work best, and what the long-term impacts are. This will be accelerated as more and more organisations start using the Skills Builder framework – allowing for greater comparisons between cohorts.

As we begin to be able to share and compare teaching approaches more fully, we might end up learning new things about what works. We might well find techniques that are more effective than the approach that we currently take at Enabling Enterprise. We are already testing out some of those alternatives or complements ourselves through innovations like Teach Enterprise as well as learning from partners.

Finally, as technological change continues apace, we might be able to do all sorts of sophisticated things that we can barely imagine at the moment. That might mean that every student has their own record of their skills development that they can draw on or update at any time. Or it might mean that students can learn individually or through virtual reality situations to hone their skills.

I hope that that all the work to date is really just the first stage of a much longer journey. Because, as the next chapter makes clear, our children and young people will really need to master building those essential skills to make the most of the future.

Chapter 17:
Ready for the future

As I write this, the future looks as messy and unsure as it surely ever has. Indeed, The Economist recently described this as 'the age of uncertainty'.

In education this really matters. Some of the youngest children that Enabling Enterprise is working with today will be only entering the labour market in 2030. They might well expect to still be there at a sprightly 70 or 75 years old, which takes us to 2085.

It is not a particularly insightful point that the world of work by then will be different. This evolution of the work place and the roles available has always been a fact of economic progress.

Despite the obvious limitations of trying to speculate on what the future holds, there do seem to be four clear trends emerging with clear implications for our children and young people. And each of those trends in turn suggests that the essential skills will only become more important – together, the case is overwhelming.

Trend 1: Automation and algorithms
Since the industrial revolution, savvy company owners have been replacing relatively expensive humans with cheaper and more reliable machines – whether windmills, weaving machines, or steam engines. It is fair to say that these changes have never been warmly welcomed. Over time, these machines have become increasingly sophisticated – to the extent where in the newest car factories, humans have been almost entirely taken out of the physical construction and moved into an oversight and safety role.

The reduction in manufacturing jobs is a long-term trend in the UK already. In 1976, manufacturing accounted for 25% of GDP whereas now it is just 10%. What remains is weighted towards automotive and aircraft engineering, where the UK, as an advanced economy, can still add value.

This is not just a manufacturing phenomenon though. The service industry makes up 80% of GDP and is also being significantly affected. Despite their irritations, self-service tills in shops appear set to stay, reducing the number of staff needed to run a shop. Call centres are increasingly being replaced by voice recognition systems to help the caller navigate to the information that they need – if their queries or bookings haven't already been made through the internet. Directory enquiries is increasingly a niche tool for those without internet access. Even the cockpits of commercial airliners have become emptier since the introduction of GPS and other navigation aids made the presence of a human navigator unnecessary. As a result, jobs in these areas are being shed.

More recently increasing computational power has moved this automation away from physical processes into the sort of information management processes that once secured us humans a wage premium and a reliable working life. Some secretarial roles were the first to go – as physical filing was reduced, executives learned to type for themselves, and calendar tools made diary management less of an art.

Now, even apparently lucrative roles in finance and the legal professions are starting to be turned over. There is evidence that financial audits might be more effectively and accurately completed by algorithms, along with finding information in commercial contracts. Indeed, a recent study by Deloitte projected that 100,000 jobs in the English legal sector will be automated in the next 20 years[155].

The next move is potentially even more disruptive – the ability of computers not just to apply algorithms to repeat processes or sort and retrieve data, but actually to learn and become better. This Artificial Intelligence is likely to bring about the next wave of automation to previously untouched fields: for example, Uber, Google, Apple, Tesla and many of the major car manufacturers are investing heavily in self-driving vehicle technology which would render professional drivers redundant. There is even talk of professions like teaching being turned upside down by the introduction of more adaptable, individualised learning approaches.

Such is the concern that a 2017 report by the International Bar Association suggested that one response might be for governments to set and enforce 'human quotas' to maintain employment levels[156].

The implications

There are clear implications from this trend for our young people. Firstly, there will be continued and increasing pressure on the least-skilled jobs as automation continues to be a more cost-effective option for firms than hiring staff. Some of the proffered solutions, like Bill Gates' idea that we should tax robots as we would a human workforce, are likely to only marginally hold back this trend. According to the Centre for Social and Economic Inclusion, by 2022 there are likely to be 9 million low-skilled people in England competing for 4 million low-skilled jobs[157].

If these repetitive roles are under pressure, then we have to look elsewhere. In 2016, Goldman Sachs commissioned a report into the future of work. The report highlighted that employment opportunities in the future would principally come from 'adaptive occupations' that played to the strengths of humans. These 'adaptive occupations' would draw particularly on flexibility, creativity and strong interpersonal skills[158]. Which we recognise as essential skills.

Some commentators have overshot on this point – presuming that if we need these skills so much, we must need knowledge less. They are right that mandating early training for a specific role is a more risky thing to do – but we still need a strong foundational knowledge. For example, David Deming at Harvard University analysed changes in the shares of jobs from 1980 to 2012. He found that less-skilled jobs like labourers, welders or machine operators had declined – as we would expect. What he found, though, was that jobs in ascendancy were those that generally required more social skills and more mathematical skills. These jobs included physicians, financial managers and computer scientists. So it is certainly not the case of wholesale replacement of knowledge – but that we also need to be building essential skills.

Trend 2: Changing nature of employment

Since I started teaching in 2007, one of the clearest phenomena has been a huge increase in flexible working and self-employment.

In the election of 2015, zero-hour contracts became a focus of debate. These are contracts where there is no guaranteed minimum number of hours for the employee and no obligation for the employee to work those hours offered. They are just one manifestation of a more fluid approach to employment.

At the same time, by 2015, around 4.6 million people were self-employed, with the level of employment in the UK at an all-time high. This is not just the self-employment of the sole trader or entrepreneur that we might once have recognised. Instead, increasing numbers of people are working part-time or having multiple jobs.

This shift is often referred to as the 'gig economy'. The most well-known example is Uber which has disrupted the transportation industry with apps that match customers seeking a ride with drivers. A big effect has been a significant increase in the numbers of self-employed drivers who turn the app on when they want to work, and turn it off again when they don't. Hermes uses a similar model of self-employed delivery drivers. Deliveroo applies the approach to a fast food delivery service where customers can order food online and pay for delivery by cyclist or motor bike.

All three of these examples have drawn the attention of regulators in different cities, who question whether the individuals engaged are really self-employed – an arrangement that usually absolves the company of certain employment obligations, such as sick pay.

In parallel to the 'gig economy', the 'sharing economy' is encouraging individuals to patch together income in new ways. One of the clearest examples of this is Airbnb, where enterprising individuals can supplement their income by turning their spare room into a guest room when they don't need it. Other opportunities include renting out unused parking spaces, or using eBay to sell on unneeded goods.

The implications

These shifts in employment are well captured in a reflection attributed to Sheryl Sandberg that 'the metaphor for a career is no longer a ladder; it's a jungle gym'[159].

The debate is whether these more varied and flexible careers are by desire and design or whether they are a reaction to a more limited range of traditional opportunities. In either case, managing these careers and varied income streams requires a much more enterprising skill set.

The ability to *aim high* will be important – as will designing pathways and intermediate goals towards achieving longer-term outcomes. At the very beginning of the book, I highlighted that as teachers we too often feel that we are providing so much scaffolding and support around students that they are losing the ability to do this for themselves. In the economy that our students are going into, this is dangerous.

Without those support structures around them, our young people are going to need to take more responsibility for maintaining their own motivation and ability to stick with things even when they are challenging. These *staying positive* skills will therefore be essential too.

Trend 3: Learning and re-learning

Given all these changes, it's no wonder I rarely go long without seeing headline-grabbing assertions about the proportion of jobs that are likely to no longer exist in the future, or which we cannot even envisage yet.

These 'statistics' can be overdone. This change has always been a feature of economic development. We need fewer cartwrights, blacksmiths or cavalrymen than we did a century ago. There are fewer miners, factory workers or seamstresses than 50 years ago. Even jobs that are nominally the same have evolved with the advent of new technology as well as management and organisational innovation.

At the same time, the expected age of retirement continues to shift further into the future. Already, for our students their state pension age will be 68. Two competing proposals put to the government hinted at an increase to the age of 70. By the time they get there, it could be higher still.

Just to hedge that view, others see that the acceleration of technology might have the effect of liberating large amounts of leisure time instead. We can hope – but ought to remember that 50 years ago, that was the vision of where we would be today.

It is this combination of progress, economic change and a longer working life that make the assertion of a more varied career seem a realistic one. Even where individuals forge careers in one particular field, technological progress is likely to continue to drive the need to retrain and upskill even within that career. New medical techniques are introduced, accounting systems built, design materials and methods improve, construction techniques change.

Forty years of clocking in and off, completing similar tasks every day and then retiring at 60 seems a near impossibility for our students.

The implications

It has always been risky to teach specific skills for employment in the context of school. Skills like using a typewriter, filing systems, the Dewey system have all become redundant well within the careers of those who originally learnt them. That is why we have focused on the broad underpinning set of essential skills, rather than industry or role-specific skills. Teaching all students to use Twitter might be equally redundant by the time they are in the workforce.

That only makes this set of underpinning skills even more important – to provide the foundation for all of the specific skills and knowledge that an individual job might require. We need young people who can be creative and solve problems in different settings with different amounts of information available. We will still need individuals who can collaborate and lead – whether that leadership is formalised in a hierarchy or not. Indeed, they need leadership skills even more when that position is not formalised.

It has also increased the importance of transferability – we need students to be able to move their skill set between different roles. After all, many processes, policies and approaches are exclusive to a particular employer – but everything we learnt from exploring the gap in Chapters 1 and 2 suggests that they are broadly looking for a similar underlying set of skills as well as the specific knowledge or experience for that particular role.

Trend 4: Jobs focusing on intractable challenges

The final trend that we should expect is that more jobs will move away from the routine (as we've seen previously) and instead focus on some of the more intractable problems we face as humanity. As Sir Michael Barber argues, 'Unless scientific and technological innovation accelerates, unless it is well-directed to the most pressing problems, unless there is also innovation in these more subtle and subjective domains, the future looks very bleak indeed'[160].

Along with his co-authors of *Oceans of Innovation*, he explores some of the key challenges that face humanity over the next 50 years. Climate change and the sustainability of our oceans are one cause for concern. According to climate science, the world faces critical 'tipping points' – around levels of greenhouse gases, for example.

Another is the threat of conflicts, driven by contrasts in ideology, economic disparities or changing balances of power – particularly between the 'West' and the 'East' as China looks to surpass the USA in economic clout. Then there is the challenge of how to sustain an expanded global population from around 7 billion to 9 billion in the coming decades.

Other commonly cited challenges are around healthcare. This is partly reflecting the challenges of an ageing population and how to provide effective care at an increasing scale as the proportion of elderly in society grows. Then there is the challenge of how to ensure that health advances are realised when affordability trade-offs are needed.

There will continue to be challenges around economic development and how to share the proceeds of economic growth equitably. Tensions around gaps in income and wealth are likely to increase, particularly as the global population's expectations of the standard of living they should expect increases beyond the economy's capacity to deliver. This is a point particularly highlighted by Kim Yong, President of the World Bank – that increased understanding of wealth imbalances and differences in quality of life between the developing and the developed world will mean that those imbalances are likely to be challenged a lot more[161].

The implications

We saw the concerning prediction earlier from the Centre for Social and Economic Inclusion that there will not be enough low-skilled jobs to go around in 2022. Conversely, they predict that there will actually be a surplus in high-skilled jobs – with 15 million high-skilled jobs available and a shortage of 3 million workers to fill them[162]. Notably, this prediction was made before the 2016 EU referendum vote which could change the nature of this challenge.

If we want to make progress in this context then we will certainly need highly educated individuals. To solve these deeper problems will require 'standing on the shoulders of giants' to make sure we are constantly advancing and pushing ourselves forwards. But that body of knowledge will be insufficient without the ability to collaborate with peers across the world, to continually learn from others, to be creative or to wrestle with problems logically. The reality of this is already visible in predominantly Asian countries. These countries, like Singapore, China, Korea, Taiwan and Hong Kong lead the PISA tests of traditional knowledge. But they are all grappling with the problem of how to equip their children and young people with the skills to take leadership in the world.

In their review, Sir Michael Barber and colleagues concluded that what will really be needed to navigate the challenges of the 21st century is an expansion in what schools teach. Students need knowledge, and they need ethics. And they also need schools to teach 'the ability to communicate, work collaboratively in teams, stand up for a point of view, see another's point of view and make decisions'. Sounds familiar.

Summary

A decade ago, I started teaching my students essential skills in order to fill a fundamental gap in their readiness for life. But these skills will only become more important. None of us can look far into the future, but there are trends which point in a clear direction.

Evolution in the jobs market is a fact of life, but jobs are being automated at a pace. Inevitably, this will undermine low-paid jobs, as is already the trend. But those whose jobs are often about the retrieval and application of specialised knowledge are also at risk – whether lawyers, accountants or even medical professionals.

We are already seeing the changing nature of employment. The days of having an employer-for-life followed by a generous final pension are now vanishingly rare. What is even more remarkable is the speed with which stable employment of any type is being supplemented or even supplanted by the 'gig economy' where individuals are effectively self-employed and work in an *ad hoc* fashion.

These shifts are going to make it all the more important that individuals can learn and re-learn as their longer careers span periods of great change and discontinuity.

While this is happening, the 21st century is bringing a new series of challenges – from conflict, environmental and climate change risks, an ageing population and mounting frictions from economic inequality. These challenges will need all of our knowledge and skills to address, whilst also calling for divergent thinking, intuition and empathy.

We can't afford to wait, but nor do we have to. We can start today.

Conclusion

I have now been on this journey for a decade.

It started with that simple sense in my classroom that there was a missing piece – a dissonance between what was going on in my lessons and what my students really needed then and what would really make the difference for them in their lives ahead.

The initial scheme of work that I developed for my students was unsophisticated – but managed to harness a couple of elements that really worked. The students visited employers who generously opened their doors to us. Back in the classroom they started their own small businesses as a route to building the skills that I thought would help them learn better in class, and set them up for whatever was coming next.

One of the key insights was that building these skills would require partnership between what happened in the classroom and beyond it. Also, I learned quickly that I could not just hope for students to implicitly absorb skills as they worked in their teams. They would also need to be directly taught.

It was in breaking those skills down into teachable parts, rather than just thinking about activities, that another key insight became clear. Once those skills were really broken down it was evident that each element could be taught, practised and assimilated and that these skills were as teachable as anything else.

This became more than a personal voyage of discovery because I saw the impact on my students: that their attitude to one another changed and that they had the skills to learn better, to take more responsibility and to benefit from learning in different ways. When their results came back, over half had achieved a top grade in the subject. There hadn't been a trade-off between boosting their essential skills and their academic achievement.

Setting up Enabling Enterprise back in 2009 was just the next step. The team grew, and we knew what we wanted to do: to ensure that one day, all students build the essential skills, experiences of work, and aspirations to succeed.

I'm not a natural revolutionary but I could see the mission needed to be bold. I realised we could not continue in the same way that we have tended to in the past – building the skills through occasional trips to businesses, enterprise activities in school or perhaps an after-school club. Because once the scale of the gap for our students became clear, these approaches were shown inadequate to that challenge.

The eight essential skills can support learning and personal development in school, and then unlock employment, entrepreneurship or higher education beyond the school gates. They matter hugely today, and are only going to matter more in the future. With technological advances and longer career spans, we will all need to be more adaptable, able to solve problems in creative ways that machines cannot, able to work with others, communicate effectively and manage our own futures.

There is no good reason not to teach these skills. They are not innate, they are not built by osmosis, and they do not lie latent awaiting the right opportunity. They are basic skills.

Because of this combination of their importance and the characteristics they share with literacy and numeracy, we need to make the leap: to place essential skills alongside those key subjects.

This initially felt like too bold a leap in thinking. It certainly runs contrary to how the English school system has thought about those skills until now.

But really the clues were there all along – when Sir Mike Tomlinson reviewed 14-19 learning he highlighted personal learning and thinking skills as being key functional skills alongside literacy and numeracy. He just didn't make the leap on measurability that would have put them properly alongside. The current government, although using the language of character and highlighting a very wide range of traits, has similarly emphasised that these skills are important.

At the same time, in the world of employment, firms often use a very similar approach to our Skills Builder framework to define career progression. Indeed, parts of the system we use were informed by exactly that way of thinking. Nor does the model of how skills are built in increments seem particularly revolutionary to some of our teachers of 4- and 5-year-olds who explicitly focus on building social and emotional skills in a measurable way.

It is the combination of these insights that allows us to conceptualise essential skills in a completely different way – and place them properly at the heart of what happens in great schools.

The principles that were explored in the third part of the book are built from a combination of experience and grounded research. This was often an iterative process. Sometimes it started in the classroom – to overcome a particular barrier or do something better. Sometimes it was instigated by us, but often it came from our teachers. At other points we took research findings and used them to refine or fine-tune the design of our activities.

Those principles underpin how all of our programmes are designed – a process that resulted in the removal of a lot of courses and activities which had taken a lot of hard work to create but failed the test of being the most effective way of building essential skills.

Over the last three years, as we have delivered more than 200,000 student programmes using that methodology, the principles have withstood that test and that pressure. And that is part of the reason why I am writing this book now.

I am also writing this now because I am humbled by what our Enabling Enterprise teachers, schools and students have achieved in partnership with our employer partners. This has only been possible due to the dedication and hard work of the exceptional team I'm privileged to call colleagues. But we cannot achieve this mission alone.

I have seen that teachers and schools are key to building essential skills. So we need to do more to designate 'specialist teachers' with expertise in every school. And we also need to ensure that everyone in classrooms has a basic grounding in those skills and how to teach them – both through initial teacher training and on-going professional development opportunities.

We can really magnify our impact if we can continue to create and use a shared language – whether we are schools, external providers, employers or government. Everyone has to give up something to do that, but ultimately we all gain a great deal more.

Alongside those two elements, there are systemic things that can be done to ensure that building essential skills is really valued. I don't believe that means external assessment, but I see that recognition from Ofsted could be transformational.

Finally, we can multiply our impact if we do more to work with parents too – something that I feel keenly as a parent myself.

It doesn't matter whether you read this book out of casual interest, as a teacher, or because you already knew of our work. We all have something to contribute and a role to play – whether we are teachers, students, school leaders, parents, employers, school alumni, policy makers or system leaders. We have the opportunity to make a transformational change in how we educate our children and young people.

Ten years on, I often think back to my class of students who started this whole journey. Some of them I stay in touch with: some have used pure drive to make it through university or college and to complete a degree; some are now finding their footing with entry-level jobs in the workplace.

They work hard, but their grades and their opportunities now don't reflect their potential.

I wish I could go back ten years earlier still, before they were the teenagers in my classroom to when they were 5 or 6 years old. They were still forming their views of the world and how they fitted in, and there was still time to build their empathy and resilience. This was when they could still build the interpersonal skills to learn from one another, the tools to set themselves goals and the strategies to keep persisting through setbacks. I want them to have built the communication skills to express their ideas and the problem-solving skills to work through challenges. I want them to have loved learning and their precious time in school.

The jobs they are getting now aren't the jobs that they could have got. I see their wealthier peers elsewhere who left school having mastered the essential skills and for whom life is much easier: who enter the workplace with the skills that mark them out as 'one to watch' and to whom the opportunities and support flow – and who naturally become the ones who succeed most.

What I wish for all of my students is that we hadn't been so quick to assume their capacity without giving them the chance to build those essentials skills. I wish that we hadn't just substituted preparation for real life with a decent grade, a handful of employability activities and hope in their character strengths.

Alongside their numeracy and literacy, we should have given them all those fundamental skills to really thrive.

Because we can.

Thanks and acknowledgements

While this book takes my voice, Enabling Enterprise has been a collaboration from almost immediately after its genesis in my classroom. In trying to craft a simple narrative the disappointing side-effect is that the huge efforts that have taken us so far are little acknowledged. It is impossible to do justice to the sheer number of people whose efforts have supported what's been achieved.

The Enabling Enterprise team has grown quickly over the years, but I have been humbled by the calibre of those who have joined us – individuals who have looked beyond our meagre offices and benefits package to see the potential of what we can achieve together. The successes that Enabling Enterprise has enjoyed are through the efforts of that team. The ideas in this book have been built through research, practice and debate among us – tested and tried over time as our thinking has evolved together.

I would particularly like to acknowledge a few colleagues who have been instrumental to the success of Enabling Enterprise over a number of years: Alice Faulkner, Simon Hill, Mike Zatyka, Maryam Ben Rabha, Chris Cuckson, Alison Gale, Alanna Hume, Sarah Ritchie, Alastair Phipps, Stephane Auberval, Samantha George, Chantelle Scott and Claire Bayley. More recent additions to the team have also made a big contribution quickly: Robert Craig, Kathryn Dann, Evelyn Haywood, Anna Garratt, Rachel Mowle, Tom Varley, James Prideaux, Louise Brannan, Amy Paull, Richard Hart and Billy Pretsell. This book has particularly drawn on some of the research and work of Alice Faulkner, Alison Gale, Sarah Milburn, Jenny Groot, Alanna Hume and Samantha George.

Our mission has brought together hundreds of schools and employers in all parts of the country – and that of course means thousands of teachers and tens of thousands of volunteers from those employers. It is these individuals who have reached so many students. My thanks go to all of them for making the programmes work on the ground.

This book quotes from just a handful of those schools directly, but I'd like to acknowledge how freely and generously many schools – and the teachers, teaching assistants, support staff and school leaders that make them up – have contributed over the years, not just to this book but to our other research, case studies and learning along the way. They've spoken at our events, welcomed me and the team into their schools and, most importantly, committed to building the essential skills of all their students.

On the employer side, it is heartening to see how many organisations and individuals have opened their doors to our students. I will remember forever the first time we took 7- and 8-year-olds into a leading law firm, and how the senior partner knelt on the floor to talk to them. Many employers have supported our work financially, or through *pro bono* support along with other Foundations.

Beyond schools and employers, the team and I have benefited hugely from the generosity of many other individuals who have shared their time, insights and experience. This has included taking part in occasional roundtables on challenging topics, or having a useful chat over a coffee. I'd particularly like to acknowledge the non-executive directors and advisors of Enabling Enterprise who, over the last eight years, have challenged, supported and championed us along the way: Cynthia Shanmugalingam, Jack Graham, Tom McErlain, Charlotte Ravenscroft, Lucy Heintz, Richard Mallinson and Honor Wilson-Fletcher.

I'm grateful to many people for finding the time in their busy schedules to sit down with me to contribute their thoughts and reflections to this book and our wider work: Dame Julia Cleverdon, Brett Wigdortz, Lucy Ashman, Gary Durbin, Claudia Harris, Paul Drechsler, Sally Lamb, Alison Helm, Vinisha Kurup, John Potter, David Weston, Matthew Hood, Chloe Holmes, Olly Offord, Sophie Gavalda and Tanya Watson. As this book has been a reflection of eight years of such conversations, I cannot come even close to acknowledging the dozens of individuals who have helped to influence what we do. I appreciate each of them.

Finally, I would like to add a couple of very personal thanks. To my parents, my three brothers, and wider family for their unstinting encouragement and support. To my son Joshua who wants to be a 'teacher of enterprise skills' like his dad. And to my wife Charlotte who originally helped set up Enabling Enterprise. We worked together to establish it over the first year and she has been living its highs and lows with me ever since. Thank you.

Appendix:
The Skills Builder Framework

The Skills Builder framework is made available with the permission of Enabling Enterprise. It continues to evolve and the latest version can be found at www. skillsbuilder.org. *This is just the headline outcomes that we seek for each skill - for much more detail in how each step is taught please see the website.* It covers:

- Listening
- Presenting
- Problem-Solving
- Creativity
- Teamwork
- Leadership
- Aiming High
- Staying Positive

Listening

This skill focuses on the students' ability to listen and understand information.

Initially, it is about the students being able to hear and recall simple instructions. They also develop the ability to record key pieces of information. As they get more skilled, the focus turns to being able to analyse the speaker in greater depth. This includes understanding the use of tone, bias, themes and implications.

Ultimately, by the time they leave school students should be able to listen, capture key information and also to evaluate the speaker and their goals.

Target for:	Student Descriptor	Teacher Explanation
Pre-Year 1	I can listen to others for a short time.	Students listen with enjoyment and respond appropriately to stories.
Year 1	I can listen to adults, follow instructions and tell you what I heard.	Students can listen to an adult, such as a teacher or teaching assistant, and recall and follow simple instructions.
Year 2	I can listen to other students and ask questions about what I heard.	Students are able to listen to peers and ask relevant questions based on what they heard.
Year 3	I can follow a conversation and tell somebody else what it was about.	Students are able to listen to multiple speakers, retain the information and give a basic account of what they heard.
Year 4	I can explain that there are different purposes to speech and how to identify them.	Students are aware that there are different reasons why people communicate (*eg:* to ask a question, give instructions, provide information, or persuade) and identify some simple language features of each one.
Year 5	I can listen to a talk and identify the key information I need	Students can listen to and respond to a talk, identifying the key information they need and retaining it.
Year 6	I can take part and respond in a class discussion	Students are able to follow and participate in a class discussion and express opinions when called upon which show they have been following that discussion.
Year 7	I can analyse how a speaker uses language and gesture to engage the audience	Students can analyse how a speaker engages an audience through language and gesture.
Year 8	I can use strategies to listen for a specific purpose.	Students begin to recognise their own skills and strategies to listen. Students can listen for a specific purpose and consider the effect of the language on that purpose.
Year 9	I can analyse the tone, emphasis and status of the speaker and their effect.	Students can recognise the tone, emphasis and status of speaker and consider their effect.
Year 10	I can ask probing and relevant questions to check and build my understanding.	Students are able to follow a speaker and to create their own meaningful, probing questions to check and deepen their own understanding.
Year 11	I can listen to different points of view and evaluate them.	Students can make comparisons between different points of view, potentially from different speakers, and evaluate them.
Year 12	I can identify underlying themes, implications and issues when listening.	Students can identify themes, implications and issues in what is being said.
Year 13	I can analyse bias when listening through a speaker's language, omissions or ambiguity.	Students can analyse bias through language, omission and ambiguity.
Year 13 *Better*	I can explain a speaker's techniques and approaches in different contexts.	Students understand a speaker's intentions and techniques and how they use a range of different approaches in different contexts.
Year 13 *Best*	I can evaluate how a speaker can become an outstanding speaker.	Students can evaluate a speaker's use of language, gesture, tone, emphasis, bias and the plausibility and validity of their point of view to make suggestions for improvement.

Presenting

This skill focuses on students' ability to communicate their ideas to others.

Initially, this is about being able to articulate themselves in small group situations, and then being able to order their points logically to convey meaning. Over time, the focus is increasingly on being able to deliver interesting and engaging presentations through thoughtful use of tone, detail and language. Strong presenters will be able to adapt their presentations to the audience's reaction.

Ultimately, by the time they leave school students should be confident presenters, able to adapt their approach to a range of contexts and audience reactions.

Target for:	Student Descriptor	Teacher Explanation
Pre-Year 1	I can speak clearly to someone I know.	Students can convey simple ideas of immediate interest to one other person.
Year 1	I can speak clearly to a small group of people I know.	Students can convey simple answers or thoughts to a wider group, for example in class.
Year 2	I can speak clearly and add detail to a group of people.	Students can share a narrative or extended answer while speaking to a group.
Year 3	I make points in an order that makes sense when I am speaking.	Students can explain ideas in a clear order with relevant detail, using conjunctions to structure their speech.
Year 4	I choose an order for my points so that the audience can best understand me.	Students are able to logically order information in a way that can be understood by an audience. Students begin to engage the audience with some presentational techniques.
Year 5	I can use formal language, tone and expression when I am presenting.	Students are able to use standard English when presenting to a group, avoiding inappropriate language or slang.
Year 6	I can change my language depending on the purpose and audience.	Students use appropriate language based on their understanding of the presentation's purpose and audience.
Year 7	I can structure my language in a way that makes my communication clear and engaging, and use examples for my points.	Students use appropriate structure and vocabulary, and also bring in examples to illustrate their key points.
Year 8	I can vary the level of detail and language to make my presentation interesting, according to the context.	Students can vary the level of detail and the language they use when presenting to make it appropriate to the audience and their brief.
Year 9	I can adapt my language, structure and gesture to engage my audience.	Students can use appropriate language, tone and expression for the context they are presenting in.
Year 10	I am able to modify my language, tone and expression according to the listeners' reaction and response.	Students are able to modify language, tone and expression according to the listeners' reaction and response to increase the audience's engagement.

Year 11	I can anticipate different responses from the audience and plan for them.	Students are also able to anticipate different responses from the audience and are able to plan accordingly. For example, by varying the mood to elicit different emotional responses.
Year 12	I can be flexible in my style during the presentation to better engage the audience. This might include changes to content and style of delivery.	Students can adapt their presentation during its delivery to better engage the audience.
Year 13	I explore different styles of presenting and consider their effectiveness.	Students begin to develop a personal presenting style, adapting the content, structure, language and non-verbal features to the audience and purpose of the talk.
Year 13 *Better*	I reflect on the effectiveness of different styles of presenting and choose the best style for me.	Students can reflect and develop their personal presenting style and evaluate the effectiveness of their approach.
Year 13 *Best*	I can deliver effective presentations in a personal style, adapted to the situation.	Students are able to creatively adapt the content, structure and style of presentation to the purpose, audience and tone of the talk with distinct personal style and flair.

Problem-Solving

This skill focuses on how students approach challenges and situations where the answer is not immediately clear.

Initially, we focus on simple, routine problems with one clear answer and this problem-solving is supported and structured by an adult. Over time, the students should be able to solve routine problems by themselves, including seeking out additional information.

They are then introduced to complex, non-routine problems. They build up to being able to identify different potential solutions and being able to evaluate the different options to reach the optimal solution.

Ultimately, by the time they leave school students should be able to approach complex problems with deeper causes and effects.

Target for:	Student Descriptor	Teacher Explanation
Pre-Year 1	I ask an adult to solve problems for me.	Students struggle to solve own problems, or need a high level of adult structuring and support.
Year 1	I know who I can ask when I need help.	Students can identify when they require adult support in overcoming difficulties and will seek a suitable adult for help with this.
Year 2	I can explain an everyday problem that I might have and get someone to help me with it.	Students can identify routine ('everyday') problems (e.g. I've lost my pencil) and ask for adult support to scaffold possible solutions.

218

Year 3	I can find extra information with help from others to help me solve an everyday problem.	Students can identify where they need extra information to solve a routine ('everyday') problem and can find that information with help from an adult or peers.
Year 4	I can come up with different ways to solve an everyday problem.	Students appreciate that there are frequently different ways to solve a problem and can explain different options in a given situation.
Year 5	I can use pros and cons to pick the best way of solving an everyday problem.	Students can articulate a problem to evaluate different potential solutions with adult support and choose the option they think will be most effective.
Year 6	I can explain the difference between everyday problems and complicated problems	Students can identify non-routine ('complicated') problems (e.g. I can't decide on a secondary school) and explain how these differ from routine ('everyday') problems (e.g. what I need to pack for holiday). They can explain why different approaches might be needed.
Year 7	I can carry out research to better understand complicated problems.	Students can seek additional information to build their understanding of a non-routine problem.
Year 8	I can look at the causes and effects of complicated problems, including carrying out research.	Students can identify extra information they need in order to consider the causes and effects of a problem and seek out that information independently.
Year 9	I can create a range of possible solutions for complicated problems and pros and cons of each.	Students can create a range of possible solutions, identifying the pros and cons of each approach.
Year 10	I can evaluate different solutions for a complex problem to pick the best one.	Students can choose between the options that they've created and use some justifiable method to do so – such as scoring and weighting outcomes.
Year 11	I can use decision trees to help solve complex problems with differing probabilities.	Students can apply probabilities of success models to appropriate problems where there are multiple interdependencies in a problem and use probabilities and outcome measures effectively.
Year 12	I can create hypotheses and test these as possible solutions to complex problems.	Students are able to generate hypotheses in answer to complex problems, and devise appropriate tests of these hypotheses to prove or disprove them.
Year 13	I can use deductive and inductive logic to explore implications of solutions I create to complex problems	Students have a solid understanding of deductive and inductive logic and understand how these can be applied effectively to problems.
Year 13 Better	I can explore combinations of inputs, outputs and outcomes (Theory of Change) to create solutions to complex problems I have analysed.	Students can tackle complex problems, such as societal ones, and devise Theory of Change combinations of inputs, output and outcomes that might provide solutions.
Year 13 Best	I can track the impact of a proposed solution to a complex problem and devise alternative routes of action as required.	Students can effectively evaluate and adapt to different results from their attempted solutions to complex problems and change tack appropriately.

Creativity

This skill is about the students' capacity to develop new ideas.

While there is some overlap with problem-solving, creative thinking does not presume a pre-defined problem. Initially, it is about the students being confident in using their imaginations to create new ideas. Over time, the focus is on the students building a range of strategies that can support their creative thinking.

Ultimately, by the time they leave school students should be confident when presented with the need to create new ideas or innovations, knowing a range of strategies and tools they can use to develop their ideas.

Target for:	Student Descriptor	Teacher Explanation
Pre-Year 1	I like to use my imagination.	Students feel comfortable with the idea of using their imagination. They might do this in the context of their own world.
Year 1	I can talk about when I use my imagination.	Students can talk about using imagination and when they use their imagination.
Year 2	I can share what I imagine through writing, drawing or acting it out.	Students can express and share what they are imagining through writing, drawing or other media.
Year 3	I can use my imagination to come up with ideas when I've been given success criteria to help me.	Students can produce ideas when they are given a simple brief, some success criteria or broad guidelines as support.
Year 4	I can use my imagination to come up ideas linked to a starting point.	Students can generate multiple ideas when they are given a stimulus or initial idea as a starting point.
Year 5	I can combine ideas or concepts to create new ones.	Students can merge simple ideas to create new ones and can identify that ideas have different components.
Year 6	I can explain what creativity is and how it is used in different settings.	Students can explain what creativity is, how it might be seen in different settings (the arts, design or day-to-day situations) and how it is used by different groups of people.
Year 7	I can explain how I use creativity in different areas of my life.	Students can reflect on the role creativity plays in different aspects of their life: in different lessons, during extra-curricular activities and at home.
Year 8	I can use mind mapping as a creative tool to help me generate ideas.	Students can use mind mapping as a creative tool to support how they generate, develop and link ideas.
Year 9	I can outline how introducing something seemingly random can support creativity.	Students can describe how a random stimulus (e.g. word, image or even sound) can spark creativity and support how they generate ideas.
Year 10	I can explain how considering different perspectives can support creativity.	Students can explain ways to take alternative perspectives into account and how this impacts creativity.

Year 11	I can explain how to maximise creativity when working collaboratively.	Students can explain how to overcome 'groupthink', which is the drive for consensus in groups leading to lack of diversity in ideas.
Year 12	I can reflect on how I have used creative tools.	Students can reflect on how different creative tools work and the different contexts in which they have used creative tools.
Year 13	I know the most effective creative tool for my way of working.	Students can reflect on how they approach creative tasks and evaluate the effectiveness of creative tool for themselves.
Year 13 *Better*	I can suggest multiple creative tools that would be appropriate for a given situation.	Students can identify the requirements of a given situation and justify more than one creative tool that would be suitable.
Year 13 *Best*	I can select the most effective creative tool for a given situation.	Students can evaluate the effectiveness of creative tools with respect to the requirements of the situation and choose the most effective one.

Teamwork

This skill focuses on the students' confidence and effectiveness in working as part of a team.

Initially, it is about the students being able to work with others in a constructive manner. As they progress, the focus is not just making their own contribution but encouraging and supporting others to make their fullest contribution too.

The highest-performing team members will understand their colleagues' strengths and weaknesses and support the team to divide roles accordingly. They should also be adept at avoiding and managing conflict.

Ultimately, by the time they leave school students should be able to work effectively in a team and evaluate the team's performance to drive future improvements.

Target for:	Student Descriptor	Teacher Explanation
Pre-Year 1	I can take turns with other children.	Students are able and willing to take turns on an activity with their peers.
Year 1	I can work with other children to do something together.	Students are able to make a contribution towards a bigger task as part of a group.
Year 2	I know why teams are sometimes better than working by myself.	Students are able to articulate why teamwork can be more effective than individual work in some situations.
Year 3	I am happy to help with different jobs in my team and take responsibility for finishing my job.	Students can take on different jobs in their team to complete the team task.

Year 4	I know how to get on well with my team and know some ways to resolve a disagreement.	Students are able to address disagreements and disputes in an effective way, and generally work well with others.
Year 5	When I finish my task, I help others complete their tasks on time too.	Students can think beyond their own part of a task and actively try to support other team members to complete their jobs.
Year 6	I help my team make decisions and I am happy to make my own suggestions.	Students can contribute to the decision-making process and are willing to put forward their own ideas.
Year 7	I recognise the value of others' ideas and make useful contributions myself.	Students can see that their peers will also contribute valuable ideas, and will be willing to compromise to reach a joint decision.
Year 8	I include all team mates in group discussions and encourage them to contribute.	Students can see the importance of including all team members in discussions and actively encourage contributions from their peers in their team.
Year 9	I can spot when I might be getting into an argument and take steps to avoid it.	Students are able to perceive when conflict with their peers might be developing into an argument and take steps to avoid it.
Year 10	I can spot when others might be getting into an argument and make suggestions to avoid it.	Students demonstrate an awareness of the wider team dynamics and work to avoid arguments in the team.
Year 11	I contribute to team meetings in a measured, valuable and concise way.	Students can make a valuable contribution to team discussions which builds on previous conversations and addresses the particular challenge the team faces.
Year 12	I can reflect on the team's progress and make suggestions for improvements.	Students can accurately analyse the performance of the team and suggest improvements.
Year 13	I can reflect and evaluate on the team's approaches to tasks and carefully influence to get better results.	Students can evaluate a team's approach, and use their influence to improve a team's performance and the outcomes of a task.
Year 13 *Better*	I'm aware of the team leader's strengths and weaknesses and actively support them when they need me.	Students can evaluate the performance of a team leader, and actively engage to support the performance of the leader, improving the outcomes for the team.
Year 13 *Best*	I understand the skills of other team members and adapt my approach to them	Students can identify the skills of other members of their team and can support other team members in areas they find difficult or challenging.

Leadership

This skill focuses particularly on the students' ability to lead others.

The underlying foundation of effective leadership understanding others, which is why the initial levels focus on the students' ability to articulate their own emotions and identify those of others.

As they develop as leaders, they need to better understand the strengths and weaknesses of themselves and those they are leading. Higher level leadership will also mean a self-awareness of their own leadership approach and how they can effectively motivate their team.

Ultimately, by the time they leave school students should be confident in taking the lead on a team task, understanding others and being able to motivate them to complete the task or project successfully.

Target for:	Student Descriptor	Teacher Explanation
Pre-Year 1	I can sometimes describe how I feel.	Students can sometimes articulate their feelings, in simple terms to a trusted adult.
Year 1	I can describe how I am feeling to my team.	Students are able to articulate and explain their feelings in a group situation, working with others.
Year 2	I can describe how my team mates are feeling.	Students can articulate how other members of their team are feeling, demonstrating a basic level of empathy and perception of others.
Year 3	I can make sure that everyone has a job and can help team mates when they need me.	Students can allocate tasks between different team members and are able to identify when their peers might need support or assistance.
Year 4	I take responsibility for my team mates completing their jobs on time.	Students can take a leadership role that requires them to divide roles between their peers, and encourage them to complete the tasks effectively.
Year 5	I can help my team come to a decision that most people are happy with and finish the task.	Students can contribute to team discussion to reach a consensus on what actions should be undertaken. Students are able to then see a simple task through to completion.
Year 6	I can make decisions to resolve disagreements between team mates.	Students can resolve disagreements between their peers when they are in a leadership position – EG: by voting.
Year 7	I know my own strengths and weaknesses and how to make my best contribution.	Students have developed the self-awareness to identify their own strengths and weaknesses, and how they can make their best contribution to the group.
Year 8	I understand my team mates' strengths and interests.	Students are able to identify and articulate the strengths and interests of others in their teams.
Year 9	I make the most of my team mates' strengths to help achieve team goals.	Students are able to apply, in a basic way, their understanding of peers' strengths and interests to allocate tasks in a justifiable way between them.
Year 10	I can see when conflict is developing, and have some ways of resolving these.	Students can perceive when disagreements might be developing and can use some basic approaches to resolve these through structured discussion.
Year 11	I understand some different ways to motivate my team.	Students understand the role of motivation in leadership and can apply some basic approaches to motivating their teams.
Year 12	I am effective in motivating my team.	Students are able to judge the appropriate approach to motivating their teams in different situations.

Year 13	I can describe different leadership styles and share which style I think I use and why	Students understand that there are different styles of leadership and are able to judge what type of leadership they tend towards. (E.g. autocratic; democratic etc.)
Year 13 Better	I know that there are positive and negative aspects of different leadership styles and am aware of the limitations of the leadership style I tend towards.	Students understand that leadership styles have positive and negative aspects to them and can outline the negative aspects of their leadership style.
Year 13 Best	I can adapt my leadership style depending on the situation I am in and who I am working with.	Students can assess a situation, identify which leadership style is most appropriate and adopt that style.

Aiming High

This skill focuses on the students having high aspirations for themselves and being able to turn these into realistic plans.

Initially, the students should be developing an understanding of the importance of trying their best and taking satisfaction in their achievements. This then underpins a growing ability to set their own goals and create steps to achieve their targets.

Students should also be building the ability to self-reflect accurately, and be able to draw out their strengths and areas for development – and to seek out opportunities for their own development.

Ultimately, by the time they leave school students should have goals for themselves, and the ability to work consistently towards achieving them.

Target for:	Student Descriptor	Teacher Explanation
Pre-Year 1	I'm learning what 'trying my best' means.	Students have started to understand what 'trying my best' looks and feels like.
Year 1	I know what 'trying my best' means.	Students can explain what 'trying my best' looks like in the context of their school and class work.
Year 2	I know it's important to try my best if I'm going to get better.	Students respond to encouragement and show pride in higher achievement
Year 3	I know how to try my best and I feel proud when I do.	Students are aware of when they are working at their best, and find this a rewarding experience that they can take pride in.
Year 4	I look for chances to something that I might find difficult and ask an adult to set me extra challenges.	Students can seek out opportunities to give themselves extra challenge to increase their achievements. Teachers will provide students with an achievable challenge.

Year 5	I can choose goals with some help from my teacher or another adult.	Students can set a simple goal that is appropriate and achievable, with the support of a teacher or another adult.
Year 6	I can set my own goal that gives me a chance to try something I might find difficult.	Students are able to approximately gauge what a stretching goal looks like and define that for themselves.
Year 7	I can order and prioritise different tasks to help me achieve my goal.	Students can break down simple goals into steps and prioritise those steps to achieve the goal.
Year 8	I can identify and ensure access to the resources to achieve my goals.	Students understand that they might need other resources (people, funds, tools) to achieve their goals and can identify those needed to achieve a simple goal.
Year 9	I can create a plan to achieve a simple goal, breaking down tasks and securing resources, independently.	Students can create a simple plan by setting a goal, prioritising tasks and securing resources.
Year 10	I can reflect on my skill set with accuracy and identify opportunities to improve further.	Students can analyse and justify their own strengths and weaknesses, and come up with sensible ways of developing themselves further.
Year 11	I can motivate myself to work autonomously to fulfil my plans and to achieve SMART targets to reach my goal.	Students are able to apply themselves to seeing through their plans over a period of time.
Year 12	I seek out feedback, including constructive criticism, to support me in achieving my goals.	Students seek wider input to achieve their goals and to chart their own progress against their plans, including both compliments and constructive criticism.
Year 13	I can create long term goals, based on my own strengths and weaknesses.	Students can evaluate their longer term plans in terms of their own strengths, weaknesses and ambitions.
Year 13 *Better*	I can set regular milestones to help me reach my long term goals and keep me on track.	Students can break down their longer-term plans into steps with milestones that keep them on track to achieve their goals.
Year 13 *Best*	I am able to modify my milestones and actions to respond to changes.	Students are able to incorporate setbacks or changing circumstances into forward planning and make appropriate adaptations to keep them on track for success.

Staying Positive

This skill focuses on the students' ability to overcome setbacks and manage risk.

Initially, the students need to build their own emotional awareness and empathy. In time, students can acknowledge setbacks and challenges but evaluate them effectively and keep progressing.

Over time, this should build into a willingness to take calculated risks and ability to overcome setbacks. Those who perform most highly in this skill area will be able to encourage this positivity in others as well as themselves.

Ultimately, by the time they leave school students should be able to face and overcome challenges positively, whilst learning from setbacks.

Target for:	Student Descriptor	Teacher Explanation
Pre-Year 1	I know that people can be happy or sad.	Students can articulate basic emotions and understand that other people will have changing emotions too.
Year 1	I know when things go wrong, people can get angry or upset.	Students can see that people might get angry or upset when things go wrong and see how this links to their own experiences.
Year 2	I know that getting angry or upset and giving up when something goes wrong does not help.	Students can articulate why it is important to manage negative emotions when they face setbacks. They might not always be able to put this into practice.
Year 3	I try to stay calm when something goes wrong.	Students can respond to setbacks calmly.
Year 4	I keep trying when something goes wrong, and think about what happened.	Students can be seen to respond positively to setbacks but also try to understand why the problem occurred and overcome that.
Year 5	I keep trying when something goes wrong and help cheer other people up.	Students continue to make an effort, even when they face setbacks, and can also cheer up their peers.
Year 6	I keep trying and encourage others to keep trying, even when thing are difficult.	Students keep trying and are effective in encouraging others to maintain their level of effort in the face of setbacks.
Year 7	I can look on the bright side in difficult situations and focus on that.	Students can evaluate a situation to identify positive outcomes and focus on those rather than the negative side of a situation.
Year 8	I can explain the positive side of a difficult situation to others.	Students can articulate a positive perspective to their peers and, while acknowledging challenges, explore them in a positive way.
Year 9	I can come up with ideas for changing difficult situations into positive opportunities.	Students can actively seek ways to turn challenging or difficult situations into more positive ones.
Year 10	In difficult situations, I choose the best way to move forward instead of giving up.	Students can evaluate the challenges in a situation and then continue to make progress in their tasks rather than giving up.
Year 11	I'm not afraid to take risks where I might make mistakes as I know I will learn from them.	Students can confidently approach risks where they might make mistakes because they know they will learn from them.
Year 12	I can assess and manage risks appropriately.	Students can approach situations that involve risks, and assess and manage those risks appropriately.
Year 13	I can effectively recognise and assess my own negative emotions and take positive actions.	Students can recognise and assess their emotions and choose an appropriate positive course of action.
Year 13 *Better*	I can choose appropriate positive actions based on the context and impact they will have on others, when I am feeling negative emotions.	Students demonstrate awareness of how their emotions and actions impact on others, and choose the best response for different contexts.
Year 13 *Best*	I can choose appropriate positive actions when I am feeling negative emotions, in unfamiliar contexts.	Students can choose appropriate positive actions for an unfamiliar context, while acknowledging that they are feeling negative emotions.

Endnotes

1.   CBI (2008), 'Education and Skills Survey', CBI

2.   UKCES (2009) *The Employability Challenge: Full Report'*, UKCES

3.   Department for Education (2012) 'How GCSE results compare, county by county', *The Guardian* [Accessed in June 2017 at www.theguardian.com/news/datablog/2012/oct/18/gcse-english-rates-local-authority]

4.   Department for Education (2017) *Revised GCSE and equivalent results in England, 2015 to 2016 -SFR03/2017* [Accessed in June 2017 at www.gov.uk/government/uploads/system/uploads/attachment_data/file/584473/SFR03_2017.pdf]

5.   The IDACI is the 'Income Deprivation Affecting Children Index'. It is provided by the Department for Communities and Local Government and measures the proportion of children under the age of 16 in an area living in low income households.

6.   Enabling Enterprise data from Autumn 2016, collected by teachers through SkillsBuilder. org accessed February 2017

7.   CBI (2008) 'Education and Skills Survey', CBI

8.   UKCES (2009) The Employability Challenge: Full Report, UKCES

9.   Lanning, J. Martin, R. and Villeneuve-Smith, F. (2008) Employability skills examined: Ten Key Messages from LSN's Quest to Understand Employability Skills, Learning and Skills Network.

10.   CBI (2016) 'Education and Skills Survey', CBI

11.   Nicholson, B. (1989) Towards a Skills Revolution: Report of the CBI Vocational Education and Training Task Force, CBI

12.   Mourshed, M., Patel, J. and Suder, K. (2014) *Education to Employment: Getting Europe's Youth into Work*, Washington DC: McKinsey Center for Government

13.   McGuinness, F. (2017) Youth Unemployment Statistics – Briefing Paper Number 5871, London: House of Commons Library

14.   Ofsted (2016) *'Getting Ready for Work: How secondary schools prepare young people for work'*, Ofsted

15.   All-Party Parliamentary Group (APPG) for Education (2017a) 'How well do schools prepare children for their future?', All-Party Parliamentary Group (APPG) for Education [Accessed on June 2017 www.educationappg.org.uk/wp-content/uploads/2017/04/Preparing-for-the-future-inquiry-report.pdf]

16.   King Solomon Academy, *Welcome | King Solomon Academy*, King Solomon Academy [Accessed April 2017 kingsolomonacademy.org/secondary/welcome]

17.   Paton, G. (2012) "Spoon-fed' students given tuition in basic skills at university', [Accessed February 2017 at www.telegraph.co.uk/education/educationnews/9180982/Spoon-fed-students-given-tuition-in-basic-skills-at-university.html]

18. Gadsby B, (2017) 'Challenge the Impossible', Teach First

19. University of Cambridge (2017) Key skills for undergraduates, University of Cambridge [Accessed February 2017 at www.transkills.admin.cam.ac.uk/skills-portal/key-skills-undergraduates]

20. University of Birmingham (2017) Undergraduate Law programmes, University of Birmingham [Accessed February 2017 at www.birmingham.ac.uk/schools/law/courses/llb/skills.aspx]

21. Careers and Employability Division (2017) Essential Skills and qualities of a successful academic, The University of Manchester [Accessed February 2017 at www.academiccareer.manchester.ac.uk/about/do/skills/]

22. Populus (2013) RBS Enterprise Tracker in association with UnLtd, RBS

23. Enterprise Nation (2014) '70% increase in number of company founders aged under 35', Enterprise Nation [Accessed February 2017 at www.telegraph.co.uk/finance/yourbusiness/11133048/More-young-entrepreneurs-launch-start-ups-in-wake-of-recession.html]

24. BIS (2015) 'Entrepreneurship Skills Literature and Policy Review', Department for Business Innovation & Skills

25. Chell, E. (2015) 'Review of skill and the Entrepreneurial Process', *International Journal of Entrepreneurial Behaviour & Research*

26. Whitty, G., Power, S. and Sims, S. (2013, 'Lasting Benefits: The long-term legacy of the Assisted Places Scheme for Assisted Place Holders', Sutton Trust

27. Social Mobility and Child Poverty Commission (2015) 'Downward Mobility, Opportunity Hoarding and the Glass Floor', Social Mobility and Child Poverty Commission

28. Speech: James Callaghan, 18 October 1976, Ruskin College, Oxford [Accessed June 2017 at www.educationengland.org.uk/documents/speeches1976ruskin.html]

29. Davies, H. (2002) 'A Review of Enterprise and the Economy in Education', Norwich: Her Majesty's Stationery Office.

30. Ofsted (2005) 'Developing Enterprising Young People: Features of the successful implementation of enterprise education at Key Stage 4', Ofsted

31. McLarty, L. Highley, H. and Alderson, S. (2010) 'Evaluation of Enterprise Education in England', London: Department for Education

32. Young, D. (2014) 'Enterprise for All: The Relevance of Enterprise in Education', London: Department for Business, Innovation and Skills (BIS)

33. Tomlinson, M. (2004) '14-19 Qualifications and Curriculum Reform: Final Report of the Working Group on 14-19 Reform', Department for Education and Skills

34. Seal Community, 'About SEAL', Seal Community Website [Accessed February 2017 at www.sealcommunity.org/node/356]

35. Humphrey, N., Lendrum, A. and Wigelsworth, M. (2010) 'Social and emotional aspects of learning (SEAL) programme in secondary schools: National evaluation', Department for Education

36. Morgan, N. (2015) 'Winners of the Character Awards announced', Department for Education [Accessed March 2017 at www.gov.uk/government/news/winners-of-the-character-awards-announced]

37. Espinoza, J. (2016) 'UK may lose out to Asian countries in developing 'soft skills' for life in new rankings', *The Telegraph* [Accessed in March 2017 at www.telegraph.co.uk/education/ educationnews/12190783/UK-may-lose-out-to-Asian-countries-in-developing-soft-skills-for-life-in-new-rankings.html]

38. NCS (2017) 'What is NCS?' NCS [Accessed in March 2017 at www.ncsyes.co.uk/what-is-ncs]

39. Whitty, G. Power, S. and Sims, S. (2013) 'Lasting Benefits: The long-term legacy of the Assisted Places Scheme for Assisted Place Holders', Sutton Trust

40. Millard, W., Menzies, L. and Baar, S. (2017) 'Enterprise Skills: Teachability, Measurability and Next Steps', LKMco

41. Social Mobility and Child Poverty Commission (2015) 'Downward Mobility, Opportunity Hoarding, and the Glass Floor', Social Mobility and Child Poverty Commission

42. UKCES (2009) 'The Employability Challenge: Full Report', UKCES

43. The Jubilee Centre for Character & Virtues (2013) 'A Framework for Character Education in Schools', The Jubilee Centre for Character & Virtue

44. Jubilee Centre (2013) 'Framework for Character Education', Birmingham: University of Birmingham.

45. Lucas, B. and Hanson, J. (2016) 'Learning to be Employable: Practical lessons from research into developing character', Centre for Real-World Learning

46. Whitehurst, G. J. (2016) 'Hard thinking on soft skills', The Brookings Institute

47. Goby, V. P. and Lewis, J. H. (2000) 'The key role of listening in business: A study of the Singapore insurance industry', *Business Communication Quarterly*, 63(2), 41-51

48. Owen, J. (2010) *How to Sell,* Pearson Educational

49. Deakin Crick, R., Coates, M., Taylor, M. and Ritchie, S. (2004) 'A Systematic Review of the Impact of Citizenship Education on the Provision of Schooling', Research Evidence in Education Library, London: EPPI-Centre, Social Science Research Unit, Institute of Education

50. Millard, W. and Menzies, L. (2016) 'The State of Speaking in Our Schools', Voice 21 and LKMco

51. CBI (2016) 'Education and Skills Survey', Pearson

52. Ashley, A., Duberley, J., Sommerlad, H. and Scholarios, D. (2015) 'A qualitative evaluation of non-educational barriers to the elite professions', Social Mobility & Child Poverty Commission

53. I CAN (2008) 'Speech, Language and Communication Needs and Primary School-aged Children' (I CAN Talk Series – Issue 6)

54. Millard, W. and Menzies, L. (2016) 'The State of Speaking in Our Schools', Voice 21 and LKMco

55. Robinson, M. (2013) *Trivium 21c: Preparing young people for the future with lessons from the past,* Independent Thinking Press, an imprint of Crown House Publishing

56. Millard, W. and Menzies, L. (2016) 'The State of Speaking in Our Schools', Voice 21 and LKMco

57. Millard, W. and Menzies, L. (2016) 'The State of Speaking in Our Schools', Voice 21 and LKMco

58. Education Endowment Foundation (2017) 'Teaching and Learning Toolkit: Oral language interventions', Education Endowment Foundation [Accessed June 2017 at educationendowmentfoundation.org.uk/resources/teaching-learning-toolkit/oral-language-interventions/]

59. CBI (2016) 'Education and Skills Survey', CBI

60. Detter-Schmelz, D. R., Kennedy, K. N., and Ramsey, R. P. (2002) 'Enriching our understanding of student team effectiveness', *Journal of Marketing Education,* 24 (2), 114-124

61. Claxton, G. and Lucas, B. (2015) *Educating Ruby: What Our Children Really Need to Learn,* Crown House Publishing

62. Webb, N. (1985) 'Student interaction and learning in small groups: A research summary. Learning to Cooperate, Cooperating to Learn', 148-172, *Review of Education Research*

63. Education Endowment Foundation (2017) 'Teaching and Learning Toolkit: Collaborative Learning', Education Endowment Foundation [Accessed in June 2017 at educationendowmentfoundation. org.uk/resources/teaching-learning-toolkit/collaborative-learning/]

64. House, R. J., Wright, N. and Aditya, R. N. (1997) *Cross cultural research on organizational leadership: A critical analysis and a proposed theory*

65. Goleman, D. (1998) 'What makes a leader?', *Harvard Business Review,* 76 (6)

66. Barnard, C. (1948) *Organization and Management,* Harvard University Press

67. Collins, J. (2001) *Good to Great: Why some Companies Make the Leap… and Others Don't,* Harper Business

68. Goleman, D. (1998) 'What makes a leader?', *Harvard Business Review,* 76 (6)

69. CBI (2016) 'Education and Skills Survey', Pearson

70. Gutman, L. M. and Akerman, R. (2008) '*Determinants of Aspirations',* Centre for Research on the Wider Benefits of Learning. Research Report 27. [Accessed in June 2017 at eprints.ioe. ac.uk/2052/1/Gutman2008Determinants.pdf]

71. Gutman, L.M. and Schoon, I. (2013) '*The impact of non-cognitive skills on outcomes for young people: literature review',* London: Education Endowment Foundation

72. Schoon, I. and Parsons, S. (2002) '*Teenage aspirations for future careers and occupational outcomes',* Journal of Vocational Behavior, 60, 262-288.

73. Dweck, C. (2017), *Mindset: Changing the way you think to fulfil your potential,* Robinson

74. Duckworth, A. (2016), *Grit: The Power of Passion and Perseverance,* Scribner Book Company

75. Department for Education (2016) 'Educational Excellence Everywhere', Her Majesty's Stationery Office

76. CBI (2016) 'Education and Skills Survey', Pearson

77. Seligman, M. (1995) *The Optimistic Child: A proven Program to Safeguard Children Against Depression and Build Lifelong Resilience,* US Imports

78. Scales, P. C., Roehlkepartain, E. C., Neal, M., Kielsmeier, J. C. and Benson, P. L. (2006) 'The role of developmental assets in predicting academic achievement: A longitudinal study', *Journal of Adolescence*

79. Sharp, C. (2004) '*Developing young children's creativity: what can we learn from research?',* National Foundation for Educational Research, Autumn 2004, Issue 32

80. Robinson, K. (2006) '*Do Schools Kill Creativity?',* TED Talk [Accessed April 2017 at www.ted. com/talks/ken_robinson_says_schools_kill_creativity]

81. Christodoulou, D. (2014) *Seven Myths about Education*, Routledge

82. Ries, E. (2011) *The Lean Start-Up: How Constant Innovation Creates Radically Successful Businesses*, Portfolio Penguin

83. Robinson, M. (2013) *Trivium 21c: Preparing young people for the future with lessons from the past,* Independent Thinking Press an imprint of Crown House Publishing

84. Ericsson. A, (2016) *Peak: Secrets from the New Science of Expertise*, Eamon Dolan/Houghton Mifflin Harcourt

85. Christodoulou, D. (2014) *Seven Myths about Education*, Routledge

86. Robinson, K. and Aronica, L. (2016) *Creative Schools: The Grassroots Revolution That's Transforming Education*, Penguin Books

87. Ofsted (2016) 'Getting Ready for Work: How secondary schools prepare young people for work', Ofsted

88. Gladwell, M. (2009) *Outliers: The Story of Success*, Penguin

89. Collins, J. (2001) *Good to Great: Why some Companies Make the Leap... and Others Don't*, (Chapter 2), Harper Business

90. James, R. (2009) *What is intelligence?: Beyond the Flynn Effect*, Cambridge University Press

91. The Duke of Edinburgh's Award (2017) 'DofE gives you the skills for work', The Duke of Edinburgh's Award 2017 [Accessed February 2017 at www.dofeskills.org]

92. Her Majesty's Government (2017) 'Take part: National Citizen Service', Her Majesty's Government [Accessed February 2017 at www.gov.uk/government/get-involved/take-part/national-citizen-service]

93. Ericsson, A. (2016) *Peak: Secrets from the New Science of Expertise*, Eamon Dolan/Houghton Mifflin Harcourt

94. Choudhry, N., Fletcher, R. and Soumerai, S. (2005) 'Systematic Review: The Relationship between clinical experience and quality of health care', *Annals of Internal Medicine,* 142

95. Ericsson, A. (2016) *Peak: Secrets from the New Science of Expertise*, Eamon Dolan/Houghton Mifflin Harcourt

96. Ericsson, A. (2016), *Peak: Secrets from the New Science of Expertise*, Eamon Dolan/Houghton Mifflin Harcourt

97. Lucas, B., Claxton, G. and Spencer, E. (2013) *Expansive Education: Teaching learners for the real world,* Open University Press

98. UNESCO (2004) 'The Plurality of Literacy and its Implications for Policies and Programmes (Position Paper)', UNESCO

99. National Numeracy (2017) 'What is Numeracy?', National Numeracy [Accessed April 2017 at www.nationalnumeracy.org.uk/what-numeracy]

100. CBI (2016) 'Education and Skills Survey', CBI

101. Christodoulou, D. (2014) *Seven Myths about Education*, Routledge

102. Department for Children, Schools and Families (2010) 'A Guide to Enterprise Education', Department for Children, Schools and Families

103. Lyons A. (2015) 'Enterprise for All', Ofsted [Accessed in June 2017 at www.schools.norfolk. gov.uk/view/NCC167511]

104. Whitehurst, G. J. (2016) 'Grading Soft Skills: The Brookings Soft Skills Report Card', Education Next [Accessed April 2017 at educationnext.org/grading-soft-skills-the-brookings-soft-skills-report-card/]

105. Whitehurst, G. J. (2016) 'Grading Soft Skills: The Brookings Soft Skills Report Card', Education Next [Accessed April 2017 at educationnext.org/grading-soft-skills-the-brookings-soft-skills-report-card/]

106. Ofsted (2011) 'Economics, business and enterprise education: A summary of inspection evidence – April 2007 to March 2010', Manchester: Ofsted.

107. The Careers and Enterprise Company (2016) 'What we do', Careers and Enterprise Company [Accessed December 2016 www.careersandenterprise.co.uk/what-we-do].

108. Young, D. (2014) 'Enterprise for All: The Relevance of Enterprise in Education', London: Department for Business, Innovation and Skills (BIS).

109. NCS (2017) 'What is NCS?', NCS [Accessed April 2017 at www.ncsyes.co.uk/what-is-ncs]

110. National Schools Partnership (2016) 'Principles and Practices for Primary Engagement in partnership with BITC', Prudential and the CBI

111. CBI (2016) 'Education and Skills Survey', Pearson

112. Fair Education Alliance (2016) 'Report Card 2015', Fair Education Alliance

113. Allen, G. (2011) 'Early Intervention: The Next Steps', Her Majesty's Government

114. Kwok, O., Hughes, J. N., and Luo, W. (2007) 'Role of resilient personality on lower achieving first grade students' current and future achievement', *Journal of School Psychology*, 45(1), 61–82.

115. Ericsson. A, (2016) *Peak: Secrets from the New Science of Expertise,* Eamon Dolan/Houghton Mifflin Harcourt

116. Early Education (2012) 'Development Matters in the Early Years Foundation Stage (EYFS)', British Association for Early Childhood Education [Accessed in March 2017 at www. foundationyears.org.uk/files/2012/03/Development-Matters-FINAL-PRINT-AMENDED.pdf]

117. Ofsted (2016) 'Getting Ready for Work: How secondary schools prepare young people for work', Ofsted

118. Duckworth, A. (2016) *Grit: The Power of Passion and Perseverance,* Scribner Book Company

119. Spielhofer, T. and Lynch, S. (2008) 'Assessing Enterprise Capability: Guidance for Schools', Slough: National Foundation for Educational Research (NFER).

120. Department for Education (2014) 'Assessment Principles', Department for Education

121. Graph shows average teacher assessed essential skill levels at the start of the academic year 2016-17. Source: Skills Builder

122. Sagor, R. (2000) 'Guiding School Improvement with Action Research', ASCD

123. Christodoulou, D. (2016) *Making Good Progress? The future of Assessment for Learning,* Oxford University Press

124. Davies, H. (2002) 'A Review of Enterprise and the Economy in Education', Norwich: Her Majesty's Stationery Office.

125. Ofsted (2011) 'Economics, business and enterprise education: A summary of inspection evidence – April 2007 to March 2010', Manchester: Ofsted.

126. Ofsted (2016) 'Getting Ready for Work: How secondary schools prepare young people for work', Ofsted

127. Mann, A. (2012) 'It's who you meet: why employer contacts at school make a difference to the employment prospects of young adults', Education and Employers

128. Business in the Community (2015) 'Destiny should not be determined by Demography', The Prince's Responsible Business Network

129. CBI (2014) 'A Better Off Britain: Improving lives by making growth work for everyone', CBI

130. Ericsson. A, (2016) *Peak: Secrets from the New Science of Expertise,* Eamon Dolan/Houghton Mifflin Harcourt

131. Ofsted (2016), 'Getting Ready for Work: How secondary schools prepare young people for work', Ofsted

132. Careers and Enterprise Company (2016) 'The Careers & Enterprise Fund 2016 Prospectus', Careers and Enterprise Company

133. Careers and Enterprise Company (2017), 'Business volunteers to support half of all schools and colleges', Careers and Enterprise Company [Accessed in April 2017 at www. careersandenterprise.co.uk/news/business-volunteers-support-half-all-schools-and-colleges]

134. Willingham, D. (2010) 'Why Don't Students Like School?', *American Educator,* Spring 2009

135. Tyrer, G. & Taylor, P. (2013), *The Literacy Leader's Toolkit: Raising Standards Across the Curriculum 11-19,* Bloomsbury Education

136. Department for Children, Schools and Families (2010) 'A Guide to Enterprise Education', Department for Children, Schools and Families

137. Ofsted (2016) 'Getting Ready for Work: How secondary schools prepare young people for work', Ofsted

138. Mann, A. (2012) 'It's who you meet: why employer contacts at school make a difference to the employment prospects of young adults', Education and Employers

139. Public Accounts Committee (2016) 'Training New Teachers 2015-16, Parliament' [Accessed March 2017 at www.parliament.uk/business/committees/committees-a-z/commons-select/public-accounts-committee/inquiries/parliament-2015/training-new-teachers-15-16/]

140. Ericsson. A, (2016), *Peak: Secrets from the New Science of Expertise,* Eamon Dolan/Houghton Mifflin Harcourt

141. Department for Education (2016), *Standard for Teachers' Professional Development,* Department for Education

142. Ofsted (2016) 'Getting Ready for Work: How secondary schools prepare young people for work', Ofsted

143. Ofsted (2015) 'The Common Inspection Framework: Education, Skills and Early Years', Ofsted

144. Ofsted (2016) 'Getting Ready for Work: How secondary schools prepare young people for work', Ofsted

145. Ofsted (2016) 'Getting Ready for Work: How secondary schools prepare young people for work', Ofsted

146. Dweck, C. (2017) *Mindset: Changing the way you think to fulfil your potential*, Robinson

147. Robinson, M. (2013) *Trivium 21c: Preparing young people for the future with lessons from the past*, Independent Thinking Press, an imprint of Crown House Publishing

148. Robinson, M. (2013) *Trivium 21c: Preparing young people for the future with lessons from the past*, Independent Thinking Press, an imprint of Crown House Publishing

149. National Numeracy (2017) 'What is Numeracy?', National Numeracy [Accessed April 2017 at www.nationalnumeracy.org.uk/what-numeracy]

150. PISA is the Programme for International Student Assessment – a set of tests administered every three years by the OECD (the Organisation for Economic Cooperation and Development) to 15 year-olds give a comparative measure of performance in mathematics, science and reading.

151. Crehan, L. (2016) *Cleverlands: The Secrets Behind the Success of the World's Education Superpowers*, Unbound

152. Hurst, G (2017) 'Schools 'should teach students to spot fake news'', *The Times* [Accessed in June 2017 at www.thetimes.co.uk/article/schools-should-teach-children-to-spot-fake-news-fxnscklk0]

153. Millard, W., Menzies, L. and Baar, S. (2017) 'Enterprise Skills: Teachability, Measurability and Next Steps'

154. Young, D. (2014) 'Enterprise for All: The Relevance of Enterprise in Education', London: Department for Business, Innovation and Skills (BIS).

155. Deloitte (2016) 'Developing legal talent: Stepping into the future law firm', Deloitte

156. Wisskirchen, G., Thibault Biacabe, B., Bormann, U., Muntz, A., Niehaus, G., Jimenez Soler, G. and Von Brauchitsch, B. (2017) 'Artificial Intelligence and Robotics and their Impact on the Workplace', International Bar Association

157. Centre for Social and Economic Inclusion (2014) 'Realising Talent: Employment and Skills for the Future', Centre for Social and Economic Inclusion

158. Strongin, S., Lawson, S., Banerjee, S., Hinds, M., Maxwell, K., and Shan, H. (2016) 'Narrowing the Jobs Gap: Overcoming Impediments to Investing in People', Goldman Sachs

159. Sheryl Sandberg, Speech at Harvard Business School, 2012

160. Barber, M., Donnelly, K. and Rizvi, S. (2012) 'Oceans of Innovation: The Atlantic, the Pacific, global leadership and the future of education', IPPR

161. Kim Yong, speech at Skoll World Forum on Social Entrepreneurship, 4 April 2017

162. Centre for Social and Economic Inclusion (2014) 'Realising Talent: Employment and Skills for the Future', Centre for Social and Economic Inclusion

Bibliography

Allen, G. (2011) 'Early Intervention: The Next Steps', Her Majesty's Government

All-Party Parliamentary Group (APPG) for Education (2017) 'How well do schools prepare children for their future?', All-Party Parliamentary Group (APPG) for Education

All-Party Parliamentary Group (APPG) on Social Mobility (2017) 'The class ceiling: increasing access to the leading professions', The Sutton Trust

Ashley, A., Duberley, J., Sommerlad, H. and Scholarios, D. (2015) 'A qualitative evaluation of non-educational barriers to the elite professions', Social Mobility & Child Poverty Commission

Banard, C. (1948) *Organization and Management*, Harvard University Press

Barber, M., Donnelly, K. and Rizvi, S. (2012) 'Oceans of Innovation: The Atlantic, the Pacific, global leadership and the future of education', IPPR

BIS (2015) 'Entrepreneurship Skills Literature and Policy Review', Department for Business Innovation & Skills

Business in the Community (2015) 'Destiny should not be determined by Demography', The Prince's Responsible Business Network

Callaghan, J. (1976) Speech at Ruskin College, Oxford

Careers & Employability Division (Unknown) 'Essential skills and qualities of a successful academic', The University of Manchester [Accessed in February 2017 at www.academiccareer. manchester.ac.uk/about/do/skills/]

Careers and Enterprise Company (2016) 'Enterprise Adviser Network, Careers and Enterprise Company' [Accessed in March 2017 at www.careersandenterprise.co.uk/enterprise-adviser-network]

Careers and Enterprise Company (2016) The Careers & Enterprise Fund 2016 Prospectus, Careers and Enterprise Company

Careers and Enterprise Company (2017) 'Business volunteers to support half of all schools and colleges', Careers and Enterprise Company [Accessed in April 2017 at www.careersandenterprise. co.uk/news/business-volunteers-support-half-all-schools-and-colleges]

CBI (2008) 'Education and Skills Survey,' CBI

CBI (2014) 'A Better Off Britain: Improving lives by making growth work for everyone', CBI

CBI (2016) 'Education and Skills Survey, CBI

Centre for Social and Economic Inclusion (2014) 'Realising Talent: Employment and Skills for the Future', Centre for Social and Economic Inclusion

Chell, E. (2013) 'Review of Skill and the Entrepreneurial Process', *International Journal of Entrepreneurial Behavior & Research* [Pg 12.]

Christodoulou, D. (2014) *Seven Myths about Education*, Abingdon: Routledge.

Christodoulou, D. (2016) *Making Good Progress? The Future of Assessment for Learning*, Oxford University Press

Claxton, G. and Lucas, B. (2015) *Educating Ruby: What Our Children Really Need to Learn*, Crown House Publishing

Coiffait, L., Dawkins, J., Kirwan, R. and Mann, A. (2012) 'Enterprise Education: Value and Direction', London: Pearson Think Tank and Education and Employers Task Force

Collins, J. (2001) *Good to Great: Why some Companies Make the Leap... and Others Don't*, Harper Business

Crehan, L. (2016) *Cleverlands: The Secrets Behind the Success of the World's Education Superpowers*, Unbound

Davies, H. (2002) 'A Review of Enterprise and the Economy in Education', Norwich: Her Majesty's Stationery Office

Deakin Crick, R., Coates, M., Taylor, M. and Ritchie, S. (2004) 'A Systematic Review of the Impact of Citizenship Education on the Provision of Schooling', Research Evidence in Education Library, London: EPPI-Centre, Social Science Research Unit, Institute of Education

Deloitte (2016) 'Developing legal talent: Stepping into the future law firm', *Deloitte*

Department for Children, Schools and Families (2009) 'The Work-Related Learning Guide (Second Edition): A guidance document for employers, schools, colleges, students and their parents and carers', Nottingham: DCSF

Department for Children, Schools and Families (2010) 'A Guide to Enterprise Education', Department for Children, Schools and Families

Department for Education (2012) 'What is the Diploma?', Department for Education [Accessed in June 2017 at webarchive.nationalarchives.gov.uk/20130123124929/http:/www.education.gov.uk/16to19/qualificationsandlearning/thediploma/a0064416/what-is-the-diploma]

Department for Education (2014) 'Assessment Principles', Department for Education [Accessed in March 2017 at www.gov.uk/government/uploads/system/uploads/attachment_data/file/304602/Assessment_Principles.pdf]

Department for Education (2016) 'Educational Excellence Everywhere', Her Majesty's Stationery Office

Department for Education (2016) 'Standard for Teachers' Professional Development', Department for Education

Department for Education (2017) 'Revised GCSE and equivalent results in England: 2015 to 2016 - SFR03/2017', Department for Education

Detter-Schmelz, D. R., Kennedy, K. N., and Ramsey, R. P. (2002) 'Enriching our understanding of student team effectiveness', *Journal of Marketing Education*, 24 (2), 114-124

Duckworth, A. (2016) *Grit: The Power of Passion and Perseverance*, Scribner Book Company

Dweck, C. (2017) *Mindset: Changing the way you think to fulfil your potential*, Robinson

Early Education (2012) 'Development Matters in the Early Years Foundation Stage (EYFS)', British Association for Early Childhood Education [Accessed in March 2017 at www.foundationyears.org.uk/files/2012/03/Development-Matters-FINAL-PRINT-AMENDED.pdf]

Education Endowment Foundation (2017) 'Teaching and Learning Toolkit: Collaborative Learning', Education Endowment Foundation [Accessed in June 2017 at educationendowmentfoundation. org.uk/resources/teaching-learning-toolkit/collaborative-learning/]

Education Endowment Foundation (2017) 'Teaching and Learning Toolkit: Oral language interventions', Education Endowment Foundation [Accessed in June 2017 at educationendowmentfoundation.org.uk/resources/teaching-learning-toolkit/oral-language-interventions/]

Enterprise Nation (2014) '70% increase in number of company founders aged under 35', Enterprise Nation [Accessed in June 2017 at www.enterprisenation.com/blog/posts/70-increase-in-number-of-company-founders-aged-under-35]

Ericsson, A. & Pool, R. (2016) *Peak: Secrets from the New Science of Expertise*, Eamon Dolan/ Houghton Mifflin Harcourt

Espinoza, J. (2016) 'UK may lose out to Asian countries in developing 'soft skills' for life in new rankings', Daily Telegraph [Accessed in March 2017 at www.telegraph.co.uk/education/educationnews/12190783/UK-may-lose-out-to-Asian-countries-in-developing-soft-skills-for-life-in-new-rankings.html]

Fair Education Alliance (2016) 'Report Card', *Fair Education Alliance*

Gadsby, B. (2017) 'Challenge the Impossible', *Teach First*

Gladwell, M. (2009) *Outliers: The Story of Success,* Penguin

Goby, V.P., & Lewis, J.H. (2000) 'The key role of listening in business: A study of the Singapore insurance industry', *Business Communication Quarterly,* 63(2), 41-51

Goleman, D. (1998) 'What makes a leader?', *Harvard Business Review,* 76 (6)

Gov.uk (Unknown) 'Take part: National Citizen Service', Her Majesty's Government [Accessed in February 2017 at www.gov.uk/government/get-involved/take-part/national-citizen-service]

Gutman, L. M. and Akerman, R. (2008) 'Determinants of Aspirations', Centre for Research on the Wider Benefits of Learning. Research Report 27

Gutman, L.M. and Schoon, I. (2013) 'The impact of non-cognitive skills on outcomes for young people: literature review', London: Education Endowment Foundation

House, R. J., Wright, N. & Aditya, R.N. (1997) 'Cross cultural research on organizational leadership: A critical analysis and a proposed theory'

Humphrey, N., Lendrum, A. and Wigelsworth, M. (2010) 'Social and emotional aspects of learning (SEAL) programme in secondary schools: National evaluation', Department for Education

Hurst, G. (2017) Schools 'should teach students to spot fake news', *The Times*

I CAN (2008) 'Speech, Language and Communication Needs and Primary School-aged Children', I CAN Talk Series – Issue 6

International Bar Association (2017) 'Artificial Intelligence and Robotics and their Impact on the Workplace', International Bar Association

James, R. (2009) *What is intelligence?: Beyond the Flynn Effect,* Cambridge University Press

Jubilee Centre (2013) 'Framework for Character Education', Birmingham: University of Birmingham.

King Solomon Academy (Unknown) 'Welcome | King Solomon Academy', King Solomon Academy [Accessed in April 2017 at kingsolomonacademy.org/secondary/welcome]

Kwok, O., Hughes, J. N., & Luo, W. (2007) 'Role of resilient personality on lower achieving first grade students' current and future achievement', *Journal of School Psychology,* 45(1), 61–82.

Lanning, J. Martin, R. and Villeneuve-Smith, F. (2008) 'Employability skills examined: Ten Key Messages from LSN's quest to understand employability skills', *Learning and Skills Network*

Long, R. and Foster, D. (2016) 'Financial and enterprise education in schools' – Briefing Paper 06156, London: House of Commons Library

Lucas, B. and Hanson, J. (2016) 'Learning to be Employable: Practical lessons from research into developing character', *Centre for Real-World Learning*

Lucas, B. and Hanson, J. (2017) Learning to be an Engineer: Implications for the education system,' *Royal Academy of Engineering*

Lucas, B., Claxton, G. and Spencer, E. (2013) *Expansive Education: Teaching learners for the real world,* Open University Press

Lynch, S., Kettlewell, K., Southcott, C., McCrone, T. (National Foundation for Educational Research) 'Outcomes for the first cohort of Diploma learners', Department for Education

Lyons, A. (2015) 'Enterprise for All', Ofsted [Accessed in June 2017 at www.schools.norfolk.gov.uk/view/NCC167511]

Malcolm Gladwell (2009) *Outliers: The Story of Success,* Little, Brown and Company

Mann, A. (2012) 'It's who you meet: why employer contacts at school make a difference to the employment prospects of young adults', *Education and Employers*

Martin Robinson (2013) *Trivium 21c: Preparing young people for the future with lessons from the past,* Independent Thinking Press an imprint of Crown House Publishing

McGuinness, F. (2017) 'Youth Unemployment Statistics' – Briefing Paper Number 5871, London: House of Commons Library

McLarty, L., Highley, H. and Alderson, S. (2010) 'Evaluation of Enterprise Education in England', London: Department for Education

McNeil, B., Reeder, N. and Rich, J. (2012) 'A framework of outcomes for young people', *The Young Foundation*

Millard, W. and Menzies, L. (2016) 'The State of Speaking in Our Schools', Voice 21 and LKMco [Accessed in December 2016 at www.esu.org/__data/assets/pdf_file/0026/13796/Oracy-State-of-speaking-report-v2.pdf]

Millard, W., Menzies, L. and Baar, S. (2017) 'Enterprise Skills: Teachability, Measurability and Next Steps', *LKMco*

Morgan, N. (2015) 'Winners of the Character Awards announced', Department for Education [Accessed in March 2017 at www.gov.uk/government/news/winners-of-the-character-awards-announced]

Mourshed, M., Farrell, D., and Barton, D. (2013) 'Education to Employment: Designing a System that Works', Washington D.C.: McKinsey Center for Government.

Mourshed, M., Patel, J. and Suder, K. (2014) 'Education to Employment: Getting Europe's Youth into Work', Washington DC: McKinsey Center for Government

National Numeracy (2017) 'What is Numeracy?', National Numeracy [Accessed in April 2017 at www.nationalnumeracy.org.uk/what-numeracy]

National Schools Partnership (2016) 'Principles and Practices for Primary Engagement in partnership with BITC, Prudential and the CBI'

NCS (2017) 'What is NCS?', NCS [Accessed in March 2017 at www.ncsyes.co.uk/what-is-ncs]

Nicholson, B. (1989) 'Towards a Skills Revolution: Report of the CBI Vocational Education and Training Task Force', Association of Colleges for Further and Higher Education [CBI]

Niteesh K Choudhry, Robert H. Fletcher and Stephen B. Soumerai (2005) 'Systematic Review: The Relationship between clinical experience and quality of health care'

Ofsted (2004) 'Learning to be enterprising: An evaluation of enterprise learning at Key Stage 4', London: Ofsted

Ofsted (2005) 'Developing Enterprising Young People: Features of the successful implementation of enterprise education at Key Stage 4', Ofsted

Ofsted (2011) 'Economics, business and enterprise education: A summary of inspection evidence – April 2007 to March 2010', Manchester: Ofsted

Ofsted (2015) 'The Common Inspection Framework: Education, Skills and Early Years', Ofsted

Ofsted (2016) 'Getting Ready for Work: How secondary schools prepare young people for work', Ofsted

Organisation for Economic Co-operation and Development (OECD) (2016) 'OECD Employment Outlook 2016', Paris: *OECD Publishing*

Owen, J. (2010) *How to Sell,* Pearson Education

Paton, G. (2012) 'Spoon-fed' students given tuition in basic skills at university, *The Telegraph* [Accessed in February 2017 at www.telegraph.co.uk/education/educationnews/9180982/Spoon-fed-students-given-tuition-in-basic-skills-at-university.html]

Populus (2013) 'RBS Enterprise Tracker, in association with UnLtd', RBS [Accessed in February 2017 at unltd.org.uk/wp-content/uploads/2013/09/RBS-Youth-Enterprise-Tracker-Summary_3rd-Quarter-2013-Final.pdf]

Public Accounts Committee (2016) 'Training New Teachers 2015-16', Parliament [Accessed in March 2017 at www.parliament.uk/business/committees/committees-a-z/commons-select/public-accounts-committee/inquiries/parliament-2015/training-new-teachers-15-16/]

Rebecca Burn Callander (2014) More young entrepreneurs launch start-ups in wake of recession, *The Telegraph* [Accessed in February 2017 at www.telegraph.co.uk/finance/yourbusiness/11133048/More-young-entrepreneurs-launch-start-ups-in-wake-of-recession.html]

Ries, E. (2011) *The Lean Start-Up: How Constant Innovation Creates Radically Successful Businesses,* Portfolio Penguin

Roberts, Y. (2009) 'Grit: The skills for success and how they are grown', *The Young Foundation*

Robinson, K. (2006) 'Do Schools Kill Creativity?', TED Talk [Accessed in April 2017 at www.ted.com/talks/ken_robinson_says_schools_kill_creativity]

Robinson, K. and Aronica, L. (2016) *Creative Schools: The Grassroots Revolution That's Transforming Education*, Penguin Books

Robinson, M. (2013) *Trivium 21c: Preparing young people for the future with lessons from the past*, Independent Thinking Press

Rosen, J. A., Glennie, E. J., Dalton B. W., Lennon, J. M. and Bozick, R. N. (2010) 'Non-cognitive Skills in the Classroom: New Perspectives on Educational Research', RTI Press publication No. BK-0004-1009, Research Triangle Park, NC: RTI International.

Roser, M. and Ortize-Ospina, E. (2016) 'Literacy', Our World in Data [Accessed in March 2017 at ourworldindata.org/literacy]

Sagor, R. (2000) 'Guiding School Improvement with Action Research', ASCD

Scales, P. C., Roehlkepartain, E.C., Neal, M., Kielsmeier, J.C., and Benson, P.L. (2006) 'The role of developmental assets in predicting academic achievement: A longitudinal study', *Journal of Adolescence*

Schoon, I. and Parsons, S. (2002) 'Teenage aspirations for future careers and occupational outcomes', *Journal of Vocational Behavior*

SEAL Community (Unknown) 'About SEAL', SEAL Community Website [Accessed in February 2017 at www.sealcommunity.org/node/356]

Seligman, M. (1995) *The Optimistic Child: A proven Program to Safeguard Children Against Depression and Build Lifelong Resilience,* Us Imports

Sharp, C. (2004) 'Developing young children's creativity: what can we learn from research?', National Foundation for Education Research Autumn 2004, Issue 32

Snape, J. (2015) 'It's Nice to be Nice', The Guardian [Accessed in April 2017 at www.theguardian. com/lifeandstyle/2015/feb/12/its-nice-to-be-nice]

Social Mobility and Child Poverty Commission (2015) 'Downward Mobility, Opportunity Hoarding and the Glass Floor', Social Mobility and Child Poverty Commission

Spielhofer, T. and Lynch, S. (2008) 'Assessing Enterprise Capability: Guidance for Schools', Slough: National Foundation for Educational Research (NFER).

Strongin, S., Lawson, S., Banerjee, S., Hinds, M., Maxwell, K. and Shan, H. (2016) 'Narrowing the Jobs Gap: Overcoming Impediments to Investing in People', Goldman Sachs

Teacher Development Trust (2014) 'Teacher Development Trust: Annual Report 2014', Teacher Development Trust

The Careers and Enterprise Company (2016) 'What we do', The Careers and Enterprise Company [Accessed in December 2016 at www.careersandenterprise.co.uk/what-we-do]

The Duke of Edinburgh's Award (2017) 'DofE gives you the skills for work', The Duke of Edinburgh's Award [Accessed in February 2017 at www.dofeskills.org/]

The Guardian (2012) 'How GCSE results compare, county by county', *The Guardian*

The Jubilee Centre for Character & Virtue (2014) 'A Framework for Character Education in Schools', The Jubilee Centre for Character & Virtue

Tomlinson, M. (2004) '14-19 Qualifications and Curriculum Reform: Final Report of the Working Group on 14-19 Reform', Department for Education and Skills

Tyrer, G. & Taylor, P. (2013) *The Literacy Leader's Toolkit: Raising Standards Across the Curriculum 11-19*, Bloomsbury Education

UK Commission for Employment and Skills (UKCES) (2016) 'Employer Skills Survey 2015: UK Results – Evidence Report 97', London: UKCES.

UKCES (2009) 'The Employability Challenge: Full Report', UKCES [UKCES webarchive. nationalarchives.gov.uk/20140108090250/www.ukces.org.uk/assets/bispartners/ukces/docs/ publications/employability-challenge-full-report.pdf]

UNESCO Education Sector (2004) 'The Plurality of Literacy and its Implications for Policies and Programmes (Position Paper)', UNESCO

University of Birmingham (Unknown) 'Undergraduate Law programmes', University of Birmingham [Accessed in February 2017 at www.birmingham.ac.uk/schools/law/courses/llb/ skills.aspx]

University of Cambridge (Unknown) 'Key skills for undergraduates', University of Cambridge [Accessed in February 2017 at www.transkills.admin.cam.ac.uk/skills-portal/key-skills-undergraduates]

Webb, N. (1985) 'Student interaction and learning in small groups: A research summary. Learning to Cooperate, Cooperating to Learn', 148-172., Review of Educational Research

Whitehurst, G. J. (2016) 'Grading Soft Skills: The Brookings Soft Skills Report Card, Education Next' [Accessed in April 2017 at educationnext.org/grading-soft-skills-the-brookings-soft-skills-report-card/]

Whitehurst, G.J. (2016) 'Hard thinking on soft skills', The Brookings Institute

Whitty, G. Power, S. Sims, S. (2013) 'Lasting Benefits: The long-term legacy of the Assisted Places Scheme for Assisted Place Holders', Sutton Trust

Willingham, D. (2010) *Why Don't Students Like School?*, American Educators

Young, D. (2014) 'Enterprise for All: The Relevance of Enterprise in Education', London: Department for Business, Innovation and Skills (BIS)